Wait and Sea

Mönchengladbach 2013

Author: H. Rade
ISBN 978-1-52-093855-4

Dedicated to:

My father who persuaded me to write this book;
My shipping company – to which I owe everything;
The grand masters of humor:
Stan Laurel and Oliver Hardy
Redd Fox
Rowan Atkinson
Tommy Cooper
Rodney Dangerfield
Jeff Dunham
Victor Borge
Tommy Cooper
John Cleese
Jim Carrey
Russel Peters
Gabriel Iglesias
Mel Blanc
Pierre Richard

and to my very special friend
Irish Super comedian Al Foran

Introduction:

I don't know what on earth came over me to write down some of the adventures I've experienced during the numerous years I've been working as a waiter on board luxury liners, and moreover a few of those events I considered adventurous and fascinating. In my view, the today's tourists who have decided to spend their more or less deserved holiday on board a cruise ship should be advised that a sea voyage probably entails far more than just enjoying delicacies, excellent performances on stage, and experiencing a rough sea. It's a matter of fact that guests on cruise ships may find themselves in quite peculiar situations.

With regard to the destinations mentioned in this book let me point out the following: our cruise ships travel to the most beautiful places throughout our wonderful world; my dear readers can gather information about the various tourist attractions and beauties of scenery either by contacting a travel agency or searching online. Instead of publishing a new guide book or promotional travel report, I have summarized the various amusing and sometimes gloomy experiences I've kept in mind during the last years and put them together in one single cruise with interesting destinations. Be assured that all these events are not fantasy, but have in fact happened. Believe it or not – in any case I wish you great pleasure in reading.

Chapter 1:   Born to be a Waiter?

Every human being is born, and you won't be astonished to learn that I was born, too – 3600 m above sea level in the highest capital of the world: La Paz in Bolivia.

The sun is always shining there as it would be too much like hard work for the clouds to move up that high. Due to the clear, but very thin air I sometimes had the impression that my brain suffered from a lack of oxygen; consequently it would not be suitable for an outstanding performance at the universities in Oxford and Harvard or at my grammar school in Zülpich near Cologne. Consequently I would have to look for an alternative path for the future.

Already in my early childhood I wondered which job would be adequate for my hidden talents so that I would not always have to rely on the services of the "Bank of Father", the easiest way of getting money.

As the son of a German father, a Bolivian mother with a Russian girl-friend – my future wife –, and an uncle and aunt with Greek ancestors, I was often rather confused during the lessons at school. I frequently did not succeed in catching the point of the teaching or in coping with the comprehensive learning material.

I got everybody's attention in class by eccentric entertainment rather than clever replies or input. If the physics teacher tried for example to explain the force of gravity, various things hovered back and forth between my hands without apparent reasons and thus dashed the teacher's theory. Whenever I gave a talk in front of the class, it would be far more reminiscent of an amusing scene from Stan Laurel, Mr. Bean, Jim Carrey or Victor Borge. This in turn quite often induced the teacher, his eyes filled with tears – either with laughter or sheer desperation – not only to give me a very bad mark, but also to send me back to my seat at the back of the classroom, while all my classmates were cheering and laughing.

What was to become of me?

One day, after a humorous performance at the teacher's desk and my fellow pupils' laughter still ringing in my ears, it occurred to me that I might combine my small comedic talent with some rather more serious activities to earn my bread and butter.

After I had left the teacher at his desk with severely increased blood pressure for the day, lost in thought I unwrapped my sandwich a) to admire it and b) to eat it. As usual, I looked at this little piece of art which my mother had prepared, as she does every day, with lots of love and which, as always, tasted fantastic. And I pondered ... Eating noisily and accompanied by the teacher's further fierce curses – the break hadn't started yet! – I started thinking seriously for the first time in my life. Finally the following idea crossed my mind: I had to find a job which combined delicious food, stimulating drinks and entertainment.

Having rummaged in my schoolbag; among a Playboy magazine and a Mickey Mouse comic I managed to find an article published in the Bild newspaper. There was a report about German personnel on board cruise liners in the Caribbean Sea who were evidently doing very well.

On that day it was impossible for me to have lunch after school. I was too excited. I called the shipping company to be advised on what to do in order to become a promising candidate for a job on one of their liners.

Mandatory were a school certificate giving evidence of intermediate level or even higher education, a passport photo that should not show too stupid a face and the ability to repeat, and if possible, translate the word "pea soup" into three different languages.

(The owner of the shipping company must have been a Cologne carnival enthusiast.)

The practical requirements could easily be achieved by training. The candidate waiter had to be in a position to carry three plates at the same time, despite the fact that he only has two arms, and be able to differentiate between a beer glass and a champagne flute.

I thought about it a little and was told by a voice in my head: *That's right up your street!*

Keeping the required school qualifications in mind, I started to be more zealous, even hard-working. Not so much towards what was being taught in the lesson, rather my ambitions induced me to hide under the school desk where I prepared myself for my future under cover of darkness.

6

I started to remember little magic tricks which I must have certainly seen somewhere on TV or on stage and encouraged my fingers to practice and finally master some of these gags

My cerebellum created brilliant, stupid jokes to accompany my conjuring tricks. Knowing that I would deal with an international audience someday in addition to German and the Cologne Low German, I gradually stored five further foreign languages in my cerebrum, which would help me in the future to correctly interpret the praises and/or insults of international spectators.

The clinking of plates could be heard now and then as I carried them in my schoolbag amongst my school books from my home to school in order to perfect the fine art of plate carrying. Without this learning material which I juggled during the breaks to the delight of one teacher (may God rest his soul!) I would never have found out my limits with regard to stacking fragile things.

When I had run out of plates, my fingers practiced increasingly more complicated magical tricks and my loose tongue parodied the grand masters of comedy. I gradually shaped up to be the perfect "waiter-entertainer".

Thanks to my enthusiasm for learning which arose from my anticipation of exciting adventures on the high seas, one day I triumphantly held my High School Diploma certificate in my hands which the principal had signed with furrowed brow. I did not care for his comment: "These marks are bad, very bad!" as I was just very pleased to have given several teachers the runaround during the past thirteen years. Some of my school-mates who were far better and more zealous than I had been did not achieve the Diploma; either they had indeed played up too much or they had not been able to pretend well enough that they had in fact learned a lot.

Despite my High School Diploma my way to the job of my dreams was still blocked as the Father State shook me straight out of my dreams of hot nights at the Copacabana. Instead I received the terrifying news that I had to join up for fifteen months – as a driver of a great big self-propelled howitzer equipped with disarmed atomic shells.

As my inner protests were in vain and ineffective, I gave myself up to fate. The fact that as I soldier almost run a General over with the tank (who had been silly enough to park his official car on the tank road) in the darkness was an acceptable part of my training and as such I consequently didn't lose much sleep over it.

Similar to my schooldays I left some officers behind with mental breakdowns, ringing in the ears and heart attacks, until they highly recommended me to say good-by to the barracks as soon as possible and once and for all.

My unintentional farewell present to the State was a howitzer which had a breakdown in the garage after I had completed my repair work. The technicians who had to take care of the tank upon my departure could never find out what this lance-corporal had done to the vehicle. It was simply out of operation and had to be scrapped shortly afterwards.

A broken tank was thus my small contribution to peace on earth … not a lot, but at least that! My military farce, however, had one particular benefit; it prepared me well for night shifts. I was really delighted at exercising peaceful activities once again.

Chapter 2:   Start of Career on the High Seas

After all this going on I wanted to focus on my "loveboat-waiter-career" and make my dreams come true.

By now it felt really good to already be a bit experienced in carrying plates and to recognize that my entire personality combined with my loose tongue had developed towards a plate-carrying entertainer. But was this sufficient for fulfilling the wishes of holiday-makers throughout the world? Wouldn't it be better to polish up my act a little first?

I was encouraged by my father. This great guy had already realized that it would be no good to try to direct me towards university as most of the time I would struggle just holding a book the right way up.

One day my father asked me to come into his work room where he encouragingly presented me the leaflet from a well-respected hotel management school at the Tegernsee in Bavaria. I was sold on this option, particularly after my counter-productive activities with the Federal Armed Forces. Moreover I had already heard about the culture of the people in this Free State.

I will never forget the moment when I once noticed an American in a station. Waving a pack of cigarettes, he approached a Bavarian and asked him: "Are you smoking?" The Bavarian eyeballed him and angrily replied in Bavarian accent: "No, you idiot, this is a traditional suit!" The American's blank look was one-of-a-kind.

(Translator's note: In order to help you to understand this joke let me point out that in Germany a tuxedo is called "smoking").

After my father had given his blessings, I was allowed to go to this quaint German region and take part in a one-year crash course dealing with all fields of gastronomy. I didn't want to do a real apprenticeship because of the usual and well known "gaping hole of emptiness" to be found in a wallet during an apprenticeship in a German hotel or restaurant. As I did not want to be used – particularly as an apprentice – I focused on my studies in the beautiful town Tegernsee.

Realizing that I was not allowed to horrify my family again with a lousy performance (as I had done at school), I worked flat out for the first time in my life.

The result was respectable: I completed the course as the fourth best of 250 hotel specialists. For the first time I held an excellent certificate in my hands which should put me in a good position to be employed on board a cruise liner.

Was the English I had learnt at school sufficient?

A school-friend in Tegernsee who was English proposed to me one day: "Come along with me to London; you'll find a job there and pick up even more experiences."

Why not, I thought to myself. It sounded quite promising to perfect my English, improve my knowledge in the other foreign languages and earn money at the same time. In the event of being employed by a foreign shipping company at a later date I would make good use of this income!

I followed my friend's advice and started working in one of the Hilton hotels in London just two weeks after completion of the course. I could demonstrate my abilities and knowledge while working in the restaurant and for room service. Beside numerous "average" guests I also waited on some celebrities and obtained a few dubious offers from rich oil multinationals and older ladies. Nevertheless I always kept sight of my goal – working as a "waiter on board a loveboat".

Exactly eleven months later my conversational English was almost perfect; furthermore I had by the way improved my basic knowledge in five other languages. On the basis of this knowledge and my good certificate I then hoped to be invited for a recruitment test on a cruise liner. But where should I send my application to?

11

Chapter 3: Application and Contract

Upon my return to Germany I went to the best travel agency I could find at that time, where I was shown brochures from cruise liners and the respective shipping companies. It made me proud to read in the employees' eyes in the travel agency "Wow! Such a young guy and already in a position to afford a cruise!" Of course I did not let the ladies and gentlemen in on the fact that I was using their agency as job center.

Having obtained a big pile of brochures under my arm, I happily hurried home. My ballpoint pen was on the verge of overheating, but within a short time I had finished all applications which I had put on paper with the help of my father's first-class wording and the perfect business English of a teacher in our neighborhood.

I started waiting – during this time I wondered whether I had done enough to convince one of these shipping companies that they simply had to complete their crew with this "Cologne reveler".

My efforts were in fact successful: two weeks later I received the first reply in a white-blue envelope. Surrounded by my family, I excitedly opened the envelope to take out its content.

"CONTRACT" was printed in capital letters on the first page. The promising text was very short, plain and simple. It was a pleasure for the shipping company to have the privilege of employing me with immediate effect as "Demi Chef de Rang" "(junior waiter). But, and that was the catch, I was asked to first go to Miami for a job interview at my own expense. At my own expense? I would have to pay the flight ticket by myself? Yes, indeed. As I was told later, the shipping company had repeatedly invited alleged job applicants to Miami, after they had submitted counterfeited curriculum vitae and job experiences to enjoy a few nice days on the beach of Miami and its amusement centers at the cost of the company. These jokers did not even think of showing up in the office. Instead, they worshipped the sun in Florida the whole blessed day to return home sunburnt. It stands to reason that the shipping company only invited serious applicants to Miami.

Chapter 4:   Arrival

My whole family gave me a helping hand, while I prepared for my journey. Mom put a lot of useful things in my suitcase such as light clothing, underwear, jelly bears, toiletries and a few unnecessary things such as gloves and turtlenecks. "It might be cold in Miami", my mother was worried.

At last the big day had arrived. All family members had come to the airport in Frankfurt to say good-bye to the leaving son. While Dad shook hands with me, Mom blew her nose. My siblings hugged their brother who was going away from home and wished him to return rich and healthy.

Up until now I have always returned safe and sound. With regard to being a wealthy man: I am now struggling with the second million. Why? Because I haven't achieved the first one yet …

"America, I'm coming", I mumbled to myself as I boarded the plane, a Boeing 747.

Until that day I had never had the pleasure of mixing among American guests in an American airplane. Did travelers from the land of opportunity behave in a different manner than the Europeans?

Well, the atmosphere on board was like that known from movies. On my left side I could glance into the first and business class, where relaxed, grey-haired business men were sipping their champagne. On my right side was the economy class, the so-called "coach class", where I squeezed into a seat which could no way be comfortable for anybody but Lilliputians.

As it was impossible to fall asleep prior to the take-off, I watched the hustle and bustle in the cabin with great interest. Particularly the row where I was sitting was quite amusing. A nice, Afro-American couple gave me a warm welcome: HE shouldering a gigantic jukebox from which rap sounds started loudly ringing out; SHE smiling at me now and then when she wasn't busy changing her baby's diaper. *The taste of the big wide world*, I thought. *Hopefully it's not a bad omen for my next few days…*

After the successful take-off the airport in Frankfurt disappeared within short time to just a little spot on the horizon. My journey to the land of opportunity had started; and my thoughts focused on Miami in the sun-state Florida.

Longing for a fresh sea breeze, I dozed off and was woken up by the smell of food which was on the verge of being served. I was impressed with the possibility to choose from six different main courses which the friendly stewardess almost perfectly read from the menu.

The offer comprised: chicken with pasta, pasta with chicken, chicken without pasta, pasta without chicken, pasta without pasta and chicken without chicken.

I chose the latter as each of these meals looked as if it had already been digested once.

For this reason I was satisfied with a packet of peanuts and had a drink which was declared as red wine, but rather tasted like burnt gravy.

"Hmm, very delicious!" I heard a person raving about the food in the row in front of me. Having identified the traveler's accent, I got up from my seat for a second. My assumption proved to be true: it was an Englishman who evidently liked the chicken with its thousand flying hours and the "noodle stodge" type pasta more than anything he had ever eaten in his beautiful home country.

Each to his own, was my last thought before I fell back asleep. I did not wake up again before our landing in Florida.

Late in the afternoon I was standing with my suitcases in the vast airport of Miami and feeling out of place. Having taken a deep breath, I called upon my very best English and asked the very first person who passed me how to get to Miami harbor.

"No entiendo" (meaning "I don't understand you") the passer-by replied to me in fluent Spanish. "This *obviously* was the wrong person to ask", I said to myself and tried my luck with a young lady who was selling ice-cream at a stall. Her answer was exactly the same as before: "No entiendo".

"My goodness, am I in the wrong movie?" I swore to myself in a low voice. "Where am I? I thought I had come to the United States of America!"

To be on the safe side, I took out my dictionary which I had taken along for emergency cases and flipped through it to letter "U". "USA" was written there, „being the abbreviation of the UNITED

15

STATES OF AMERICA: population of 300 million. National language: English."

Only sometime later I found out that particularly in Miami a large percentage of the inhabitants come from Cuba, Mexico, South and Central America.

Aha, I thought, *instead of going by taxi to the shipping company, I will ride a donkey which is patiently waiting for me outside the airport.*

My assumption proved to be wrong. Where I expected a donkey, a young man aged about 22 (just as I was at that time) joined me. Telling me about his rather severe communication problems, he asked me in an accent that reminded me of "Crocodile Dundee" whether I knew which country we were in and whether the plane that had left Frankfurt might have missed its destination. I worked it out that he must have been on board of my plane. As I found out later, he came from "Down Under", in other words from Australia.

Due to his orientation difficulties he asked me kindly to help him. He showed me his folder which contained the same contract as my folder. He was also heading to the shipping company where the personnel manager was expecting us on that day! What a coincidence!

Being glad about this we decided to have a cup of coffee to discuss our situation and celebrate our chance encounter. Both of us couldn't help smirking shortly after, because – despite the fact that we were in the heart of America – the name of the restaurant we had gone to was "Sol". (Meaning "sun"); its owner's name was Emilio Sanchez Rodrigo Jimenez.

The waiter who cared for us was an extremely business-minded Asian with Chinese-Cuban accent, very polite and helpful. When he understood – after having served the espressos – that we were heading for the harbor he offered to take us downtown to the shipping company with his motor-driven rickshaw at midnight at the end of his shift; if we paid him twenty dollars plus a night hazard bonus of 300 dollars. "Going by rickshaw is far more refreshing than going by car", he explained.

As it was, however, still the morning and our job interview at the shipping company was scheduled for the afternoon, we had to reject his offer, but promised to take up his offer when we were in Miami

16

again in the forthcoming year although it seemed that this guy had smoked a few Colombian kumquats that day!

Time pressed now. The bosses in the office would most probably not approve of us showing up late on the very first day.

As expected, the taxis were waiting at the parking lot – honking and with running engines; no sign of donkeys and rickshaws!

After a while we caught sight of a "yellow cab" labeled with "We speak English". We highly appreciated this way of informing us of the driver's knowledge in the language typical of the United States of America.

Having put our luggage into the trunk, we snuggled down in the leather seats of this great big "gas guzzler" type car. At that time the cab companies had no problem with the huge gas consumption of these vehicles.

Awaiting a generous tip, the driver politely introduced himself to be Jose Manuel Santos. Shortly after he directed his "battleship" to a six-lane interstate towards the center of Miami.

Six lanes are a must, because in America you get your driving-license already at the age of sixteen. Consequently it may happen that some of these teenagers are unable to look over the steering wheel due to insufficient body height and need to execute risky driving maneuvers, when they try to evade obstructions.

We passed gigantic skyscrapers, ballparks and football stadiums, until we finally reached the harbor of Miami. Already from afar we were mesmerized by the tremendous silhouettes of the cruise liners which either entered the port or were prepared for leaving.

This was very interesting for a country bumpkin like me who so far only had the chance to watch the container ships on the rivers Rhine and Moselle and the canoes on the rather unknown Neffelbach in the Eifel.

I marveled at the red-white giants of the "Carnival Cruise Line" – also known as party boats –, the white-colored ships of the "Norwegian Cruise Line" with its legendary "SS Norway", the former "France" which unfortunately had to be scrapped a few years ago for reasons of age, the ships of the "Royal Caribbean Cruise Line", the today's "Royal Caribbean International" with its beautiful ships in dazzlingly white and dark-blue, the interesting white-blue ships of "Princess Cruise Line" and numerous other more or less spectacular ships which either entered or left the port. In the early days of my career the shipping company's office was accommodated in a rather plain building in front of which the taxi driver dropped us off. It was evident that this office building was a port of call for international people who either had already taken regular employment there or were still waiting – just as me – to be hired.

Chapter 5:   Recruitment Test in American

A voluptuous lady with lots of jewelry approached us, gave us a warm welcome and took us to a modestly equipped hall where numerous diverse freshmen, like the two of us, were rather pale and nervously squatting on their chairs. They were all excitedly listening to the lady who introduced herself and one of the operation managers who would run the recruitment test. I managed to keep myself under control this time and was listening without distracting the man with any comments or magic tricks.

According to the operation manager we would have to take an English and fitness test in the course of the next two days in addition to today's job interview. They were aimed at finding out which of the applicants had all the necessary skills for working on board one of the luxury ships waiting in the port.

Afterwards we were asked to put the copies of our curriculum vitae and reference letters on the table in front of us. Shortly a pile of papers was ready to be collected from each table.

Everybody - except one short Korean – produced the required papers. When the manager asked the Korean for his papers, he looked at him in a dumbfounded manner and started stammering. Shortly afterwards it turned out that he was working as cleaner in this building and had erroneously blundered into our group. The friendly manager sent him back to his job.

After the reference documents had been collected, they disappeared in a dusty drawer, accompanied by the comment: "These scribbles aren't of great importance! Paper doesn't blush and doesn't provide evidence of the quality of your work and your ability to meet the guests' requirements on board the cruise liners!"

This was okay with me, particularly as, compared to me, the other applicants had produced far more documents of evidence for their supposed professional experience; they now looked rather disillusioned.

Afterwards the manager turned again his group of new employees and stared at us over the rim of his glasses. He advised us of the daily routine on board and – reading from a control book – the comprehensive obligations and tasks of a waiter. To fulfil them, the fitness of an alpinist evidently was required. In this moment a few applicants certainly felt that they were in the wrong place, and it was immediately rather clear to me that this job would be somewhat different from the activities of a European waiter.

I was to be proven quite right …!

The first hurdle to be cleared was a language test. Every "junior waiter" had to get up and introduce himself in English: name, home country, native language, marital status – "preferably single". In the first instance we had to give reasons for which we felt called us to aspire to such a noble profession. All replies were almost the same: "I like to be with others", "I enjoy travelling" or "I want to earn money." All those wishy-washy reasons were proudly announced, which if we had been applying to German companies would have led to us being given the good advice to go home and decide for another job. In the USA such things are, however, handled in a more open-minded manner. The reasons seemed to cut ice, although I had the impression that the manager stopped listening closely after the introduction of the fourth future waiter. Probably he was already thinking about supper and the following baseball game.

His bored facial expression, however, changed when the waiter applicant Burmi got up to introduce himself. To be more precisely – he had already got up, which wasn't obvious at first glance as he was only about one meter fifty seven tall. Gawping through his thick horn-rimmed glasses, he was standing there like a delinquent condemned to death who had been allowed to consider which company should sponsor his last cigarette. Having rattled off his curriculum vitae, he was just on the verge of sitting down again, when the manager asked him to also explain why he had applied for the job. Looking around embarrassed, he replied almost tearfully: "I have applied to you to be as far away from my wife as possible. She always beats me up."

Murmuring and snorting could be heard in the hall, but everybody tried to control themselves. But when Burmi even pushed up his sleeve and thus revealed some large bruises as evidence of his abuse at home, we all burst out laughing. The manager smirked and seemed to realize that Burmi would be a faithful and loyal colleague. If you don't dare to go home where could be better than on board a ship?

21

I thought to myself: *My God, guys like Burmi are the just the right types to satisfy demanding guests on cruise liners – a tragicomedy on legs.*

No-one in the hall – except the operation manager – were proven right with regards to Burmi. The boy took advantage of the opportunity to escape his hell on earth. He replaced his large horn-rimmed glasses with contact lens and turned out to be a really good waiter. He talked to his wife on the phone only one more time. I was nearby when he gave her the good advice to go to hell. I could not help but laugh, because the moment he mentioned the word hell, one of my favorite jokes crossed my mind: The story about the Lord of Hell who – accompanied by rumbling and sulfuric stench – enters a church during a mass. Afraid, all believers run into the street – with the exception of a short, wrinkled, old man who remains sitting in the first row, staring at the altar. Hovering towards him, the devil snaps at him: "You there, aren't you afraid of me?" Looking at the devil, the wrinkly man sadly replies: "Afraid of you? Are you joking? I've been married to your mother for thirty years!"

Apart from the fitness test scheduled for the next morning, the tests of the newcomer brigade was completed for this afternoon.

An eventful and strenuous day was behind us, however it was still far from being over …

The lady at the front desk gave us another warm welcome, congratulated us and gave us a few bus tickets to go to the hotel.

Great, I thought, *it's really time for a good dinner and a comfortable bed to stretch out those weary limbs.*

The bus started to move; fifteen minutes later it stopped in Miami Downtown in front of a building with the sign "HO EL".

At that time the company evidently was very young and not yet financially sound so it could not always afford the very best accommodation for its crew. This has, however, changed in the course of time. Nowadays great importance is attached to the employees' board and lodging as only satisfied employees are productive. The lodging house of which I am talking about now was an exception and is in no way representative of the fantastic American hotels and their excellent service well-known from radio and TV.

22

Having entered the "HO EL", we looked around. In addition to numerous crew members also "ordinary" guests were in the lobby. We happily queued in front of the reception desk.

Some minutes later we had checked in, took the lift to go to the third floor, put our suitcases down in the rooms and ran down again. Our stomachs were growling; we were all curious about the variety of meals and drinks offered by the kitchen and waiters of this house.

Shortly after we had sat down on the bare chairs with sparkling eyes, awaiting the food which was to be explained and served to us. A shuffling, bored waiter approached us, put some warped knives and forks, which had been wrapped in paper napkins, on the table and was about to advise us by heart of the chef's recommendations without reading them from a menu. His words were a real blow. "Chicken or pasta?" he asked tiredly. "Chicken or pasta", we replied glassy-eyed, questioningly looking at each other.

"Wow", I said to myself. "That's what I call efficiency." Obviously the chicken and noodles left over from the plane had been collected; and were now being fed to starving waiters.

We looked at the waiter who all of a sudden had a strange smile on his face as if he wanted to say: "I won't have a lot to do today, will I?"

"Okay, what's it to be?" he asked once again. "Chicken or pasta?"

My loose tongue was the first which answered: "Bring us a city map which shows the shortest way to Mc Donald's!"

The guy seemed to be prepared for this request because our wish did not surprise him at all. After he had disappeared in the next room, he returned directly with a photocopied map of the nearby area.

Without speaking, one after the other got up. Fortunately McDonald's was not far away, as Miami is a rather dangerous place in the USA at night time.

McDonald's was of course okay! Hunger is the best chef! Moreover you only had to pay once for the beverages and can swig as much as you want to. As this kind of offer was unimaginable in Europe at that time, it was twice as much fun for us.

Nothing happened during our walk back to the "HO EL"; the mere thought of a comfortable and cozy bed lent us wings.

Upon our arrival at about midnight we were surprised at the numerous guests who were still waiting at the reception to check in. *A popular hotel*, I thought to myself. At this moment I did not know that the lodging house would severely go down in my estimation within the next two hours. I will refer back to this later!

After I had quickly bought a beer from the vending machine which should help me to sleep better, I took a shower in my room. Afterwards I was happily sitting on the edge of my bed and refreshed with the amber nectar in my hand. Duly arrived in the United States of America, a warm welcome, a nice dinner and fast asleep now – it just couldn't have been any better. I expected visions of my new job appearing in my dream; a job for which I had been preparing for many years and of which I was already very proud.

Being at peace with the world and myself, I dozed off ...

At this point I intended not to keep my dear readers in suspense any longer and start reporting of my embarkation; but before that I first have to tell you about another event. It is stuck in my mind and shall be a warning to everybody who likes to choose the cheapest accommodation for their holiday.

I don't know how long I had been sleeping – it couldn't be more than just half an hour when I was awakened by a tickle at my foot. *Oh, very cute!*, I thought, *a baby cockroach on my naked toe!* It was sitting there, playing with its small antennae and staring towards me. I carefully wiped it off with the ankle of my other foot without hurting it; after all these animals also love living. It fell onto the floor and disappeared under the bed. It evidently held my rescue operation against me, because shortly after it showed up again – with support! By the look of it they had to be twin brothers; they bore a striking resemblance to each other. Now I was watched by two cockroaches which evidently enjoyed nibbling at my toe.
All of a sudden I was wide awake because I remembered a biology lesson I had paid attention to instead of practicing my magical tricks.
We were taught by the teacher. "Wherever a cockroach shows up, its brothers and sisters won't be far away. And next to these cavorting brothers and sisters, their watchful parents will also be around."
I carefully lifted the mattress. Voilà – all blood relations of the cockroaches were there! Several parents including their children, uncles, aunts and even the grandparents with their little grand-children were happily running across the cockroach countryside - excuse me! Across the bed linen countryside probably looking for something to eat.
Instead of counting sheep I now counted cockroaches and found a total of sixty-two in and under my bed. There was sufficient food for them. Particularly the old cheese under my bed which had been lying there for at least one year seemed to be a much sought-after delicacy and gave reason to a never ending celebration.
My God!, I thought. I am not very demanding and do not tend to complain. It doesn't bother me, if there is a hair in my soup as long as it's a clean hair! And I am one of those people who only smile if

they are presented a wine glass showing the red pursed lipstick mark of a female guest. This mini-zoo was, however, just a bit too much.

I went back to the corridor and rummaged the box rooms of the evidently underpaid chambermaids and found right away what I was looking for: a large jar with screw-cap for chasing the cockroaches in my room. It took only ten minutes to collect most of these little insects, pile them into the jar and make them as comfortable as possible.

Unfortunately the jar was not large enough to accommodate all these cute little beings!

I put on my clothes and repacked all the things I had just taken out of the suitcases. But not before checking that none of the clever cockroaches had escaped from my trophy collection and tried to nibble at my jelly bears.

Carrying my luggage in my hands and the mini-zoo under my arm, I entered the lift and went down to the lobby. *Fine*, I thought, *there are still quite a lot of guests at the front desk who are trying to book a room for the night. I'd like them to witness this particular drama.*

As I did not intend to stay in this palace for another second, I did not queue, but veeeeeery slowly approached the reception desk step by step, balancing the jar, clearly visible, on the palm of my hand like on a tray.

I could feel that the guests who – being very tired till that moment – had all been looking forward to a bed in an acceptably clean room. But now all tiredness had gone. They started whispering in various familiar and unknown languages, while they curiously turned their heads towards me.

"Are you the manager?" I asked a pot-bellied, bespectacled fat guy behind the front desk.

"Yes, I am – manager and owner", he replied. "What's the matter?"

"It's a matter of check out!" I answered in a loud voice, while I thumped the jar onto the reception desk with a bang. "I check out because my room is already occupied by these ones!" I pointed to the jar where the clearly visible cockroach family enjoyed being stared at by curious and disgusted guests. The manager gaped, lost for words. Beads of sweat got stuck in his bushy eyebrows.

As is proper for a well-behaved gentleman like me, I put my room key on the desk, lifted the jar, turned again to the dear audience and apologized for the interruption. I kindly asked them to continue checking in; as otherwise the cockroaches – being alone in the room – would be bored. In order to add zest, I pretended to drop the jar. An outcry could be heard among the crowd of guests. Everybody was suddenly in a hurry to either return the room key to Porky Pig behind the reception desk or to turn on the heels and immediately leave the " HO EL".

I made use of this hustle and bustle to go outside and get into a taxi. "Where do you want to go to?", the taxi driver asked me. "First of all let's get out of here! Go to a hotel which is not too expensive and free of cockroaches, please!" I determinedly replied. The friendly taxi driver, who to my surprise was actually American, laughed. I told him about what had happened in the HO EL", which made him roar out with laughter.

"Well done", he remarked. "It's about time to teach these hotel dudes a lesson. You are not the only guest who has had such an experience in this building."

He then asked me for the reason of my journey. Upon my answer he nodded approvingly and returned: "Cruise liners, a good working-place in a great atmosphere. I have already cruised twice in the Caribbean and am already planning my next cruise with my family." I was pleased to hear that, as it confirmed to me that I had made the right decision.

Shortly afterwards, he stopped in front of a very good hotel and explained to me that this lodging house was a contracted hotel of the shipping company. Consequently it would be possible to book a room at a quite favorable price upon presentation of the employment contract. He was right: affordable luxuries including breakfast – and without further incidents!

As the night was rather short due to the just described incidents, I was glad that I did not need to show up for the medical test until 10 a.m. the next morning. Moreover my pocket money was running short; it was time to go on board the cruise liner in order to escape from the world where I had to pay everything by myself.

The entire waiter brigade of the previous day were there. A doctor put us through our paces. All of us were handed over a certificate with the comment "healthy" which we had to present to the ship's doctor at the time of embarkation, the so-called "sign on". "A bus will come here at 3.00 pm to take you to the ship!" a female person shouted to our group as she held up a list of employees.

The time had come. Off we went! This was the point of no return! Reverently we boarded the bus; the door closed behind us with a hissing sound. As the bus with its passengers had started moving, we experienced this transfer with mixed feelings and faster beating hearts, while we were pressing our faces at the window panes to catch sight of the luxury liner as early as possible.

Within less than five minutes the bus stopped in front of a snow-white and royal blue cruise liner which was waiting for us and eleven hundred passengers. We were proud of being among the cruise pioneers, although we first had to undergo the American customs and immigration office control procedure. We were to be checked very thoroughly so that nothing forbidden was taken on board.

To prevent boredom the friendly lady with the list of employees distributed a little brochure with some technical details regarding our luxury liner. In addition to length, width, height, motor capacity and further information we were advised of the fact that due to the great popularity of this ship during its first years on the high seas there had been a waiting list of two years for the chance to cruise on this liner.

The company realized that they could be losing a lot of money, unless they took appropriate counteraction. The shipping company was, however, too young to place orders for new ships. Therefore an already existing technology was applied: the ship was put in dry-dock and separated in the middle; a pre-assembled intermediate section comprising of 150 additional cabins was integrated and then all parts assembled again.

The "stretched ship" which originally could accommodate 750 guests, had now been modified and offered cabins for 1100 travelers and the entire crew.

We had just finished reading our brochure, when the friendly lady waved us through the customs and immigration office to let us know that our luggage and passports were in good order and nothing else stood in the way of our embarkation.

Chapter 6: Safety on Board

There we were! Standing in front of our new, floating working-place, we eyed this magnificent vessel up and down. "Hopefully we won't experience the same as the crew on board the Titanic", said a colleague next to me who was thinking aloud. At that time I was too enthusiastic to worry about negative headlines of cruise liners. I, however, have to admit that later on the idea of safety on board an ocean liner occasionally came to my mind, particularly in the event of rough seas and reports about terror attacks.
In this context I would like to refer to two amusing first-hand occurrences at the time of the safety instructions. Please note that our shipping company spares no expense in installing computer-controlled detectors which correspond to the latest state-of-the-art technology. Moreover only professionals with first-class references are employed as safety personnel and door guards to completely ensure the safety of our guests and the crew. Let me tell you about only two instances which happened on the gangway in the course of my longstanding career, which, however, were rather more amusing than threatening.

The people from the Philippines are usually short and fine-boned, hardworking, dutiful and artistically inclined. But these Filipinos, who guarded the gangway that we were just going up, looked as if they had already been in the boxing ring with Mike Tyson. A back like Schwarzenegger during his performing career as movie hero, vice-like hands and a look which would have frightened off a pit bull terrier and induced it to take to its heels! Whenever I pass these well-toned security guards, even nowadays I remember that evening many years ago. About midnight the ship, on which I had been working most of the time during my career, berthed in Playa del Carmen in Mexico. Everything was fine, the sea was smooth and as usual the security guards had taken guard at the foot of the gangway. As only now and then a call with safety instructions was received from the bridge, a quiet evening was expected.
All of a sudden a loud "splash" interrupted the silence and the water in front the ship was disturbed. "A big fish", one of the guards

commented. Upon another "splash" one of his colleagues remarked "Must be a shoal of fish".

Both of them were, however, wrong. Suddenly two heads and two arms appeared at the surface of the water. Two human beings could be seen swimming the crawl with powerful strokes. Fast as lightning they reached the ship and skillfully climbed up the gangway.

There they were: two young, rowdy Mexicans, probably from Acapulco, in underwear and with soaking wet hair. They grinned at the dumbfounded security guards. "That was great!" they cheered in Spanish and ran past the men who still did not know what to say.

"Now let's jump down from the very top, where the captain is!" they shouted as they tried to return to the ship. Too late! After a button had been pressed at the bottom, two doors closed at the top and at the same moment the two little, wet Mexicans were fidgeting in Manolo's arms, the brawniest among the security guards. It was funny to watch them writhing in his grasp without being able to escape.

"Yes" was always my truthful reply to the frequently raised question whether a ship also accommodates a prison – and this place was exactly where our two divers were now being taken. At their sight Wilhelm Busch, the German story teller and poet, might have said: "Transporting them is very hard, towards the officer, passing the guard."

Wrapped in thick woolen blankets, they had to stay in prison, until their furious parents picked them up. The head of the family was recommended to ensure a proper behavior of the little imps for the rest of cruise, as otherwise the stay on board would finish far earlier than scheduled for the entire family. This was one of the two instances I mentioned earlier.

The second event that I still remember vividly, happened on the romantic Mediterranean island Mykonos. Our ship berthed in the small, comfortable harbor; the sun was just setting after a beautiful, cloudless day. Two assistant-waiters, who had been off on that day since lunch time, had passed out on the beach at 40°C after a private boozy session. They only woke up again, when the deafening "TOOOOOT" of the ship ready to leave soon drowned their snoring.

In record time they came running from the beach which was of a distance of about 1 km, hoping the ship's departure would be delayed that time, but all efforts were in vain. Wearing sandals and with sun-burnt faces they were standing in front of the ship, staring at the battened down hatches. It seemed as sure as eggs are eggs that their waiter career would end on the beautiful island of Mykonos!

Two ropes still connecting the ship at the polder with the dock offered them the very last way out and invited the two waiters to a venturesome climbing tour.

Less than two minutes later the duty officer on the bridge caught his breath, when his short telescope presented him a peculiar picture: two extra-large, spidery creatures with bathing sandals and scorched eyebrows slowly, but surely made their way hand over hand up the rope, turning their heads to estimate the distance which still separated them from the ship's rescuing railing.

Both of them were convinced that they were not being observed by anyone in the dusk and really put their backs into it. Another three meters – two meters – just one last meter – "Good evening, gentlemen!", the dull voice of Manolo, the giant Filipino, was heard. "What are you doing there? Practicing for the next Spiderman-movie?"

Frightened to death, both of them looked back to the water and thought about jumping into it; but at the very same time Manolo's vice-like hands had already seized them and lifted them on board. The man, who was usually very friendly, took the two assistant-waiters by the arm and led them to a pile of towels next to the swimming-pool. Both waiters were allowed to choose a towel and put it around the shoulders.

"Congratulations!" Manolo said to them. "You are invited to a private audience with the captain."

Everybody knows that the captain's invitation is generally accepted with pleasure – but not, if you have to show up on the bridge wearing a towel and sandals! As neither tea, coffee, milk nor pastries wered offered to either one of them, it didn't bode very well.

The welcome did not take long; to be more precisely it took thirty seconds.

The captain entered his office, eyed the two gallows birds up and down and showed them a photo of two individuals who were playing like Tarzan at the lianas in the evening sun. "Is that you two?" he asked. "Yes, captain", they replied. "We were climbing there because the door wasn't open, although we had knocked at it several times!" The captain ignored their impudent reply and instantly finished the meeting, saying: "You are fired!" They were not allowed to work again on board the ship; instead they were once again standing on the gangway the next day waiting to go home.

I am frequently asked "Have guests ever missed the ship, because they have enjoyed a shore excursion too much or because they have been stuck in a traffic jam?" My truthful reply is always "This happens now and then". "And what happens to the latecomers in such cases?" "Well, first of all they get themselves all worked up towards the captain who had the cheek to set sail according to schedule instead of waiting for them. Afterwards they call a taxi to either go to the travel agency or directly to the airport, because they have to do their best to catch up with the ship in the next port." "It stands to reason", they confirm nodding. "And afterwards?" "Afterwards", I continue. "Afterwards it will be very expensive. As you know, flight tickets can generally only be bought at favorable prices if you order them some time in advance. If you, however, show up at the airport wanting to be at a certain destination the next day in order to continue a cruise, the cashier will rub his hands together and quote a price which is almost as high as the charter price for a cruise liner. Swearing, the latecomer will take out his credit card to pay the exorbitant price. After the credit card has been swiped, it will be so light that it is almost hovering. Having gained another experience, the latecomer – in a bad mood, but also a bit relieved – will hopefully be at the gangway in time the next morning and request to board."

Dear reader, please always bear in mind that a cruise liner is neither a bus nor a taxi which will wait for you! Arrival and departure times are strictly regulated and need to be followed for financial and of course for safety reasons.

It is important to know that the "zero-tolerance-law" is applicable in addition to numerous rules which the guests and the crew have to respect. Prior to the start of a cruise the employees and passengers will be made familiar with these rules. They simply say: "Behave yourself; otherwise your cruise will be finished at the next harbor!" Nobody – neither guest nor employee – can do what they like. All public facilities are monitored by numerous cameras; moreover a considerable number of safety personnel are on duty round the clock. Once I was involved in an event in which the cruise finished for the guest directly after his first evening. An older British hothead had decided to take his fury out on me and struck me with a napkin, after his travel agency had not been able to reserve the desired table in the restaurant. I think he was living in Australia and as is with several other guests he was not able control himself. Maybe he wouldn't have flipped out so, if he had read the tolerance law. The management was forced to send him out of the dining-room, accompany him to his cabin and monitor him. At this time the man was already very furious, but he went totally berserk the next morning, when he was sent packing and told that he would have to bear all costs including his flight ticket back to Australia by himself.

He raised such a hell at the gangway that he was once again put under lock and key and led off handcuffed. Nobody knows what happened to him afterwards. Hopefully he did not start an argument with the American authorities as in that case his next cruise may not take place before the year 2081.

Chapter 7:   On Board

Let me talk again about my first days on board!
Having passed the security checkpoint, together with the gang of new waiters I went on board the gigantic ship which would turn out to be my second home. We were welcomed by the crew purser – the officer for the employees – and led through various corridors until we had finally reached a staff room. There we received extracts from the "Behave yourself-catalog", the cabin key and a blue-checked small cloth jacket as uniform with a plastic nameplate. My nameplate was labeled: "Johannes – Busboy".
"What's a busboy?", I asked the purser. "This is your job title", he answered. "You will be working as a busboy in the restaurant." I was dumbfounded.
"Why on earth is a busboy employed in the dining-room?" I wondered.
Even my parents were slightly shocked when I went home for the first time during my leave with this job title in my papers. In the first moment they believed that it was my job to offer soft drinks and snacks to the passengers in the bus in which they had been picked up from the airport.
"Don't worry!" the purser laughed. "Busboy is the American term for assistant-waiter."
It took a load off my mind because I had already imagined myself working on the motorway: Wearing the cloth jacket and a silly cap, I would have to distribute sandwiches and coke in a bus during the day and in the evening wearing a blue overall – I would have to scrub the company's vehicles in the yard.
Now it was time to check the cabins.
With a smile on his face which did not please me at all, the purser recommended to us: "Make yourself at home as far as possible."
When we opened the doors to what would be our accommodation for the forthcoming six months, we figured out right away the reason for his smiling face, which spoke louder than words: a small room approx. 5m x 6m in which six male adults should make themselves comfortable (at that time no waitresses were employed). At our disposal were three loft beds for six persons, a small table, two small chairs, at least one wardrobe for each of us and a small

sink. It was only possible to see one side of the face at a time, as the mirror was too small for reflecting both sides in one go.

The little cabinet mounted above the mirror in question was in danger of collapsing after four tooth-brushes had been deposited in it. Furthermore the sign "Shared showers and toilets 30 meters on the right side" did not bode well. It would all take some time to get used to ...

That's the way it was. Still today I reply to the guests' question about the size of my cabin with the following sentence: "If the sun is shining in then I have to get out!"

Considering this barely furnished lodging, its sparkling cleanliness was a comfort to us as the company attached greatest importance to excellent hygienic conditions.

By the way: since the mid-eighties all shipping companies set new benchmarks regarding the crew accommodation. All single and double-berth cabins are equipped as standard with shower, toilet, TV, video system and nowadays also with internet connection. The cabins are still small, but excellent, so that living in them is quite pleasant. Our company's motto is: "Only a satisfied crew is able and willing to deliver first-class performance!" Quite a lot of other companies throughout the world should follow this example.

There was a knock at the door. The friendly purser was standing outside, advising us of good news: Lunch would be served shortly and we were to gather in the canteen to eat and to hold our final meeting before starting work.

There was no need to tell us twice. After we had gone astray several times, which can often drive you crazy in a hull, we finally managed to find the canteen where a really good lunch was served in buffet-style. Those days the food was already great but it is continuously improving still today. It is frequently whispered behind closed doors that the home-style cooking prepared by the numerous exotic chefs in the crew-galley is simple, but quite often more delicious than the food offered to our guests. I, however, do not share this opinion as many of the recipes are not intended for the average eater.

If the chefs are Indian, a fire extinguisher is to be held ready to release your tongue from the pain caused by the hot food. If the chefs are Filipinos, all blood will be absorbed by garlic. If the meal is prepared by a French chef, it will have a promising name, but its portion is so small that it is hardly visible on the plate. If an English chef demonstrates his culinary skills, all food will taste the same.

The main point was that the crew could always eat a large piece of bread after a hard working day or a hard night shift, which we also did at that moment to give ourselves a great start for the first appearance in the smart restaurant.

Afterwards a very intense and interesting meeting took place which was headed by the purser. "As soon as we leave the port, your life starts to get serious, guys", he explained to us. "Your job is simple: None of the guests' wishes will remain unfulfilled. Although it sounds easy, it is difficult. Only the best of you will keep a stiff upper lip and earn a lot of money."

Feeling intimated, I swallowed hard. My colleagues evidently felt the same way in view of such encouraging forecast. All of us stared at Burmi who was sitting apart and cleaning his horn-rimmed glasses.

He will probably be the first who has to go home, we all thought, but none of us had assessed him correctly. In particular he proved to be much-loved and very popular with the guests and the crew due to his excellent work and stayed with the company for 15 years.

In order to get to know each other, to enhance the prestige of our team and at the same time to teach us respect towards the superiors, after the meeting we shortly came into contact with the highest ranking officers of the ship who introduced themselves one after the other. First of all the "food & beverage" manager, followed by the hotel manager, the "staff captain" (captain's deputy) and – last but not least – the captain himself did us the honor. He looked exactly as you imagine a captain to look: tall, very neat and smartly dressed, with a white beard and a soft voice with a Norwegian accent.

He told us about his life, made us familiar with the safety arrangements of the ship, explained to us once more what was allowed and forbidden on board und wished us all the best for the

39

forthcoming contract period so that all our dreams would come true in the future.

"Phooey, … dreams, what's that?", one of my roommates, a grumpy Italian called Enzo, grumbled, while all of us got ready for the shift. "This job doesn't grant you much time for dreaming. Maybe you get nightmares, but nothing else!"

"Um", I replied. "What about the money? Is it true what the manager told us upstairs?" "That may very well be, but not necessarily", Enzo muttered, while he shaved his face with the razor blade. "It depends on you. If you do a good job and the guests like you, you'll line your pockets. If, however, you do a bad job, you will be flying back home in next to no time!"

I swallowed again. Knowing that I had neither done an apprenticeship nor gathered a lot of experience – except the course at the hotel management school and my brief spell at the Hilton hotel – combined with my funny character and my loose tongue, made me nervous. Nevertheless I was highly motivated and willing to do my utmost.

5.00 p.m., another 1.5 hours till the countdown. Last self-inspection. Shaved? Check: shoes cleaned? Check: fingernails filed? Check: hair done? Check: everything okay? Let's go to the restaurant!

Once again we went astray in the corridors until we nervously entered the lift to the dining-room.

The lift first stopped in the galley where numerous chefs of various nationalities prepared   dinner   for 1100 guests under the direction of head chef Helmut from Austria and the sous-chef Kirk Patrick.

It was a great sight: everybody was at their posts and fulfilling the particular task which had been allocated to them.

"I see, the newcomers!" an Indonesian chef shouted and friendly waved to us with his scoop. "Welcome to the world of never ending work and few breaks!"

Trying to ignore his comment, we headed for the dining-room around the corner. There was a hustle and bustle with dozens of waiters and assistant-waiters who were busy laying the plates for the dinner. While helpers in different uniforms were carrying soups and appetizers to the buffet, others were listening to the instructions from a maître d' who obviously was in charge of coordinating all the work. The entire scenario was similar to the well-known anthill in which everybody has his specific job to do.

An English head waiter called Michael spotted his rookies and approached us at a smart pace.

"You're the new guys?" he asked in a rough voice. We nodded dutifully and answered in the affirmative. "Okay!", he replied. "Go to the office! The maître d'or is waiting for you."

As the office was small, we all had to stand close to fit in.

There he was – our boss, teacher, lawyer, minister and big brother all in one: maître d'or Mr. Tevser from Turkey, one of the shipping company's most splendid managers. It was impossible to pull the wool over this man's eyes with his photographic memory, his incredible powers of recollection and his phenomenal knowledge of human nature. He spoke to us in a low voice; his words were well-considered, formidable and indicated great competence.

Having welcomed us, he explained the work proceeding and work routing in the restaurant and asked us afterwards to take a seat at a table outside. We did as we were told and noticed a quick wave of Mr. Tever's hand towards a head waiter. Within five minutes all head waiters were gathered at our table to give us another warm welcome.

"They are your immediate superiors whom you have to obey in all respects", Mr. Tevser advised us.

"The word of these gentlemen is law. Do a good job so that no problems occur!" and with these words, the maître d'or returned to his office.

The head waiters read our names from a list to make sure that nobody was missing.

"Gentlemen", the Italian Adriano, the direct assistant of the maître d' continued, "I will now announce the numbers of the tables for which you – together with the allocated waiter – will be responsible for in the next week." His voice was rough, but cordial; he further explained: "In order to avoid difficulties and mishaps in serving, you will only practice this week by waiting on selected employees who are entitled to enjoy the same service in the dining-room as the guests. At these tables you have the possibility to demonstrate your skills without the guests breathing down your neck."

Our group took a deep breath; all of us were obviously relieved.

41

"Just a moment, please", the head waiter Adriano eyed me. "Are you Johannes from Germany?" Slightly concerned, I answered in the affirmative. "Happy birthday! We already need you today for the guests at table 18. This small group from Germany wishes to have a German speaking waiter – and you are the only one. Come on then!"

This announcement made me break out in sweat and my hands started trembling slightly. Having pity on me, my colleagues smiled at me and disappeared towards the staff station with a grin on their faces.

"Don't panic!" Adriano comforted me. "The most experienced busboy will now brief you with a short training so that everything will work like a charm. Always bear in mind that you are the only newcomer who is allowed to wait on guests directly this week and therefore has a chance to make good money, while your colleagues will only be earning low wages without any tips for their work."

His encouraging words did not help a lot at this moment. Considering the fact that the restaurant would open in only 20 minutes I wondered which kind of training I could do.

Dolphin, a slightly older busboy who – carrying a tray on his shoulder – had already covered several thousands of kilometers in various restaurants throughout the world and for this reason came scurrying over with a stoop. He evidently was not very pleased to have to teach me service practice on a cruise liner at the very last minute and therefore focused on the most essential explanations.

"Here are your breadbaskets, your dressing bowls and over there your dressing spoons", he instructed me grumpily. "You will find the glasses somewhere in the galley next to the coke vending machine; the cups for serving the coffee are still in the dish-washer. Good luck!" The training was herewith finished.

Perfect instructions!, I thought to myself. *This is a restaurant where you can learn a lot and where you are given a first-class helping hand! Okay then, let's start!*

Shortly afterwards, and in my opinion far too early, the doors of the restaurant were opened. Hordes of guests were rolling in like an avalanche in search of their tables while some of them were flailing their arms and arguing vigorously. It was incredible to witness how hungry people behave. Within less than ten minutes they had all taken their seats and were waiting, holding knife and fork in their hands.

Also my tables – not only one! – were occupied by hungry guests in less to no time. Their stomachs were grumbling as they had not eaten anything since the lunch buffet three hours ago.

My "station" comprised of two tables with eight guests each. At the left side American guests sat down, while German guests graced us with their presence on the right side.

Looking around, I realized within a short time that 95% of our passengers originated from the United States and there were only a few guests from other countries. There were some English on board who – behind the Americans – rank second among the nations addicted to cruises. Also participating in this cruise were some Canadians, quite a lot of Norwegians and the Germans at the already mentioned table, who I was allowed to wait on due to my mother tongue.

At that moment I experienced true American friendliness for the first time. While there was polite and expectant silence at the German table, the Americans had again jumped up from their seats to shake hands in all directions and introduce themselves by announcing their names and home countries.

I had never seen anything like this before and was surprised when a gentleman turned to me as well, shook my hand and shouted: "You must be our waiter – what's your name and where do you come from?" "Johannes", I replied with hesitation, "I was born in Bolivia, my father is German, my mother Bolivian, my girl-friend Russian and now I am in the United States of America. I am your busboy."

My introduction was followed by astonishment and the hearty laughing of the gentleman and the other guests at the table, a warm welcome which meant the world to me in this moment. Feeling relieved, I laughed with them. "Really nice to meet you", the American continued. "May I have a glass of water?" Before I could give an answer, I felt a heavy hand on my shoulder. It was Enzo, my waiter and roommate, who pushed himself to the fore, introduced me once again and explained the service procedure. Afterwards he gently pulled me to the table of our German guests and whispered: "Come on, introduce us to them and explain to them how we work here! I don't speak German!"

The guy has some nerve!, I thought after having been in the restaurant for half an hour, he wanted me to stand in for him. Before I had to show my ignorance, I was interrupted by one of the German gentlemen and with a wave of his hand he said with a smile "We speak English, your waiter can explain everything to us."
Being a bit relieved, I – smirking – generously waved my hand and let Enzo go first. I noticed that Enzo hated nothing as much as losing time at the workplace. His guests had to brace themselves for service at speed and with the precision of a Ferrari. "Water and bread for all guests!" he hissed at me, before he turned to the guests to take the orders. "Water and bread?" I repeated, looking around. Where to find it? The good, old Dolphin had in fact not shown anything to me.
"Do you need help?" I heard a voice behind me. Turning around, I looked into the friendly looking face of an Indian busboy with a thick hammer nose. His name was Harry. He told me to follow him. "Come on, I'll show you what you have to do", he said and shook his head in the typical Indian manner. I was very pleased to make use of his willingness to help me, as I still had no idea what I had to do. Enzo did not help me a lot – or to be honest – he did not help me at all, because he was far too busy talking to the guests and gaping at the ample bosom of a pretty woman at the German table. *Italian through and through,* I thought, *always focusing on the most essential.*
Harry led me to the galley and taught me how to prepare the bread, iced water, iced tea and dressings and how to convince the coke-vending machine to spit out its valuable contents without any resistance. After some further good advice he sent me back to my station in the restaurant.
It was high time to finally start contributing to the service. Enzo had meanwhile stopped dreaming of bosoms. He had been brought back to earth and – looking rather grumpy – was busy taking care of his guests.
"I give you five minutes to serve the water, bread and the dressing!" he snarled at me in Italian hoping that I – contrary to the guests – would understand him. Arguing in front of passengers never goes down well and indicates disharmony in the service area. Enzo

gawked flabbergasted, when I came back at him in quite good Italian, which he had not expected at all!

I, however, was happy that my studies under the school-desk had already proven to be useful, if only for cutting a waiter down to size.

But now we jointly focused on the service without any further superfluous words or interruptions, as a great deal was demanded of us.

Enzo was an incredibly fast waiter without making mistakes and talking a lot so that I struggled to keep up with my tasks. There was simply too much new things to learn and digest.

Water – for example – is a major aspect in the American service. Everywhere in the United States and in all American restaurants – no matter whether they are expensive or low-priced – the waiter first of all introduces himself to the guest by name and afterwards serves him a glass of iced water. Without being specially requested by the customer, this water is refilled again and again so that you never eat without drinking. The same applies to coffee. The American likes drinking coffee not only in the morning while having breakfast, but frequently also has a nice cup of coffee for lunch or dinner. It's quite interesting to watch an American enjoying a filet steak with mushroom sauce and sipping his cup of coffee at the same time.

The most popular beverage in the United States of America, no matter whether it is for breakfast, lunch or supper, however, is iced tea which – either sweetened or unsweetened – is a must for every meal. All waiters on a ship with American guests always have a carafe filled with this refreshing soft drink at hand in their stations.

A further important difference between American and European drinking habits is the attitude towards the respective drinking vessel and its contents. In Europe – for example – you pay an average of two Euros for a cup of coffee and only order the next cup, if you need more caffeine and can afford the additional expenditure.

In the United States of America you pay approximately one dollar for a cup of coffee; all other non-alcoholic drinks are only slightly more expensive. Compared with the European attitude towards the filling level of a drinking vessel the subtle difference is the following: in the United States of America a glass or cup once or

45

twice raised to the mouth for sipping is considered empty and must be refilled by the waiter right away. Any other behavior is an example of bad service.

It took an entire evening until I had realized it. As the saying is: "When in Rome, do as the Romans do."

All tourists going to the United States of America will like the service of low price and large quantities, as the slogan "Think big" is still valid for the food!

With these new experiences in mind, the first evening in the service area was quite harmonious. I got great praise from the guests who evidently had become aware of me being a newcomer without a lot of experience.

"How long have you been working with this company?" one of the German guests asked. "Two days including tomorrow!" I truthfully replied, and even on this day the answer was rewarded with laughter. More and more I got the feeling that I was working in the right place. Of course I did not know at all what would happen in the future, but at that moment I felt generously rewarded for my courage and preparations.

The current feeling of happiness, however, did not last long because my waiter Enzo suddenly approached with eighteen – I re-counted them indeed, eighteen main courses with plastic covers which he, slightly teetering, seemed to carry around on his shoulder quite easily. Without grimacing his face with exertion, he put them down in the station. "These plates must be made of a very light material", I assumed and had to satisfy my curiosity immediately. I wanted to know what was going on.

The moment was opportune as Enzo was busy taking away the superfluous silverware from his tables. I asked him whether he would mind if I tried to lift this tray. "Go ahead, little Hercules!", he encouraged me with a wave of his hands and a smile which made me anxious rather than happy. I placed my hand under the tray, seized it with my left hand, slightly bent my knees and ... and ... I was very embarrassed ... ! I didn't even manage to lift the stack ten centimeters. Being frustrated and with a face reddened by exertion, I put the shaking matter down again.

46

"Ladies and Gentlemen", Enzo shouted, drawing his guests' attention to my efforts, "may I introduce to you the German Hercules?"

Everybody laughed, which slightly cheered me up. But deep inside I was now a bit afraid of the job. At that time my body weight was unfortunately only 95 kilos so that I was nicknamed "Toothpick". The idea that my weak muscles would never enable me to carry around such stacks on my shoulder crossed my mind.

Then Johannes, the toothpick, was jolted out of his thoughts and instructed by the waiter to help him serve the main courses.

Doing quite a good job, I forgot the gigantic stack of plates and my fine-boned build which would never be suitable for weightlifting.

"What's the matter? You were impressed by the few plates I have just carried in?" Enzo asked me shortly after. "That's no big deal at all. Have a look at the station over there with the three tables in the corner. Our champion is responsible for them. By the way – there he is coming with his main courses. Go there and count them!"

I needn't go there; Omar, the Turkish waiter, was seen from afar. As it was clearly visible from the distance, he cheerfully headed for his station with four stacks comprising six main courses each – in other words with twenty-four plates – on his shoulder which he put down in front of his guests without any great effort. Some passengers were so enthusiastic that they videotaped the "coup de main", while Omar was walking through the restaurant with his stack on his shoulder. I had never seen anything comparable in a restaurant before.

The world collapsed in me. I could not believe at all what I had just seen. "I will never be able to handle it; after all I am not Hulk Hogan", I mumbled to myself. "I'll never make it!"

"Only focus on your job!" I heard a voice behind me. It was my head waiter who had realized the pure horror in my eyes at the sight of the leaning tower of Pisa which should have been in Italy instead of on a waiter's shoulder. According to Adriano "Your body will change in the course of time and automatically adjust to this hard work. We, the management members, will never allocate a station to you which does not correspond to your power. Therefore stop comparing yourself with waiters who have been working in this job for many years. They don't serve as a rule."

47

These words were very helpful to me. I regained my peace of mind, suppressed all negative thoughts and thanked Adriano. It was a great feeling to be encouraged and helped in return for my efforts to do a good job.

My bad mood disappeared once for all, when I was asked by my waiter what I would like to eat after I had done my job. Enzo explained to me: "Just like the guests, the restaurant staff are allowed to select a lot of food from the menu and eat it at the end of our working day. Only lobster, large prawns and filet Mignon are reserved for the guests." "Never mind", I replied, "who wants to eat lobster every day?"

This was really great! After the tables had been laid for the midnight buffet, we were sitting in a corner of the restaurant, chatting, getting to know each other and enjoying the same delicacies as the passengers. Although the food was not freshly cooked, but microwaved, it still tasted fantastic.

The Indian busboy Harry, who had been kind enough to give me a helping hand, had also sat down at the table and crunched his Indian rice with spicy sauce, pita bread and vegetables prepared by one of our numerous Indian chefs. While he enjoyed eating with his fingers, he told me about his life on the high seas. He had already been on board for two years and pointed out to me the importance of closely cooperating on a ship. I fully agreed with his explanations and was happy to have a colleague who would allow me to join his team. Only later would I experience his understanding of teamwork.....

"Where are we going?" I asked Toni, an Irish waiter. Giddy with excitement I had not raised this question till that moment. All of a sudden I became aware of the fact that a guest, who could not remember the exact travel route, might address me and expect precise information. "To Cozumel in Mexico", Toni replied. "Afterwards to the Caribbean islands Jamaica und Barbados, then we'll pass the Panama Canal and last, but not least we'll go to the Cayman Islands. Before we arrive again in Miami, we will spend a few days on the high seas. Tomorrow we will travel across the Atlantic Ocean so that the passengers can acclimatize and recover from the stress of doing nothing."

This all sounded brilliant. I was totally happy and as proud as Punch to be allowed to contribute to making our passengers' holiday an unforgettable experience by serving them delicious meals. Having a job in which I could not only visit the most magnificent places of the world, but also fill my empty wallet with money, was probably the most wonderful idea I had ever had to date. For this reason I vowed to myself to make the best of it …

I went outside on the crew's own deck. It was a starry night and I was looking for the Southern Cross in the night sky which I had read about in my faraway home. The ship was pitching, while the sea was rushing due to the rotating propellers. Compared with the gigantic diesel engines and gas turbines which are nowadays used to drive our huge ships, the small motor at that time originated from the Stone Age. At least it was humming and loud enough to greatly impress me in those days.

Looking up, I recognized some night owls who were walking across the upper decks with their cocktails in their hands. Just like me, they enjoyed the warm Caribbean air. Suddenly I became aware of the fact that I had not as yet seen anything of the interior of our cruise liner – except for the dining-hall. I decided to inspect the ship in detail in the next harbor. Right – I was looking forward to a long, interesting walking-tour to get to know everything.

I felt so good with myself and the world around me that I had not realized how quickly the time had passed. At 7:30 a.m. breakfast would have to be served and I wanted to be among the first in the restaurant. Therefore I hurried to our cabin, set the alarm to 6:00 a.m. and switched off the light. Even the snoring of my three roommates wouldn't prevent my deep sleep now. Having thrown a last glance at the clock that showed 2:00 a.m., I had already fallen asleep.

It seemed to me as if I had shut my eyes only for a short while, but the alarm signal told its own story: 6.00 a.m., time to get up and get ready for the day! My fellow lodgers didn't spare a thought of getting up so early; the daily program was already a matter of routine for them, which allowed them to stay in bed as long as possible.

I jumped down from my top bunk bed and – bang!!!
I crashed into a cabinet with a hard blow.

My room-mates immediately woke up and looked to see if I was okay. "Take it easy!" one of them dozily coughed. "Remember you are no longer on dry land; and this nutshell is pitching up and down quite heavily."

When one was right, one was right. In fact, in the early hours the ship had turned from the yesterday's smooth, hotel-like building to a game ball for the sea god Neptune. Although it is amusing reading it, a physical disaster seemed to be looming.

Feeling totally giddy, I staggered towards the shower cubicles hoping that the clear, alternately hot and cold water would improve my poor state of health. No chance! I continued feeling sick, which then even worsened.

"Terrific!" I said to myself. "You are quite seasick." What next? It was impossible to report sick on the first morning. My manager would laugh at me. I felt lousy not only because of my seasickness, but also because of the unnerving crew's comments. The others had meanwhile got up and of course realized what the matter with me was.

"Ah well, look at you!" said the first. "You have a face like a Swiss cheese!" "A very good morning!" this was the second's voice. "How are you on the seven seas?" Both were topped by the third: "For breakfast I recommend pickled herring from yesterday's buffet with honey!" he cheerfully shouted from his cabin. Talking like this was a fatal error on his part: due to his recommendation, I instantly puked the herring and yesterday's leftover food precisely at his feet. The sneering disappeared from his ugly face, but he was helpless. It was his fault to have wormed the fish of the evening buffet out of my body with his comments. Now he stared at the pool of vomit on his carpet; the idea of having to clean up the mess obviously did not please him at all.

Once again I staggered towards the shower cubicle where I stayed for the next twenty minutes. Thank God, I was a little bit better, but still not fine. With a towel wrapped around my hips and bathing slippers on my feet, I returned to the cabin making a detour to first pay a short visit to my tormentor with his superfluous comments.

I could hear them, which means him and his roommates swearing from afar. Evidently all of them had witnessed from their beds what had happened.

50

"Any progress in that cleaning?" I asked with interest. "May I bring you another bucket of water? I also have some good perfume in the cabin which I can lend you." Eying me with bloodshot eyes, my tormentor pretended throwing the vomit-soaked cloth towards me.

"The next time you should think first before making comments to a seasick person!" I mentioned and let the cleaning squad continue working on the carpet.

As soon as I had returned to my cabin, staggering, I put on my uniform, while the ship continued pitching up and down. Ignoring the queasy feeling in my stomach, I put on my friendliest smile and went upstairs to the restaurant.

Many busboys were already busy laying the tables for the breakfast. When I searched for the other newcomers I was advised that two of them couldn't get up due to severe sea-sickness. *Chalk up one for me!* I thought, but the ship did not stop bobbing up and down.

Note for all those who are already seasick while reading this: The technology of side stabilizers for cruise liners which keep the ship balanced in heavy seas wasn't yet sophisticated in those days. Consequently sensitive people were at the mercy of the sea and frequently suffered from dizziness and nausea. Thanks to the laterally extracted and retracted stabilizers a modern ship nowadays ploughs through heavy seas without any significant motion, which enhances the comfort for everybody on board.

Feeling miserable again, I was now standing in the galley and desperately trying to contribute to the breakfast service by filling little bowls with heaps of butter and jam so that they could be collected by another colleague and placed on the tables in the restaurant.

Bravely fighting against my weaker self, I tried to think straight. I didn't want the manager to see me in this way. I neither could nor wanted to pass out.

But it didn't help at all. All of a sudden I was overwhelmed by the wretchedness at full force and had only one thing in mind: "Get out of here!"

Thank God I already knew the door to the weather deck and was outdoors after two or three giant leaps.

51

While the last remainders of my stomach contents poured out into the sea, I clutched at the railing to prevent my body being washed overboard in addition to my vomit – environmental pollution en masse!

Crouching down in a corner of the promenade like a picture of misery, all I wanted to do was die.

An older gentleman – evidently a pensioner with the experience of at least fifty cruises – was easily jogging around in a tracksuit and as he saw me he stopped right in front of me. "Seasick?", he asked. I nodded silently. "Do you know why the ship is pitching up and down so severely?" he continued asking. "Why so?" I replied with difficulty. "Is there any other reason beside the rough sea?"

"Of course!", he answered mischievously. "There are too many honeymooners on board, that's why the ship is bobbing up and down." Laughing at his joke, he left me behind on the deck and continued jogging.

I forced myself to smile, but I liked this explanation. To this day I still use it to make guests laugh who aren't feeling very well, although it's not always a success.

The door opened and my head waiter appeared. He had been looking for me, but sympathized with me and gave me two pills and a glass of water. Furthermore he recommended that I fill my stomach with light fare, as soon as I felt better. "A full stomach and a can of Sprite or Ginger Ale are the best remedy for seasickness", he explained to me. "A full stomach is important for your general well-being, while the carbonic acid in the soft drinks stabilizes your sense of balance." Keeping this advice in mind, I have never been seasick again.

By order of the head waiter I took the pills and lay down. The pills took effect and only half an hour later I was my old self again. Stopping in the canteen for a moment, I had two bananas so that my stomach could report "feeling fine" to my brain. Shortly afterwards I patted my waiter on the back. Enzo had been at work already for long and was quite happy to see me. He was worried that he would be the only waiter for the fully occupied station. Ensuring a good service, however, always required two waiters…

We were lucky: only the table with the Americans was occupied. The German guests either needed more sleep or preferred the buffet at the swimming-pool upstairs.

I was cordially welcomed at the table. They wanted to know whether I was fine again and whether I had been a victim of the rough seas for the first time. Encouraged by these well-meant words, I started to thank them by serving them with particular zeal.

Serving the breakfast particularly to Americans, I considered as the next challenge. Utmost concentration was required.

Contrary to the German breakfast which consists of rolls with jam and a boiled egg, the Americans feasted in the lap of luxury: pancakes with fruit, eggs "Benedict" for the ravenous, cold salmon, hot herring, cold and hot cereal, oven-fresh pastries and omelets with various sweet or savory fillings. To complete all these delicacies I poured fresh coffee, tea or hot chocolate and served exotic juices, which made the guests forget the rough sea.

While serving these treats, my mouth was watering. After all I knew quite well that we – the waiters – were allowed to try all these dainties after work. *Well*, I thought to myself, *thanks to this selection I will grow big and strong and will soon be able to carry the same heavy stacks of plates like all the other waiters.*

In the course of time more and more German guests sat down at the table. Surprised at the wide variety of food on the menu, they raised the slightly confusing question: "What do you recommend, please?" Although I had seen all these delicacies only fifteen minutes before for the very first time, I painted a rosy picture of them. Consequently also the German guests ordered a lot and dug in. Enzo, the waiter, threw a few grumpy looks at me, as he had to go to the galley repeatedly to bring in supplies. But I didn't care. In this moment it was quite clear to me why the pop band "Supertramp" had entitled its most successful album "Breakfast in America". The table with all the treats looked appealing and welcoming and all guests enjoyed the meal.

That morning I unfortunately did not have a chance to eat much as the break between the second breakfast session and the first lunch session was only thirty minutes. I did not like the thought of not being able to try at least one of these treats and therefore hurried into the already closed galley. I told the chefs that a guest had

53

arrived late and had ordered French toast with fried potatoes and bacon. Although I was not sure if the chefs had believed me, I got what I asked for.

The gentlemen in the galley knew of course that the guests had to be satisfied – and strictly speaking – I was a guest as well. I was a guest in the United States of America, the headquarters of my company, and a guest in Mexico, our actual destination. Therefore I too was entitled to satisfaction.

Having thanked the gentlemen in their white aprons, I disappeared with my prey to a corner of the dining-room. The French toast with bacon and maple syrup was excellent! I told myself I would serve this specialty to my family in Germany during my first home leave.

Chapter 8:   About Harry, Heroes and Lobster

The break was over within next to no time; now it was time for moving chairs. "Hey, partner!", I heard the voice of the hammer nose – the Indian Harry – who I remembered as helpful guy. "Nice to welcome you again in the restaurant!", he shouted cheerfully. I was also happy to see him. Being called "partner" by him made me proud – at least at this moment ...

Work started. The lunch was served in buffet-style and had to be prepared accordingly. To make way for the buffet, everyone was allocated a number of chairs, which had to be moved to various spots in the restaurant. Everyone was responsible for moving and correctly placing about 30 chairs each.

Panting, moving and carrying the rather heavy seats, I started transporting them to the respective place.

About ten minutes later, when I had already transported approximately ten chairs, I tried to find an explanation for twenty-five chairs still being at their original place in my station. *That's an odd thing*, I thought, *maybe I have miscounted. Whatever, keep going.* After I had moved another ten chairs, I recounted. Thirty minus twenty equals ten according to Cocker, which was also confirmed by my calculator. Nevertheless twenty of these damn chairs were still at their original place pretending to have never been moved.

As everybody was sweating and busy preparing his station for the buffet, my colleagues only had time for a shrug.

"Why do you work so slowly?" I was chided by the head waiter. "Chairs too heavy?" *My first ticking-off*, I thought, *very embarrassing.* To make up for the lost time and to be eventually finished with this work, I now carried two chairs in one go. This time I did not forget to turn around and: Bingo! As quick as lightning, hammer nose Harry came out of nowhere and moved two chairs from his station into mine instead of carrying them to the defined place which was further away. Now I realized to whom I owed the head waiter's ticking-off.

When Harry became aware of having been caught during his bustling, he cheerfully shouted: "Such team work is a great thing, isn't it?"

I would have liked give him a kick in the backside, but I controlled my temper and only replied: "Yeah, you're right, it's perfect! If more people like you were living on earth, world peace would be foregone conclusion!" Shaking his head, Harry nodded with a smile. He obviously had interpreted my sarcasm as compliment – the rat!

Less than two hours had passed since breakfast when the doors of the restaurant were opened again for lunch.

The guests were rushing in as if they had reached the saving oasis after they had been wandering in the wilderness for weeks. The buffet was immediately overcrowded.

It was my job to help those guests carrying their plates which had been packed so full that they couldn't be carried by the guests themselves. In addition to this assistance I accompanied the guests to their table which a head waiter had allocated to me. It worked quite well. We, the busboys, led the guests to the tables, and the waiters served non-alcoholic beverages, wine and other spirits.

Within half an hour the dining-room was so full of people that further guests had to queue up in front of the door. Well, that's what you get if you are silly enough to stay away from the restaurant for more than two hours after breakfast. In this case you have no option but to hope for a full guest being able to get up and make room for a waiting guest. There were hardly any problems or complaints because queuing up and waiting patiently is common in the United States of America and Great Britain. In most top-restaurants in the USA you first have to wait in a lounge or at the bar, until a manager or head waiter is gracious enough to signal by waving his hand that it is your turn to spend a lot of money in the respective restaurant. Sometime later I myself had been queuing up for two hours to try the most famous USA roast chicken in the "Knottsberry Farm" restaurant in the Californian Disney Park. Of course I did not queue up myself; instead I sent my wife who was extremely crazy about this roasted bird. I, however, enjoyed taking a ride on the Ferris wheel, the ghost trains and rollercoasters until my better half signaled from afar that it was our turn to enter the restaurant.

The chicken was very delicious, but our buffet in the restaurant "Zauberflöte" on board the ship was a bit of all right as well. In addition to the wide selection of cold and hot meals, salads with dressings, of which I had never heard of before, various pasta dishes were prepared by three head waiters on their mobile flambé-tables. A delicate scent of garlic filled the entire dining-room, spreading throughout the ship it lured the guests into the restaurant. The waiters were standing around the busy head waiters to have the plates filled, which they afterwards served to their guests either as first or main course.

It was not surprising that this appetizing smell continuously drew large crowds of hungry guests. Sometimes the last guests in the queue even had to wait in the casino which was adjacent to the restaurant. Now and then they inserted a few coins into the one-armed bandit either to fight boredom or to hope for winnings which would allow them to complete the selected menu with a particularly precious juice of the grape.

Enjoying the hustle and bustle in the restaurant, I was once again very proud of being a small part of this properly functioning service procedure.

Even the maître d'or forced himself to leave his office and watched the "operation lunch buffet" like a hawk. He gave instructions to his head waiters and during his round he made time for all new waiters who were busy with the buffet. Coming up to me, he asked after my well-being. Except for having been seasick for two hours I was full of praise and happy to be told that I could always contact him in case of problems. "Do your utmost!" he said to me. "This is a hard, but also highly satisfying job which can enhance your career. But above all – and always bear it in mind – stay away from the casinos! There are waiters working on board our ship who have been hoping for the big win for years and to-date still have not been successful. They have neither a house, a reasonable car nor a considerable bank deposit to call their own. Don't forget, steer clear of the gambling dens!" At first I did not get the meaning of these words, because there were no casinos on the islands we were heading for. At home I had been in such gambling dens only very few times due to lack of money. At a later occasion I would, however, remember quite well these words of my boss …

For now I was glad that the boss of the restaurant had exchanged a few positive and friendly words with me and again focused on my work.

One of the head waiters released me from the job of carrying the guests' heavy plates with food to their tables and instead made me responsible for one of the salad buffets.

What I had to do now was quite simple. I had to carry prepared salads in large ceramic bowls from the galley to the buffet, return the empty bowls after lunch time, wash them up and put them back onto the shelves.

Of course I was most eager and thus brought numerous large bowls to the buffet so that the guests could choose from a great variety of salads and would never find empty bowls.

While I was bustling around, time flew. Lunch was over and I started removing and clearing up the buffet. Twenty-one heavy ceramic bowls had accumulated and were now waiting to be returned to the galley, cleaned and put away.

Damn, they were really heavy, which I had not realized on my way to the buffet. Nevertheless I lugged them – at first only one, later two bowls at one go and always bearing in mind that this exercise would be helpful to increase my muscle size.

I recounted. As eleven bowls were again back on the shelves, nine bowls were still missing.

It was as if I was struck by lightning when I returned to the buffet station, because I could not believe what I saw. As if by magic sixteen salad bowls were smilingly waiting there to be returned to the galley.

"Harry, the hammer nose!", I cursed. "Only he would be so bold!"

The other buffet, where Harry was just cleaning the floor and cheerfully whistling, was only forty meters away. "Hey, partner!", he once again shouted when he noticed me. "I thought you might need some more salad so that your guests will have enough to eat. Don't forget – I am your partner and ..." "Who needs enemies with friends like you!", I ranted at him. "That's the last time that you deposit your stuff on my station only because of you being evidently too weak to go into the galley. I will ignore it this time because you've helped me. Should you, however, try again to force your donkey work on me, you will be for the high jump!"

This was the end of our small-talk and "The crafty Harry" with his distinct sense of teamwork, had to collect and dispose of his salads on his own. While he was carrying the bowls, his unhappiness at

my not appreciating his friendly way of cooperation could be easily read from his face
Moreover it was evident that his brain was quite fried from hatching a dirty trick. This didn't bother me a lot as I was no body's fool, I had learnt a lot during my military service.

Note: Harry is only one of the most peculiar waiter characters described in this book and just a foretaste of other bizarre guys I had the pleasure to work with throughout my career. I will tell you about them later.

After the dining-room had finally been cleaned and emptied, the brigade of waiters spent the two-hour break till dinner either in the sunshine on the crew deck or in bed in the dark cabin. Everybody rested in one way or another to charge up his batteries for the next stressful dinner.
I decided to use the break for both options. Walking on deck in the sunshine and sea-breeze would do me good and sleeping afterwards for an hour would give me the required energy for the evening.
I looked for a crew lift as only the passengers were allowed to use the normal lifts.
I headed for the pool deck to catch some sunshine and to watch the bustling crowds of people in bikinis and bathing trunks. After I had pressed button number 8, the lift started to move.

Note: Nowadays you have to go to the fourteenth, fifteenth or sixteenth floor, if you want to pay a visit to the pool deck of our mega-cruise liners. Activities such as swimming competitions, mini golf, basketball, table-tennis and climbing at climbing walls take place so high above the sea that the company thinks about offering skydiving to fearless guests. Upon payment of a moderate extra fee you can even borrow a parachute which is guaranteed to open. If you do not want to pay this extra fee, your motto should be: "No risk, no fun!"
Dear reader, be assured that this was a joke. The shipping company would never offer any activities which jeopardize the passengers' health and well-being.

I started sweating when wearing my woolen jacket and cloth pants I was on the pool deck for the first time to see what was happening there.

A jolly and cheerful atmosphere was prevailing. As it is typical of an outdoor swimming pool, people were running around half-naked, lolled on their sunbeds or enjoying a cocktail at the bar.

"One day I will go on such a journey with the family", I told myself. "Everything looks great; and you never have to go far to do what you would like to. The refreshing pool here, bars and lounges everywhere, the casino three floors down and always the possibility to return to the cabin to take a rest from the stress of a cruise."

But for the time being there was no talk of resting. A lot was going on around the pool. It seemed as if almost all thousand guests were there in order not to miss one of the funny moments in which the passengers forgot their everyday life and dignity to make fool of themselves.

One of these ludicrous activities seemed to be in full swing at that moment: amid applause and jubilation of the crowd a dozen gentlemen in swimming-trunks walked out of the changing cubicle and headed for the swimming-pool. Yelling was heard over the hand loudspeaker, when the cruise director, who organizes all activities and shows on a ship and is thus quite similar to a circus director, presented the wild, marching horde to the amused audience and gave instructions in a deafening manner.

The group had to line up at the edge of the swimming-pool, first one after the other, afterwards next to each other. After that the cruise director explained the sensation the audience was curious about.

"Ladies and Gentlemen", roared out from the loud-speaker, "may I introduce to you the participants competing for the most erotic legs? They have come here from all parts of our beautiful world to present their shapely, thoroughly fit legs which nature has blessed them with. Let's hear it for them, give it up for them, ladies and gentlemen! Look at them more closely. This gracefulness, this attractiveness!"

"I've heard enough", I told to myself. "It's time for a close inspection."

I cheekily cut my way through the gaping crowd, until I was standing directly at the pool.

The man with the loudspeaker had babbled about gracefulness and attractiveness, but even with the best will in the world I could not see anything bearing a likeness to something attractive and graceful. A few individuals showed themselves on the catwalk whose legs had not been blessed by nature at all; rather the ravages of time had left their mark on them. The pronounced bow legs of the first candidate looked as if he had just descended from his donkey after a ride of 2.000 kilometers. The legs of candidate no. 2 were so hairy that he could have starred in the movie "The yeti is alive". The legs of the third candidate were of different length. Due to his legs which were extremely twisted backwards, candidate no. 4 looked to the north, while his feet were moving towards the south. The shortest of the fools seemed to be closely related to the Popeye family; the only difference being that his legs instead of his arms were thicker at the bottom compared with their top. Candidate no. 6 only had three toes to each foot. The most courageous of all candidates – no. 7 – only had one leg, which, however, did not keep him from taking part in the competition.

Upon the go-ahead for the presentation, the crowd went wild cheering the participants on. The gentlemen turned around, showing themselves from all sides, held their ugly legs up and caressed them with the palm and back of the hands. While they let their hands wander on their more or less bootylicious butts, they shook their hips in the rhythm to the music which had just started. Only the movements of the one-legged candidate were limited. He was hopping around and moving his arms like a bird which had dropped down from a nest and was not yet strong enough to fly upwards again.

"Stop, stop!", the cruise director shouted. "Please stop and stand still, gentlemen! Thanks to all participants for their excellent performance. Now it's time for the finale. The candidate who presents the most beautiful leg by holding it up outstretched in the most erotic way will be selected by the audience as the winner of our today's "sexy legs-competition". Come on, gentlemen. Listen to my command, then turn around to the audience and hold your leg up. Ready, steady, go!"

Following his instructions, all participants were standing at the edge of the swimming-pool a few minutes later – with an outstretched leg and waving arms – trying not to fall into the water.

Finally the one-legged man appeared who also turned to the audience. Upon the command "Leg up!" blaring from the loudspeaker also he held his leg up horizontally. Unfortunately no further leg was left to stabilize the man so that he plunged backward into the water with a loud "splash". This was no doubt what he intended to do to make the audience laugh with this performance; his plan worked out. The people were applauding and screaming with pleasure, admiring the man's courage and unanimously selected him as the winner of the competition. He was presented with a bottle of bubbly and a medal. His performance had been recorded on the cruise video which is taped every week and offered for sale to everybody.

My short break in the sunshine was over; my curiosity about the offers on board to keep the passengers happy was satisfied for now. I silently went into the cabin not waking my snoring roommates and took a nap for the last hour.

Spick and span I entered the galley at 5:30 p.m. to prepare my station. Thanks to Harry who was next to me, filling the glasses with ice and ignoring me, everything was done more quickly and trouble-free. The station was prepared for the service in a matter of minutes.

Making the final preparations, waiter Enzo polished wine glasses and made small-talk with his neighbor about the fair maidens in general and his wife in particular. According to Enzo she was waiting at home and in good hands there. "Organization is everything", he commented. "A waiting wife at home and a waiting lady in every harbor. Only when you get that in order can you call yourself a real sailor."

"Yes, you are right", waiter Chris from England standing next to us added. "If you think everything through and don't be as stupid as our colleague Bruno from Spain!"

As this memory made Enzo and Chris burst out in loud laughter, I had to ask what the matter with head waiter Bruno was. After all it was important for me to learn what might happen on board and in this job.

"This idiot", Chris explained, "got involved with a racy lady from South America during a cruise. He turned her head and swore fidelity to her after have a little too much to drink. Usually such romances on board aren't for real and are over after a few days. In case of our Bruno, it however, took quite a different course and he had some bad luck. The lady somehow managed to figure out his phone number and address in Spain. Well, one day while Bruno was on home leave the lady in question was standing in front of his house, with a small suitcase to remind him of his vow of fidelity. Fortunately our fair-weather friend was sitting at the galley window and drinking coffee at the moment the fair lady came upstairs to his front door.

The cup dropped from his hands at this sight and at the same time the vision of a divorce lawyer flashed before his eyes. In the very last minute he managed to save his marriage by running out, taking the former beloved by her hand, pulling her into his car, flooring the gas pedal and heading for the airport.

During the car ride a stage-ready drama must have taken place. Consequently Bruno first had to have the demolished rear-view mirror and the smashed car radio repaired in a garage on his way back home so that his wife wouldn't become suspicious later.

In the end the lady took a flight back to her South-American home, but only after Bruno had paid for her return ticket in first-class and promised to finance her a car at her home. The racy, love-crazed woman hustled a total sum of 25.000 dollars from our Bruno.

Bruno has never told us how he explained the missing amount on the account to his wife."

We all giggled again. Of course, such a story before the dinner eased the atmosphere. After all it's always a good thing to welcome the guests with a smile on your face.

We were well prepared for a celebratory evening on board. All passengers had got dressed to appear in the most elegant style and the best light: the gentlemen in tux, the ladies in long ball gowns, their children in small suits and dresses. Everybody seemed to be in a very good mood as the captain had just invited them to a cocktail party where more or less high-proof drinks had already put most of the guests in the right mood for dinner.

Even the Germans sporadically let out a few roars of laughter at their table; the service personnel in their red gala uniform were welcomed with acclamations and friendly gestures. The relaxed atmosphere was fine and good, but could not hide the fact that we had a hard evening in front of us. The waiters had to be highly ambitious as they had to personify the speediness of a weasel, a circus director's organizing ability, the vigilance of a meerkat, a friar's submissiveness, a gourmet's experience and the sensitivity of a star violinist.

"This week we are lucky", Enzo said. "Not a single bad apple among the guests who intentionally wants to give us a bad time." "What do you mean?", I wanted to know. "It's very simple", he replied. "Most of the passengers have come here to enjoy themselves and have a good time. Apart from them there are also the so-called "complaint professionals" who haven't come here to spend an unforgettable holiday on a cruise liner. Quite the contrary – these are persons who have already taken part in several cruises and are unable to find any peace of mind unless they can criticize everything and everybody. You know what I mean? Oddballs who get up in the morning, look at their ugly, jaded faces in the mirror and take their anger about their odd appearance or relationship problems out on the crew, preferably on the waiters. Be sure that you will get to know some of these types. I particularly dislike those who complain about our excellent food on board." I fully agreed with Enzo. The meals on board a four-star liner are magnificent. Unfortunately many passengers, however, often forget that they are not dining in a restaurant in which around 80 guests are being entertained per evening. They instead are provided with food from a galley brigade which daily prepares approximately 10.000 main dishes in an arrangement, with such flavor and at a speed which would make many restaurants on land look very small indeed.

Many passengers are of the opinion that the money they have paid for the cruise is totally spent on the catering. They're miles out, dear reader. Do you know for example the costs for fuelling a ship? Between 500.000 and 2.000.000 dollars depending on the ship size! After about ten days the ship needs to be refueled. On average a guest only plays 7 to 10 Euro per day for the catering on a reasonable cruise liner, that's all. In return the guest is offered breakfast, lunch, afternoon tea, dinner and a midnight buffet – everything in a quality that leaves nothing to be desired and gives very few occasions to complain. Okay, even our galleys have sometimes offered a dry fish or a tough piece of meat, which is quite normal considering the scope of meals. Such small things are corrected by the waiter or head waiter with a smile and within a few minutes. But unfortunately there are always some professional fault-finders among the guests who cannot be pleased. Customers who do not understand that you can't go to McDonalds and get a bag filled with a filet steak and béarnaise sauce for one Euro. The demands they make on the waiters on board cannot be fulfilled. For instance they ask for caviar, goose liver pâté, truffle and roast saddle of venison. In the event of such demands and when they moreover order a coke or soda pop instead of a good and expensive wine which would have somehow justified their desire for luxury appetizers, I always put on a gentle smile and explain that such desires go beyond our scope. I recommend them to book their next cruise on board the "MS Europa", "Crystal" or on a liner from the "Seabourne" or "Seadream" shipping company where such delicacies are included in the standard offer. "Never heard of them!" they mostly reply awkwardly. "But thanks for the information, I will bear it in mind." "All right", I then think, "just reading the price list for these cruise liners will make you feel dizzy and you will soon be a good boy and return to us."

A rather uneasy situation occurs at the table, if the guests describe our meals simply as "bad" or "boring". Doing so, they see a different side to me. In these cases I always thank them for their honest critic and leave the restaurant for some minutes. Afterwards I return to the table of the "complaint professional" who mostly expects to obtain at least a bottle of wine on the house in compensation for the criticized food. Far from it! I look directly at the person who is oh! so terribly dissatisfied, and say: "Pardon me, Madam (or Sir), I have just talked to the head chef. He also appreciated your frankness. I've informed him that you yourself must be a gourmet chef who can distinguish good food from bad food very well. The head chef would like to know the specialties you serve to your guests at home. Kindly let us know what you chef at home to impress your own guests. He will then consult with his sous-chef and prepare the specialty you require. We want you to feel at home here."

The addressed person generally glazes over with a furrowed brow and starts contemplating. The first beads of sweat appear, while they look to their table-neighbors who excitedly wait for the reply of the wannabe gourmet. They slowly open the mouth: "Well, er, ahem, er ...", tormented they start talking and the stop abruptly. Gotcha! Nobody had expected the waiter and head chef to react to the complaint in this way. Being aware of the fact that many people often live off fast food and pizza at home, have never visited a starred restaurant, and that only the simplest of fare – if at all – is prepared at home, the embarrassed guest sips at his glass of soda thinking of some sort of clever retort. "Take your time, our head chef is a master of patience". These are my last words addressed to the guest; usually not a sound is to be heard afterwards. In the course of time you also get used to this type of person and are no longer stuck for an answer to put them in their place. Constructive criticism is, however, always highly welcomed, Ladies and Gentlemen; but only for good reason; otherwise it makes no sense.

But now let me again refer to Enzo, who was busy distributing the meals to the tables in next to no time.

Hot escargots in garlic butter, French pâté, prawn cocktails and other delicacies were accurately served by him with Italian charm and without a single mistake. While the sommelier filled the wine glasses, I was very busy with my side orders, ice-teas, coffees, juices, cokes and soft drinks. The guests were offered a choice between duck breast with red cabbage, pasta in truffle oil, filet Mignon with green asparagus, halibut with wild mushrooms and a fancy vegetarian meal as main course. There were guests who ordered several appetizers or main dishes in one go, as the portions were not as large as in many American and German restaurants; moreover the appetite was considerably stimulated by the sea breeze. Nevertheless there is always sufficient food for all on board. You can reorder as much as you like until you are truly full. You never have to worry, whether there is still sufficient money left in the purse to pay the additional food. Quite a few guests who I have served during my long career on board the cruise liners audaciously made use of this "all-inclusive service" and scoffed more food in one week than they would have scoffed at home in a month – as the saying goes: "I have paid for it; therefore I'll chomp away irrespective of my health!"

Once a guest put away a pile of ice-cream, after he had provoked Enzo by saying: "I don't believe that you can manage to serve an ice-cream sundae which will leave me fully satisfied!" He looked a right idiot, when Enzo placed a pyramid in front of him comprising of 20 scoops of vanilla ice-cream and asked: "How would you like to eat the ice-cream – with a liter of chocolate sauce or a kilo of whipped cream?" "Neither nor", the rather horrified man replied. He gobbled up the ice-cream, on the one hand as it tasted very good and he was loudly cheered on by his fellow diners and on the other hand because he did not want to make a fool of himself. Though he hurriedly left the dining-room shortly before he could scoff up the last scoop. He wasn't seen in the next two days. When he dared to go back to the restaurant again, he always had a bottle of digestive bitters in his jacket pocket.

After another man had made a silly bet with a fellow diner, he ate two complete ducks. He won the bet, but had to spend the night and the next day in hospital, which was really expensive.

In short, there were quite a few guests who – victim of their greed – gambled with their health. I must tell you in detail about the worst occurrence of this which I will remember for as long as I live:

In February 1996 our cruise liner left the harbor of Miami and as usual the restaurant doors were opened for the guests' first dinner. A family who had been allocated a table in my station headed for me. All family members were slightly to considerably overweight and very loud while walking across the restaurant. When they found the allocated table, the father – a hulk with a weight of at least 130 kilo – left the family and approached me, saying: "When will lobster be on the menu?" I was slightly confused because usually a waiter is addressed with the words "Good evening". His wife was all smiles, announcing: "Well, my husband, he is a master of eating lobster; it's the only reason he takes cruises."

She fondly embraced his enormous hips, squeezed his chubby cheeks and pecked them.

The chair which the proud man had sat down on next to his full-figured wife and his well-fed children was one of the so-called

68

champion chairs. They are always held available for slightly overweight customers and used every day. The double seat, chair legs made of iron and missing armrests were a blessing for the obese, as their hands were granted a lot of room for shoveling food into their mouths.

I have to forestall that I had already advanced from assistant-waiter to waiter by that time. Therefore I was unfortunately responsible for the well-being of this light-hearted family. It was with dual pleasure that I watched these persons tucking in. Every family member wanted to top the others with regard to the quantity of eaten food. Biting off huge pieces and gulping them down quickly, the father demonstrated how to defend his position as biggest eater of the family.

The guests in the direct vicinity witnessed this internal competition which was combined with loud laughter and jabbering. After three days the other guests were so terribly upset by that they asked my head waiter to call the family in question to order and calm them somewhat.

Although the man did his best, he was not very successful. The family stubbornly and loudly continued, insisting on their right to be allowed to eat as much as they wanted. I had to run into the galley again and again to provide them with more food. I served three main courses for every family member and even a fourth for the man of the house who raised a cheer from his family with this great performance.

I shrugged off the humiliating toing and froing between the restaurant and the galley. Obedient helpfulness which is frequently exploited is part of the waiter's job. Also in case of humiliation the saying "The guest is king!" applies.

The family members, rather full and satisfied, got up with difficulty and came over to me. "When will lobster finally be offered?", the mistress of the household asked in a slightly annoyed voice. "Four days are already over without lobster having been offered yet!" "Tomorrow, Ma'am!", the head waiter promised. "Tomorrow you'll be offered lobster. The head chef has worked overtime fishing only for you to make sure that enough of these little animals will be available for you and your family."

The woman evidently did not realize the sarcasm in the head

69

waiter's voice and was satisfied with his reply.

"My sweetheart will demonstrate to you how many lobsters a really exceptional eater is able to consume; the dinners up to now were only the beginning."

Oh, dear!, I thought remembering Wilhelm Busch. *O dear, O deary, when the end comes sad and dreary!*

The next evening the lobster champion was among the first guests in the dining-room.

"I hope that the chef is true to his word!", this is how I was greeted by Daddy Eat-a-lot. Panting, he sat down on his champion chair and tried to put the napkin around his neck. As this was, however, far too thick, his wife gave him a helping hand and – standing behind him – tucked it into the collar of his shirt.

The whole family had hardly sat down when they started asking the first questions, whether enough lobster would be on board for the father and whether I had fished the lobster by myself. "Of course, I have fished the lobster by myself", I replied. "Didn't you see me last night when I was standing at the railing with a fishing-rod in my hand?"

My answer caused laughter at the table and also at the next one where my comment had evidently been overheard.

The service started with my assistant-waiter who served water, bread and ice-tea before I distributed the menu.

Then the fun started. Locking horns with each other over something, the children insulted each other by using swearwords which were totally out of place in a restaurant. Being engrossed in the menu, the parents did not bother about the kids at all. In the end a guest from the neighboring table who was fed up with the noise got up and gave the squabbling brats a piece of his mind. The parents had not expected this reaction. Before they had a chance to say anything, they were also told off: "Shut up! If you are unable to have your kids under control, I'll take over. Alright, keep your mouths shut now and eat; otherwise I'll call for the security guards!"

While the parents were lost for words, an evil grin appeared on the children's faces. It was now so silent that I could take the orders.

The mother and the children ordered as usual: first course, soup, salad, main course and dessert; they, however, asked for two lobsters instead of one on every plate. Afterwards it was the father's turn. Propping himself on his elbows, he looked up to me: "Are you ready?", he asked. "Yes, sir, I am", I replied. "What can I do for you?" "Okay", he continued. "I'd like to have two lobsters as first course, two further lobsters instead of the soup. As I don't like salad, I'll order another lobster. Regarding the main course I am not sure. I first have to see how large the lobsters are." He tried to make a joke when his fingers were wandering across the menu and finally stopped at the main courses. "I think I tend to have lobster tonight. One large lobster as main course, please; a smaller one instead of the vegetables and a very small one instead of the potatoes." "All of the lobster are the same size", I calmly replied. "Lucky me!", Daddy Fatso triumphed. "Maybe I'll get enough to eat today to be full!"

"You can count on that", I grinned although I did not feel like smiling. In that moment I already was fully aware of the fact that, unless I was assisted by the head waiter, the service for the other guests would suffer from this monster. Listening to this order, the children and the mistress shouted for joy as if the famous Benny Hill would have cracked a joke.

The order had been overheard at the neighboring tables; comments such as "impossible" or "unbelievable" caught my ear. "That guy is a bit strange, isn't he?", a guest asked me at my second table when I took the orders there. "Do you think they also eat like this at home?" "You never know", I replied, "but obviously lobster is their favorite dish there as well."

As quickly as possible I returned to the galley to get the dishes with my notes on my pad. I had lost a lot of time and needed to hurry up to start serving very shortly. The mouths of the minors had to be stuffed before they start raising hell again. The tray was considerably overloaded when I returned to the table. Only thanks to the helping hand of a head waiter I managed to put down everything on my station without problem.

Without saying anything Mom and Dad Eat-a-lot pitched into the shrimp cocktails and quiche. The kingpin was craving for the two first lobsters and almost pricked my fingers with his fork, when I placed the shellfish in front of him.

I then started placing the appetizers on the second table in an elegant and appealing manner as I had been taught in the school of hotel management. Ladies first, followed by the gentlemen.

Only a few seconds later when I was just serving the last appetizer, I heard the champion's voice. "Finished! I would like the next lobster!" Turning around, I did not believe my eyes. Porky pig had scoffed down the first two lobsters in less than two minutes and now looked as if he was starving.

"You are astonished, aren't you?" his wife said, smirking. "Well, hardly anybody matches him when it comes to eating lobster."

She was indeed correct; that was certainly a record time that had not existed before in this particular discipline.

Heading for the galley to get the guests their second course, I hoped that my corpulent guest would have eaten enough. But nothing had changed. Everybody enjoyed their soup, while the esteemed gentleman gulped the next two lobsters as if he had not eaten anything for days.

Next the salads with Asian sauce followed. The dressing for our champion comprised of at least one liter of liquid butter which he had spread across his shellfish during the course of the dinner and which increased his cholesterol level to an undreamt-of-value.

It was time for the main course. The guests enjoyed pasta with steamed scallops, baked tilapia, grilled rump steak with herb butter, coq au vin, and an exquisite vegetarian dish with Indian spices. Thanks to the superb quality of the food which pleased everybody, the delay in the service which could not be prevented was – thank God! – forgotten.

Our record eater evidently was satisfied as well. Four lobsters lying side by side and garnished with plenty of liquid butter and some lemon slices were shining a luscious red on his plate, before they disappeared down his mouth never to be seen again. His appetite seemed to be infinite. All the other guests looked on.

Afterwards dessert was served. While everybody was looking forward to lemon cake, chocolate mousse and pina-colada-tart, only one person didn't seem to be impressed by these delicacies.

"Don't make me laugh!", said Fatty while wiping the sweat off his forehead. "I am not one for desserts. Instead, just bring me another two lobsters!" He ordered in such a loud voice that all the guests at the neighboring tables overheard and covered their faces with their

72

hands. My head waiter who was also listening, suggested accompanying me to the galley where all areas except the dessert station had most probably already finished work. The head chef was not at all pleased when he was advised of our wish, but he managed to motivate one of his chefs to remove another few shellfish from the oven which were originally scheduled to be offered as part of the midnight buffet.

Returning to the station with my tray, I looked rather strange: balancing delicious desserts and cakes in my right hand, and holding a large plate – wrapped in the fine scent of garlic – in my left hand. With the help of the above mentioned chef my head waiter had attractively arranged all lobsters available in the galley on the plate and put them in front of our champion, saying: "That's it; no more lobsters available!". The greedy-guts had already looked at his watch to gesture that he had to wait too long for his dessert to be served.

I had already stopped counting how many lobster I had meanwhile served to our hungry guest. But I could clearly see that he in fact had difficulty trying to scoff the remaining lobster. He evidently was entirely possessed by the idea to eat as much as possible in return for the money paid. He did not even bother that the eyes of all the other guests where on him, wanting to witness the impending drama.

It must have been lobster no. 13 or 14 when our thick master turned entirely pale in the face. Trying to get up, he grabbed his heart and collapsed on the table with a loud bang. There was a dead silence, only his wife and the children were obviously not aware of how serious the situation was. They giggled, believing that father wanted to show off. Only when blood was dropping on the tablecloth from his hand which had been hurt by shattered glass, did they start shouting. My head waiter came running as quick as lightning and radioing the code "Alpha Alpha" for the acute emergency case. The wife and children shook the inanimate body, before two dauntless guests laid the man on the floor to perform the heart massage. Doctors, nurses, the staff captain and three officers arrived within minutes. While they cared for the family members and tried to calm them down, our lobster king lost the struggle for survival on the floor. This man who had dedicated his life to eating lobsters had died of a massive protein shock and a severe heart attack at the same time.

I have to admit that it was not a pretty sight, although I had the feeling that some guests at the neighboring tables whom the family had annoyed all along were not of the same opinion.

When the dead man on the stretcher was carried out of the dining-room, he was accompanied by sardonic grins and black humor. "Saint Peter knows that you are coming and has already cast a net to catch the glorious lobsters". I ignored this comment from the neighboring table to the right. "I wonder which food will be offered at the funeral party?", this question was raised at the neighboring table to the left. "Shrimps", somebody shouted, "because all lobster reserves of have already been eaten!" The British accent of the guests who mocked the dead man could easily be picked up. Their laughter was contagious. I also started laughing, but shut myself away in the galley to avoid any trouble with serious passengers who were shocked by the events.

I have never again met the rest of the family. They left the ship in Mexico the next morning and went home by plane.

I was told that lobster soup was served as lunch on the plane on their return flight. Whether our family might have asked for a second helping? We will never know.

On board I was of course faced with the sarcasm of the other waiters. "Hi, Johannes!", Alberto shouted at me, Alberto was the biggest of all the waiters – well actually! – the biggest of the entire crew of our ship..,.

"How much tip did you get? Will you have lunch with us in Mexico tomorrow? We've found a nice restaurant where particularly tender lobster is served."

Well, that's typical of my colleagues who are always friendly and never at a loss of words.

The saying "punishment follows swiftly" held true for the above mentioned big eater Alberto on that day. He prided himself on eating a normal sized steak within less than one minute. This was true indeed; the Argentine gulped down five to six steaks every evening and sometimes also for lunch in a time which a normal person needed to eat only one piece of meat. He often got into trouble with the chefs and particularly with the head chef, because the other waiters frequently complained of there being no meat left for the crew because of Alberto. After he had emptied the container holding with the leftover steaks which were designed for the crew, he would scoff them down in a dark corner of the restaurant. It worked fine until Alberto couldn't even wait until the food was released by the head chef for the crew after their job had been done. As already said, it happened on the same day on which our guest had died after he had gorged like there was no tomorrow. In the evening Alberto collected the main courses for his guests.

Keeping an eye on all the filet Mignon being arranged on the plates, he waited for the moment in which the head chef was busy with the vegetables on the first plate. In less than a second Alberto reached for the meat, stuffed the whole filet from the last plate into his mouth and started chewing. He had to be ready, before the chef would realize a filet was missing. He almost paid with his life for the idea to swallow the meat with just a few bites. All of a sudden he started gasping, turned blue and collapsed on the floor. The filet had gotten stuck in his throat and entirely blocked the windpipe. Acting with a great power and caution at the same time, a strong Jamaican waiter managed to set Alberto on his feet and squeeze the meat out of his throat using the Heimlich maneuver.

The doctor confirmed Alberto to have been very lucky because a 250g steak stuck in the throat could easily have been the death of him. Although Alberto usually wasn't a religious man, he crossed himself twenty times and promised to improve.

Chapter 9:   Iced Coffee

Prior to entering the port of Cozumel, the waiters prepared for dinner. Everybody was in high spirits since a shore leave was always bound to be interesting. I was really looking forward to a refreshing bath, diving in Cozumel's crystal-clear water, relaxing in a local music bar during happy hour over a tequila... In other words, simply enjoying all the services lavished upon the guests. What could possibly go wrong ...?

Everything did run smoothly - at first. Enzo, the waiter, served the meals and drinks, and while assisting him, I regaled the guests with clever and silly anecdotes as well as stories of my schooldays and military service.

But then it happened: one of our friendly American guests asked me to serve him an iced coffee with dessert.

"Iced coffee?" I repeated, slightly astonished at the request. Once my brain had realized that the ordered beverage had to be the equivalent for the German 'Eiskaffee' (Translator's note: cold coffee with lots of vanilla ice-cream and whipped cream). "Yes, please," the guest, a kindly older gentleman from Texas, confirmed. "And make that decaf!"

"Enzo," I said, "one of our guests would like an iced coffee." "So what?" he answered. "That's nothing unusual. Many Americans like to drink iced coffee. But before you go to get it from the galley, please serve the regular coffee and tea and refill the water glasses."

I followed his instructions and then headed for the galley to prepare the ordered specialty in the way I was familiar with. "Iced coffee, iced coffee," I repeatedly mumbled to myself. I needed a tall glass, strong decaf coffee, vanilla ice-cream, whipped cream, a bar spoon and a drinking straw. It was rather troublesome to collect all accessories as I still did not know my way around in this environment. Moreover, the bar was located at the furthest end of the galley.

Just the same, I did my utmost to carry out this mission. Knowing the importance of cooling down the coffee to an ice-cold temperature, I diligently shook it in a shaker from the bar which I had filled with ice cubes. After I had put two scoops of vanilla ice-cream into the glass, I poured the cold coffee over it. I then asked the astonished pastry chef to adorn it with a sumptuous whipped cream topping and finally - the crowning glory - to decorate this delicious arrangement with a few chocolate sprinkles.

It looked exactly as I knew this much-loved specialty from Germany should appear and put it on my tray to serve it to my guest.

"Have you started working as a bartender?" I was asked by my colleagues as I – balancing the tall cocktail glass – headed for my station. I was puzzled. Why did they ask? Had they never seen an iced coffee?

Indeed, neither they nor my guest had ever seen a proper iced coffee! Everyone was agog with surprise when I proudly placed the delicacy in front of him.

"What on earth did you order?" the Texan's wife asked with interest. "What is this beautiful confection?" other guests at the table were eager to know. Even Enzo was perplexed. "What is that?"

"And what is this supposed to be?" I heard the head waiter's voice behind me.

"Iced coffee," I sheepishly replied, while a feeling of uncertainty crept up on me. "Why do you ask? Have I done something wrong?"

In the meantime, the friendly American smiled at me, clapped his hands and explained, "I hadn't expected anything quite like this, but it looks great. Can't wait to try it!"

He poked around the glass with the spoon, took a sip through the straw and clicked his tongue. "Delicious! Very delectable!" he commended. While lifting the glass, he shouted: "Does anybody else want to try it?"

While the glass was being passed around, I felt a tug at my jacket. As I turned around, I was confronted by my stone-faced head waiter. "Come here!" he hissed at me. "I need to explain something to you."

I had to follow him behind the counter where nobody could see us and was taken to task for the second time.

"Do you realize what you've done?" he asked me.

"The guest did not order anything but an American iced coffee, which means a glass of regular coffee with a few ice cubes. In the United States it is quite common not only to drink iced tea, but also

78

iced coffee. So in that case, the glass is filled with coffee instead of tea. I surely hope that not too many guests will acquire a taste for it, otherwise we'll have a real problem on our hands."

"You're the real problem!", the harsh voice of the head waiter was heard behind us. After he had evidently witnessed the whole scene, he gave my head waiter a good scolding. According to the maître d': "You are responsible to ensure that nothing the waiters are not familiar with is being served. Your instructions are what determine whether your team does a good job. I don't want to have to deal with a mistake like this ever again and now it's up to you to sort things out!"

While my head waiter had to endure the reproaches of his superior, I peeped around the corner, hoping that the dust had settled regarding my "iced coffee."

Quite the contrary! I watched the friendly Texan as he stood at the neighboring table with his iced coffee and extolling its virtues.

A cold shiver ran down my spine because all of the guests the old chap allowed to sample the cursed iced coffee were totally gaga over it.

I could barely muster up the nerve to return to my station, but the head waiter who had just been given a severe reprimand tried to bolster my spirits. "Come on, we'll get through this!" he assured me. "Maybe we'll get lucky and the guests will be satisfied with just this one and only iced coffee."

Quite the fanfare awaited me when I returned to my station, "Look! There's our hero who created this amazing drink!" "All of us are totally hooked on your masterpiece. Can we please have another seven of your coffee specialty?" "And another three for us, please," the guests from the neighboring table added. "May we also try two of these delicacies?" other guests asked me.

"Dammit!" my head waiter cursed in a low voice. "The shit has really hit the fan now!"

The entire scenario was pathetic. My poor superior had no choice but to frantically ask for help in the galley, at the bar and in the bakery. A few colleagues laughed uproariously when he described the problem; nevertheless they sympathized and were willing to rescue him in order to complete such a tall order. While I again chilled another few liters of coffee, I imagined what would happen

79

if 200-300 guests acquired a taste for German iced coffee. Beads of sweat appeared on my forehead and I again felt as though I were suffering from sea-sickness – but a thousand times worse than the day before.

Help came from our resolute head waiter who had stayed in our neighborhood to watch the spectacle. All of a sudden he appeared in the doorway to the restaurant. He stared at the tray with the twelve iced coffees, gave the head waiter withering looks which made our blood run cold, and accompanied us to the station. For the first time in my career I witnessed a manager who determinedly cracked down on a potentially threatening situation by defusing it in a skillful and charming manner. Making use of his vast experience and wisely selected words, he explained to the guests that, effective immediately, this special version of iced coffee would no longer be served, as this product had found its way to the enthusiastic audience purely by accident, due to a certain inexperienced German assistant waiter. It would, however, be taken for granted that every interested guest would be entitled to the recipe for this German specialty – of course with the automatic guarantee it would make the perfect addition to a party at home.

It took a load off my mind and I vowed to myself to first ask a colleague for feedback in the future before taking a chance at something so foolhardy.

And that was the end of that – at least for me. This episode had consequences for my head waiter, however, who was rewarded by the head waiter with the extra task of "training new waiters" prior to the start of the cruise.

On this particular night I lay awake pondering. *Boy, oh boy,* I thought, *you've been taught a lesson you'll never forget. It is, in fact, quite different here than in Europe and even more so than in Germany. Always listen, pay attention and never stop learning – that's the order of the day.* No doubt about it!

Chapter 10:   Porridge in Mexico

The next morning we were awoken by bright sunshine. Although the cabin was tiny and ugly, it featured a small porthole which not only enabled a few rays of sun to find their way indoors, but also allowed us to look out.

Snow-white beaches, palm-trees and the most magnificent water you could imagine enhanced the true feeling of a cruise. "Cozumel, Mexico, here we come..." A colleague from a neighboring cabin who was getting ready for work suggested, "If you don't have to work at lunchtime and feel so inclined, you may join us in our visit to the city and the beach afterwards." I was naturally delighted at this prospect. "That would be fine," I laughed. "How do I find out whether I have to work at lunchtime or not?"

"Ask your waiter!" I was told. "If the guests from last week gave him a good rating, you might get the chance to go to the beach. Otherwise you will be one of the lucky ones on hand to help out and serve about 1,000 guests during the lunch buffet. Who is your waiter?" my co-worker asked. "Enzo," I replied. "Very good," he answered. "Most of the time he manages to coerce the guests into admitting that he consistently provides the highest level of service. He frequently gets five stars." I didn't know anything about this rule and decided to ask Enzo, who was working upstairs in the restaurant.

But first of all we had to focus on the breakfast buffet. Every waiter was not only busy with his own station, but also served other guests who helped themselves at the rich buffet and were afterwards accompanied to the tables by assistant waiters such as myself. Once the guests arrive at the table, the waiters are prepared to serve them to their heart's desire.

During a rare moment in which there wasn't a single guest at the buffet, and I recognized that Enzo didn't have a lot of side duties at his station, I scurried over to him to find out about these five stars and the day-off situation.

"Well", he explained to me, "at the end of a cruise a card is handed out to every guest on which he or she rates the cruise by checking off certain items pertaining to the cruise's staff, facilities and services. Various categories are rated, for example: friendliness of the ship's crew, the shows, the excursions, the food in general, the bar service, the wine service and the food in the restaurant. It is up to each guest to select one out of the five ratings on the card which range from 'excellent' to 'very bad'. This rating is of great importance to us: the better the rating, the more leisure time is granted to the waiters and assistants during lunchtime, when most of the guests are on an excursion. At the end of the cruise, the waiter with the highest number of 'excellent' ratings gets a reward from the head waiter's office. What's more, he or she is also granted leisure time over lunch during the next cruise which he or she may use for a shore leave or for taking care of private matters. "Um," I said, "this means that the guests with this assessment card have us, the employees, over a barrel. They can either heap lavish praise on us or potentially put us out of work, can't they?" "That's right," Enzo replied. "It has occasionally happened that guests found fault with something at the very end of the journey and had entirely forgotten about the positive experiences they previously enjoyed, thanks to the employees' efforts. They checked off the option 'very bad' on the card, added a nasty comment and consequently put an innocent, hardworking family man out of work. Last time it happened to a cabin waiter. He was accused of having stolen a diamond ring, although he maintained his innocence. No employee in his right mind would ever steal something from a guest and put his work at risk. On their last day on board, these bizarre guests who bitched about the cabin waiter in question - both verbally and in writing - on board, showed him no mercy. After they had returned home, they called the ship and the shipping company several times to learn whether the villainous employee had gotten what he deserved. In the end the waiter was fired. A day later the ring was retrieved from the drain pipe of the toilet. After a great deal of commotion it came to light that the daughter of this family had accidentally dropped the ring into the toilet. Considering its value however, she did not have the courage to admit her guilt during the hearing out of fear for her parents' anger. The accused cabin waiter consequently refused the attempts for reconciliation and excuses from all parties involved and went to court over the incident. This matter became really expensive for the company and these dear guests as such happenings are exactly what famous

83

American lawyers are waiting for."

I listened attentively as Enzo continued, his voice barely audible: "We are constantly under great pressure and are not allowed to make severe mistakes. Every time God sends easy-going and uncomplicated guests to my station, I say a quick prayer of thanks." "Well?" I asked curiously. "How many stars did you receive last week?" "Five stars!" Enzo laughed. "I actually get five most of the time. Go and spend a nice day in Mexico after breakfast! Be back on time tonight, though, because your guests and I need you."

As I looked outside again, my heart leapt with joy. For the first time I would have the opportunity to breathe in real Caribbean air and possibly even take a swim in the inviting water. "Quite agreeable, isn't it?" Enzo - who had read my thoughts - added, "Being on the Caribbean Sea and getting paid at the end of the week!" I couldn't agree more. I happily returned to my work and helped the guests who had filled their plates with delicacies at the buffet find a comfortable table where they were offered the beverages for breakfast.

You might believe that breakfast – which is the most important meal of the day for some – is usually a rather boring affair as you often have to cope with grumpy, tired guests. Yet this time of the day a few alert but very strange individuals also show up who transform a simple breakfast into a stage-ready spectacle which you'll never forget.

On one such occasion I took notice of an older lady who did not help herself at the buffet, but was obviously looking for something different. She caught sight of me and before I could offer her my help, she harshly asked me, "Do you work here?" "Yes, I do!" I replied. "I am at your disposal to help, Ma'am." "Don't babble, Sir!" the lady replied. "Get some hot food for me!" "Hot food? What exactly do you mean?" I asked in astonishment. "We always serve cold and hot meals."

"Sir!" she bellowed at me. "Can you tell what country I'm from by my accent?" The answer was on the tip of my tongue straightaway. Considering her upper class accent and tone, "Iron Lady" Margaret Thatcher immediately sprung to mind.

"England," I promptly answered.

"Quite right," the lady replied, bursting with pride. "Do you also know how we – the English – like our meals?"

At this moment I did not see the point of her question, but fortunately I still had her original inquiry about hot food in mind.

"Hot?" I answered tentatively. "You're exactly right," she hissed, "hot, very hot! Since I've been on board, I've never had any hot food, everything is either lukewarm or cold!"

Nonsense!, I thought. I always see our guests blowing on their meal to cool it down so that they can actually eat it. This old hag with the huge wart on her nose is off her rocker!

A male guest who was standing behind the warty-faced guest and had witnessed the conversation was bemused by the situation at hand and smiled at me over her shoulder while he gesticulated with his hands to convey he agreed she was crazy.

"Okay," I said in a friendly manner, "this morning I will make it my responsibility to serve you hot food. So, may I take your order, please?" "Porridge!" she replied demandingly. "At your service, Ma'am. Why don't I accompany you to your table and then I'll serve you some hot porridge." "I hope so!" she snarled and sat down.

I quickly asked a colleague where to find the porridge. Shortly thereafter I was standing in the galley in front of a large bowl filled with steaming hot porridge. To assure myself of the correct temperature, I took a tablespoon and sampled it. "Hot!" I confirmed to myself and scooped the porridge from the bottom into a pre-heated soup bowl. Convinced my efforts would be praised to high heaven, I served up the steaming meal to the lady, but what I ended up with was quite the opposite! "This is as cold as ice!" she shouted and provokingly stirred the porridge with her finger which, of course, is less sensitive to pain than one's mouth. "Could I eventually get the hot porridge I ordered, please?" she snapped at me.

All of the other guests at the table stared at me. I felt like a fool for not being capable of serving such a simple meal. Full of shame, I removed the bowl from the table and carried it back into the galley.

"Do you need some help?" I was asked by my old bosom buddy, Harry.

"No, thanks!" I replied. "I'm wise to your kind of 'help'. I'll get the dirty end of the stick again and unintentionally end up doing your

85

work." "Don't worry," Harry laughed. "I only wanted to suggest that you use the salamander heater and microwave." Well, all right, Take his advice, since you don't want to keep your esteemed guest waiting any longer than necessary.

Shortly thereafter the microwave signaled that the time was up, I had set it to two minutes, although the porridge had already started to simmer after twenty seconds. Using a napkin, I put the bowl onto the plate and hurried back to her table. "That took ages!" the old crone spat. "I nearly starved." *Right*, I thought, *you've evidently lost considerable weight during the four minutes I spent in the galley.*

I served the porridge, wished her an enjoyable meal, then turned on my heel to go back to the buffet.

"It's still cold!" the old biddy loudly cawed behind me. I didn't believe my ears, but turned around and gaped at the spoon which she had just taken out of her mouth. "Sir!" she shouted. "Do I actually have to go the galley with you and show you how to make a proper bowl of hot porridge?"

I looked at her with surprise and bemusement. The other guests who had barely noticed me only a few minutes ago were now sitting at the edge of their seats, perversely enthralled by the spectacle that was unfolding.

I heard the sound of giggling then realized it was none other than Harry, who doubled over with laughter behind the buffet.

"You needn't stare at me!" she growled. "All I'm asking for is …" "Yes, I know," I interrupted her. "Hot porridge." "That's right!" she said. "Before I faint, preferably." "Just you wait, you old bitch!" I mumbled. "This is the last time you embarrassed me in front of everyone. Now you're going to get what you deserve!"

"Harry!", I hissed towards the buffet. "I need your help!" "Come along!" he grinned. "I'll talk to the executive chef." He returned within a minute, proudly brandishing a utensil for making crêpes, in other words: a pan which gets extremely hot within seconds. Afterwards he took a bowl to fill with fresh porridge oats and said, "Follow me and pay attention!"

He led me to a high-capacity salamander heater in the furthest corner of the galley. It was so hot that my face had already reddened at a distance of two meters. Putting the bowl into this extremely hot galley utensil, he said: "I hope it won't melt;

otherwise we'll get into trouble with the galley boss." "Don't panic," I replied, "these bowls are solid and heat-resistant."

A moment later, Harry placed his crêpe pan on the stove. After the pan had immediately become red-hot, he poured the freshly prepared porridge into it. He continued stirring until the seething sludge was more akin to boiling lava than something a human being would actually eat. From afar it looked as if a blacksmith had been busy at work. The porridge which my Indian pal, Harry, who was wearing special gloves, poured from the pan into the red-hot bowl closely resembled liquid iron cascading into a mould.

"You can carry it," Harry instructed and handed me a metal tray which he had picked up in the meantime.

Paying careful attention so as not to burn myself while pouring the lava, I carefully trod behind Harry. Harry loudly warned a group of waiters who were perilously close to the approaching danger.

I had almost managed to place the boiling lava in front of my waiting lady without an accident, when a droplet of the seething porridge spilled and landed on my wrist which later required treatment with burn ointment.

Ignoring the pain, I put down the mini volcano in front of the lady and said: "Please, Ma'am, please be careful, the oatmeal is extremely hot!" "Hot, hot!" she disdainfully replied. "What do you whippersnappers know about really hot food? Nowadays nobody takes the time to sufficiently heat food. Everything is pretty hectic and most of the time the meals in the restaurants are cold!"

Her harsh words sounded very silly to Harry and I, yet we were curious whether our joint attempt to appease her would be successful or backfire. We moved back behind the buffet to watch her reaction to the extremely hot meal.

What happened next is something I will never forget.

Observing the small, glowing lava mount, the guests sitting to the left and right of the "hot-air grandma" carefully backed their chairs away to avoid getting injured by hot spatter. My lady, however, seized the spoon with her right hand, while she held the bowl with her left one.

"She'll start crying any minute, now," Harry whispered and shook his head. But what happened was nothing we could have expected.

"I can't believe it!" I groaned. "The wrinkly old prune grabs the bowl as if it has been taken out of the fridge." That's how the porridge episode continued. 'Red-hot grandma' touched the bowl with her fingertips and afterwards held it with three fingers. Any normal human being would have suffered from second- or third-degree burns to their hands, but as a side effect of her long-time obsession for hot food my old hag seemed to be immune to heat.

Firmly holding the bowl with the lava, she dipped the spoon into it and put it - without blowing on it even once – into her mouth. No reaction, nothing, nothing at all!

We caught our breath. She raised her spoon before it disappeared again into the ultra-hot porridge.

Everybody watched the old lady in disbelief, as she ate the scalding hot porridge spoonful by spoonful without so much as batting an eyelash.

Emerging from the buffet, I positioned myself in front of her. "Everything okay with the temperature, Ma'am?" I asked, hoping to be showered with praise. "Yes, thanks!" she answered, taking me by complete surprise. "Tomorrow I'll come back again expecting the same."

"That's really nice to hear, Ma'am," I said with affected politeness, "we are all looking forward to your visit."

"That's the way they are, our dear guests", Harry explained while both of us returned to the buffet. "Every week we get a few strange individuals among our guests who give us a hard time and commandeer us around but only leave a lousy tip. And it will never change," he sighed.

The rest of the morning passed without incident. The guests came and went and enjoyed the breakfast specialties. Everybody prepared to disembark the ship after breakfast and visit the island of Cozumel. More precisely, not all guests felt the need to go ashore. Some were more interested in learning when the lunch buffet would be served. After all, they didn't want to miss anything.

Most of the travelers had booked an excursion to the Mayan ruins and were patiently waiting in a queue outside at a small buffet which had been set up by the bar staff. There they received their provisions comprising two large sandwiches and a bottle of mineral water. The more athletically inclined bustled in the lounges and corridors, checking and preparing their diving gear to spend the day

88

in Cozumel's crystal-clear waters which rank among the most beautiful and most interesting diving paradises on the planet. Other tourists looked forward to their excursion to one of the numerous hotels to attend a crash course in snorkeling in the hotel pool before perfecting their new skills in the sea. The daredevils among our guests borrowed a small motorbike to explore the island on their own. Tourists are advised against borrowing motorbikes as they would never pass a safety check. Now and then I've also made use of one of these vehicles and – thank God! – always returned to the ship safe and sound. But accidents with these clattering scooters are a daily occurrence. Therefore, if you borrow a two-wheeler on any island, please be careful! It is a rewarding sensation to feel the breeze on your face, go shopping in a foreign city, visit the famous Mayan ruins and, afterwards, relax on one of the numerous beaches wearing new swimming trunks for the first time. The contrast between the turquoise sea and the snow-white beaches by the Mayan ruins is a breathtaking sight to behold. You truly believe you're in a paradise created by the aliens that the controversial author and researcher Erich von Däniken is always raving about. I recommend that all tourists combine a trip to Mexico on board a cruise ship with a visit of the Mayan ruins! It is incredibly worthwhile!

In the late afternoon – when all tourists have returned from their excursions – it seems they all follow the same unspoken rule: either frequent the bars of Mexico or the bars on board the ship and enjoy a few delicious cocktails or Mexican beers while recounting the events of the day. A trip to Mexico is only perfect if you experience the hustle and bustle in the lively bars.

The Mexican guests who board top-quality cruise ships are usually very genial customers. In fact, they are often very wealthy, not at all arrogant, always friendly, amusing and easy to please. I often remember one such Mexican family whose patriarch – I called him "Don Mexicano" – was 80 years old, but still very alive and kicking. On the first evening he beckoned to me and with an earnest expression on his face, asked me, "Are you our waiter?" "Yes, I am," I answered. "Okay, look here," he continued, "this is my family: 26 adults and 12 children. I rule the roost and you are responsible for all of us being satisfied, capito?" "I'll do my very best," I replied.

"Fine," the patriarch whispered, "listen to me carefully. We would all like to have caviar as our first course every evening. Well then, what are you waiting for?! Go to the galley and ask the chef to get down to business!" "With pleasure," I answered and looked at my head waiter who had overheard the patriarch's orders. He waved me to a corner and said, "This is a guest who got cheap substitute caviar free of charge on board another ship and now probably expects to receive the same product here to impress his family. We'll take the wind out of his sails, just you wait. I'll be back in a minute."

Five minutes later he stood at my table with the champagne bar menu in his hand. When he tried to introduce himself, he was immediately interrupted by Don Mexicano. "Where is our caviar? We are hungry."

"Have a look, Sir!" the head waiter answered, bringing him the menu. "Please make your selection; all three types of caviar are at your disposal: Beluga, Sevruga and Osetra at a price of 80, 90 and 120 dollars per ounce. Which kind would you like to have for your family? We are all at the ready to fill the plates."

The patriarch was visibly dumbfounded. He had indeed expected the substitute caviar which is usually used as trimming in the galley and of course served free of charge. He stared at the head waiter, and was on the verge of pointing out the mistake. The entire family, however, was not at all interested in the predicament grandfather had gotten himself into. The family members seized their knives and forks, then - banging on the table - shouted: "Caviar! Caviar! Caviar!"

Knowing full well that he did not have the option to cancel the order, Don Mexicano wiped the sweat from his brow and pointed a trembling finger at the cheapest of the three caviar types which was priced at 80 dollars per ounce.

"May we also serve you and your family a few bottles of champagne?" the head waiter asked.

Don Mexicano determinedly shook his head. "No, thanks, we are not very fond of champagne."

"We don't like champagne? Since when?" his wife interrupted him.

She evidently had not realized that the caviar had put a tremendous dent in their cruise budget and turned to the head waiter with a smile on her face. "Six bottles, but only the best champagne, please."

A group of proud waiters holding plates filled with caviar materialized in front of the family shortly thereafter. The bar manager leading the waiters bowed to the patriarch out of respect and waited for a sign of permission to serve the extravagant meal. So far, no one had ever ordered twenty-six portions of caviar, accompanied by Dom Perignon champagne! Don Mexicano who was expected to be happy to bestow such generosity on his family was instead pale-faced and extremely ill at ease. I had the impression that he was forcing himself to smile to hide the fact that he was actually gripped with terror.

He was visibly nervous while waiting for the bill. At the end of the ordeal it was delivered on a small silver tray - a piece of paper with long columns of numbers.

Grimacing as he had most likely never before, Don Mexicano took out his credit card, his hand now trembling more severely than before. He would have loved nothing better than to run away. While he signed the bill, I turned to the bar manager and announced in a loud voice: "The gentleman would like to have the same first course for the entire family every evening!" The grandfather immediately started gasping and vigorously shook his head to the point it threatened to fall off. It took a whole meal before he managed to explain to his family why no more caviar would be ordered. During the following cruise Don Mexicano was very careful about ordering luxury food.

Chapter 11:   Bling and Casinos

On this particular morning, hard work had also come to an end for me. I could take my time and decide what to do with the rest of the day. Although I was enticed by the sun, beach, and sea, I wanted to first of all follow through with my plan and become properly oriented on the ship as well as get acquainted with all of the cruise liner's various activities, including the multitude of amenities offered.

Usually the employees are not obligated to participate in such activities, but I didn't mind. Pretend you've gone astray, I told myself and headed for the next excursion on the ship.

I was very curious to know where our dear customers spend the time between meals and what they get up to. At that time I had already realized one thing: a good waiter must know what is going on aboard his ship and should be able to reply to questions which do not directly pertain to eating and drinking. In other words: a waiter must be a 'fountain of knowledge' when it pertains to his workplace. As I curiously started my excursion, the beach and the sea, the motorbike and snorkeling as well as the cocktails at a hotel bar would just have to wait.

My first stop was one of the most interesting attractions ubiquitous on any ship which have cast a spell over the money-grubbing human beings right from the beginning: the casino. If you were accustomed to the cool, often rather boring elegance of most of the European casinos, you would be confronted with a quite different atmosphere here. On a cruise ship, you would be drowning in lights, signals, sounds and speaking one-armed bandits that cordially welcomed and fascinated mere mortals.

A casino provides endless opportunities to either multiply or gamble away hard-won savings within seconds. My dear reader, in most instances you will certainly be aware on your own whether your cash will be multiplied or depleted. In any case we observe a few of our most appreciated guests every week who – intending to increase their fortune - pay a short visit to the gambling den. Afterwards they wipe the sweat off their foreheads, which clearly indicates that they have suffered considerable losses. I still remember a couple who entered a jeweler's shop at the same time as I did during one of my shore excursions. They were looking for a particularly beautiful Mexican piece of jewelry. To be more precise: she was looking for it, after the master of the house had donated too much of the cruise budget to the casino the previous evening. Standing in front of a large mirror, the wife held a magnificent, golden necklace with an exclusive pendant in the hope of leaving the shop with this pretty bauble around her neck. "Have a look, sweetheart," she sighed affectionately. "What do you think of this majestic golden piece?" "Very beautiful," he replied, "but a silver necklace is also typically Mexican, Look, this copper-colored one would go very well with your complexion."

"You and your damn gambling!" she snapped at him. She was obviously wise as to why her husband prefered jewels made of silver or bronze to the golden necklace she had selected. "I'm already aware we're flat broke - once again. I'm going back to the ship now, excursions and shopping aren't fun under such circumstances!"

Due to the casino visit the couple unfortunately was not only strapped for money when it involved a pleasant shopping spree, but also for the bottle of wine ordered over dinner which the wife in particularly looked forward to.

"One chamomile tea, please!" the husband requested that evening. "I've got problems with my stomach." "Liar!" his wife hissed. "You've got problems with your wallet - which is empty. Now we have to swig tea and water during the entire cruise. What a great holiday! If I ever see you in the casino again, I'm divorcing you!" With these words she left the restaurant.

Whenever I hear or read the word 'casino', I cannot help but think of – among others - my waiter colleague. I' want to tell you briefly about his unique 'unlucky in luck streak'

Similar to many waiters on the ship, Paulo was addicted to gambling and therefore regularly paid visits to every casino in the Caribbean, whether in Puerto Rico, Antigua or St. Maarten. This individual was unable to pass a gambling den without helping the owner of the gambling hell become a bit richer. There was no doubt that his vice would someday be his doom, but nobody could anticipate that it would happen in such a bizarre fashion…

94

On this particular day we cast anchor in Grand Cayman, an island I will refer to later and on which gambling is prohibited even today.

As Paulo and I didn't have to work at lunch time, we decided to spend the day at one of the gorgeous beaches. Heading for the cabins to pick up our swimming trunks, we - being bone idle - took a shortcut. Against orders, we crossed over to the casino which was exactly opposite the dining-room. Casinos are always closed while in port, since gambling is only allowed at sea. On this particular day, the one-armed bandits and roulette machines were flashing, blinking and ringing for no apparent reason and immediately turned my friend Paulo's head.

"Look!" he whispered. "The machines are switched on, I have to!" "You don't have to do anything," I admonished him. "You know quite well that we have no business here and that we are not allowed to gamble!" "Just one coin," Paolo begged and pleaded, "just one little coin. Nobody is on board; everybody has gone to the beach."

"Quite a lot are still here, though," I reminded him. "Don't forget that the management and especially the casino managers are not asleep!" I tried to restrain him by grabbing his sleeve, but I was helpless against his addiction. Having reached the first available machine in a single bound, he inserted the coin into the slot. To avoid any noises, he did not pull the lever, but pressed the button to activate the rollers of the bandit.

The first seven showed up, then the second seven appeared. "Oh no!" Paulo stammered. "I can't believe it!" The incredible feat most gamblers await in vain for years had just happened: the third seven turned up on the display. Jackpot!!!

I made my escape as quickly as possible. The ringing of the bells, the wailing sirens and the whimpering of the happy unlucky fellow echoed throughout the ship. The curious masses came running from all directions to see what had happened. The casino manager was also among the interested crowd. Stony-faced, he first stared at the slot machine and then at the lucky devil.

"The show is over!" he rose to speak. "You can leave the casino now, Ladies and Gentlemen. And to answer your question in advance: no, the casino is not open. The machines were only switched on to carry out their weekly inspection. You, Sir," he pointed to Paulo, "you will come with me to collect your winnings."

"Have I really won? May I keep the money?", Paulo asked in disbelief. "Yes," was the reply in a chilly, British accent, "but instead of money you've won a free flight back to your home in Portugal. You can pack your bags immediately and leave the ship. The captain and the staff have already been advised accordingly. Your discharge papers will be handed over to you shortly!"

That's the way it is with casinos and gambling addiction – things can so easily go wrong. To be honest, I also have to admit that there are always guests who win a lot of money in the casino or during the daily bingo which they use to either splurge or invest in the next cruise. As already mentioned, a game after a delicious dinner is always very entertaining – in moderation. I'll tell you later about another person who was hopelessly addicted to gambling.

97

Chapter 12:   Indian Curry bring bring!!

The first session on the third evening of our cruise had almost come to an end, when a strange scene caught our guests' attention and caused all heads to turn towards the aisle next to the tables.

Two waiters were helping a colleague who obviously was not well and tried to take him towards the exit. 'Not well' was probably not the proper term, not to mention a slight understatement because the sickly waiter's face alternately resembled a bizarre mask, a forced smile, and the next minute he seemed to laugh and cry while his head was shaking uncontrollably. "Ha ha, he he, curry curry!" he giggled. "Curry curry, bring bring, ha ha he he bring bring!" "What's the matter with him? Is that guy alright?" the guests wanted to know. "Depending on how you look at it," a waiter colleague vaguely replied. "This week he was the lucky devil who had the honor of waiting on our Indian guests. Well, it was bound to happen – just look at him! He went nuts!"

"Why?" they wanted to know. "Is there anything peculiar about Indian guests? They're so friendly, endearing and very polite." "That is certainly the truth," the waiter laughed. "Nevertheless, a waiter who has to take care of more than three or four Indians at dinner time should always take a valium beforehand!"

"What do you mean?" the stymied guests asked in response to the waiter's odd remark, whereupon he elaborated. "Let me explain! By pure chance, the unfortunate soul is my roommate and he regaled me with his tale of woe two days ago when he returned to the cabin, sweating and dog-tired." The waiter continued with a vivid narration of his colleague's ordeal.

"What an evening!" my fellow waiter gasped. "*Sixteen* Indians who have seemed to have forgotten they were on holiday in another country and acted as though they were having dinner at a restaurant in Bombay." "It's no secret, all the staff are familiar with this strange behavior," I answered. "Yes, of course, but these guys were really over the top," he explained while he wrung his aching hands.

"Every time you have to take care of these exotic guests, you hope they will actually order what's on the menu and that the service will go smoothly. But on this particular occasion it was exactly the opposite."

"Let me guess," I replied. "Have they been taking liberties with the menu?" "Absolutely!" he confirmed my assumption. "Yet I never give up the hope of one day taking a 'normal' order from Indian customers, serving them in the usual way and finishing work on time."

Then my colleague got really wound up…

"With the slogan, "We'll work it out somehow" as my guide, I confidently presented the menus to my guests on the first evening and was quite vocal in recommending the "usual" menu items. I even tried to make them as tempting as possible.

"Let's start with the beverages!" I suggested in a friendly manner. "What would you like to drink? A cocktail, a good bottle of wine for the grown-ups and perhaps some apple juice and lemonade for the kids? What may I bring you?"

"*Mango lassie* for all of us," one of the mothers replied. "We don't drink any alcohol." *Great,* I thought to myself, *no extra money from wine and spirits, nothing but strange beverages that are more trouble than they're worth.*

"Oh yes, please!" the children cried out. "*Mango lassie, mango lassie*—bring bring!"

Since my only exposure to *Lassie* was from a TV series starring a collie which, as far as I could recall, ate ordinary dog food and didn't drink mango juice, I didn't have the slightest idea what these Indians had ordered to drink.

"Which lasso?" I asked while I was looking around, searching for an experienced head waiter to help me out of this predicament.

"No! Not *lasso*," the mother corrected me. "*Mango lassie* is mango juice mixed with yogurt and Indian spices. But it must not be too viscous. Dilute it with some agave juice, if possible."

I heaved a weary sigh after I had noticed that head waiter Massimo had witnessed everything and gestured for me to take care of the "*lasso.*" He disappeared towards the executive chef's office. Upon his arrival he crossed himself three times, took a deep breath and entered the office where he was welcomed by the chef at once. "My fellow Indians! Am I correct in assuming they've shown up for dinner?" the cook asked Massimo, though it was obvious he already knew the answer. I replied with a silent nod. "I am sure that the waiter will do his best to take orders from the menu provided with

99

no wacky substitutions," Massimo said. "But I am not sure whether he will be successful."

He was absolutely right. While he was still consulting with the executive chef, I was busy singing the praises of our appetizers, soups, salads and main courses in the slim chance I would be able to take a regular dinner order – without success, as it turned out.

"Well, what would you like to eat this evening?" I asked amiably and resolutely while simultaneously trying to avert the unavoidable. The Indians who had so far politely listened to my recommendations smiled brazenly, but shook their heads at my menu suggestions and asked, "Where is your executive chef from? What is his native country?" I was of course wise to their point. "China," I replied with an impudent smile to match theirs. While everybody started laughing at my reply, the Indian grandfather spoke up. "China? Nonsense! We know a lot about your executive chef: he is Indian and his name is Anil. We made sure to inform ourselves of this detail before the cruise began."

"Okay," I admitted. "You're right. He is the executive chef, the master of a brigade of more than 80 chefs who always do their utmost to prepare 12,500 main courses every day to our guests' liking." I sent another hurried prayer up to heaven requesting that the Indians please refrain from ordering food which an ordinary mortal cannot even pronounce and to not exploit the fact that the chef was one of their compatriots. But my plea seemed to have fallen on deaf ears.

"Twelve thousand and five hundred main courses per day!" the Indian patriarch exclaimed. "Fine, now they will have to prepare 12,516. May we order now?"

"Yes, please do," I answered. "Which appetizers would you like to start with?"

"Well, we would like to have four portions of *jurg malai tikka* which is chicken; eight portions of *jingga varuval* which is a dish of wok-fried prawns with Indian spices and *kozhi-65* for the children, but with less garlic." "Great!" the children were excited. "*Kozhi 65, kozhi 65*, bring bring!" "Less garlic," I replied, writing it down on my notepad. "But more cumin," the father requested. "Cumin is good for the bronchia!" "Cumin from the north or south of India?" I asked diligently. My remark incited laughter from the entire table.

"We appreciate your sense of humor – it's splendid!" one of the male guests commented. "If you like, you may try our food later because you're so cute." "Oh, thanks! You're too gracious. I'll take you up on your offer because when I was a child I had problems with my bronchia." Well," the man answered, "you can now put our order in with the chef and serve the appetizers." "Bring bring!" I said and handed the order over to head waiter Massimo who had just served the *mango lassie* which all family members slurped and swallowed in record time. Looking at the order form complete with appetizers, Massimo shook his head and disappeared into the galley to ruin the executive chef's day. "Oh, my goodness," Anil said. "I can manage it, but I surely hope this will be the one and only order like this." "Are you kidding?!" Massimo asked. "So far they have only ordered the appetizers! The waiter is taking their order for the main courses." With a loud sigh Anil entered the galley to advise his brigade that they would again have to prepare additional Indian food although they all had their hands full with the preparation of 1,000 main dishes.

"May I please take your orders for the main courses now?" I asked, turning to my guests again. "No main dishes yet," the father explained. "First we'll have soup." "I see," I said. "Which soup would you like, duck consommé or our specialty, a Mexican potato soup?" The guests all stared at me as though they didn't understand a word I'd said. "*Tamatar rasam,*" the ordering family member replied. "And some *mirchi* which is similar to a chili!" "It sounds quite exotic," I remarked. "Is it necessary for the chef to climb a tree to pick the *mirchi*?" "Ha ha," they all laughed. *Ha ha, hell,* I thought and turned to the waiting Massimo. "Massimo," I instructed him, "go and get some *tamatar rassam* and *mirchi. Mirchi mirchi* bring bring!"

The head waiter once again disappeared into the galley like one of the Three Wise Men about to announce the arrival of the Messiah.

"It will take some time until our chef can find the *mirchi* and to prepare the soup." I told my guests. "In the meantime, may I ask you which main courses you would like to order? What about our stuffed turkey roulade, salmon in saffron sauce or the prime rib – don't you think you might like it?" "Of course, we will order now," the grandfather assured. "Please be so kind and serve two portions

101

of salmon, two portions of turkey and one portion of pasta fagioli with cream cheese sauce." I was inwardly jumping for joy at the prospect of having escaped with only a slap on the wrist and was looking forward to finishing work on time which made me very happy – at least for about 15 seconds until a chorus of the dear children's voices jolted me out of my reverie: "But we would like *kolhi milakko* and *vardesta curry* to eat, please Grandfather, please!!" *"Kolhi milakko* and *vardesta curry?"* the grandfather replied. "Okay, darlings – and you," he turned to one of his grandchildren and reprimanded him, "if you again show up unshaven at the table tomorrow, you won't get any *shahi tukra* for dessert! Got it?" The chastised grandson winced. *No shahi tukra?* he thought. *I'd better clean up my act!* "Waiter, three times *vardesta curry* and *kolhi milakko*. The executive chef knows how to prepare the meal. We would also like two portions of *raichi chotto chathacho*, which is lamb with some extra *karuvepillal*. This is a curry leaf which adds the necessary zest to the meal. Do you know what I am talking about?" "Of course I do," I replied. "My mom prepares this food for me at least twice a week, but she usually drizzles some lemon juice over the meal." "Really?" he asked. "No, not really!" I answered, slightly stressed. "Unfortunately, I neither know what you're talking about nor do I have any idea how to even write these orders on my notepad. What's the correct spelling for the digested curry?" "No, it's not *digested* curry," I was corrected by the father. *"Vardesta curry* – var-des-ta, have you got it now?" "I think so. And what's the spelling of *curly mikado* or whatever you call it — the meal you mentioned a few minutes ago?" Some of the children started giggling. "Really!" one of the adults blurted out. "Not *curly mikado*, but *kolhi milakko*." "Got it," I said. "And how do you spell *chathachokaruvepillal?*" "Just as it is pronounced. Now please be so kind and get the food we ordered, we are hungry." "Yes, of course, yes, yes, I bring, bring!"

"Oh, there you are, Mr. Massimo, hello!!" I shouted as I turned around to face the already frustrated head waiter. "Keep it down," Massimo said sternly, obviously wanting to escape the notice of the demanding guests and their noisy children. He had been standing behind me and had witnessed the spectacle.

"Look, there is that nice juice waiter from before!" the children cried. "Another round of *mango lassie*, please. This time with some peppermint, please. It tastes so good like that!" "Does it?" Massimo asked. "Yes, indeed!" he was told. "You should try it." "I will," Massimo promised, "maybe in the year 2046!"

"Ha ha!" the whole table erupted into laughter. "The two of you are very amusing," one of the family members expressed who was wearing a turban. "Well," Massimo interjected, "now I'll go to the galley and make our executive chef's and his brigade's day with your elaborate order. I don't think they've had much fun today till now."

The executive chef Anil accepted the order without protest and went into the pantry to look for the necessary spices and ingredients.

Our guests had to wait for an hour until the meals they ordered were finally brought to their table.

"That sure took a long time!" one of the older Indians remarked. "What was the matter – was there a loss of power in the galley?" "No," Massimo replied. "We were rather short of star anise for the *junk malai* ..." "*Jurg malai*," he was corrected. "Yes, for the *jurg*. This is why it took a bit longer."

"I see," the man realized, "but I hope that it won't happen again."

By this time my fellow waiter had to stop and catch his breath before resuming his extraordinary tale.

"And then worse came to worst!" he exclaimed "What happened next?" I asked. "Considering the fact that I had to help out in room service after dinner until the early morning, I didn't want to spend the whole evening and possibly half the night in the dining room. I went to the pastry department to discuss possible Indian desserts with Anil and the head baker which could be offered without an endless discussion at the table about exotic desserts beforehand.

While my guests enjoyed the main courses (I have to admit that they smelled great) and my busboy dutifully ensured everything ran smoothly, I memorized four exotic Indian desserts which the baker had described. I wrote them down, learned them by heart, rewrote them, and repeated them once more before returning to my station. By the time I approached their table I was full of pride and a lot of self-confidence according to the old adage, "practice makes

103

perfect." The Indian guests had meanwhile eaten more or less of all the food on the plates; considering the extra large order it would have been impossible to eat it all in one sitting. After all, it is always better to order too much than too little. The totally sated members of the Indian clan looked at me contentedly and listened attentively as I emulated a top salesman while enthusiastically recommending the desserts I had just been taught and which the baker started preparing. "Ladies and Gentlemen," I cleared my throat, "I am proud to announce our array of Indian desserts which the head baker is preparing at this very moment. First of all there is *rasmalai* as well as *jalebi*, you may also order *halwa* and – to top it all off – *gulabjamun*. As you know, it is very popular and will require a bit more time to prepare. May I take your orders now?" "Three portions of vanilla ice cream without whipped cream, please!" the Indian grandfather replied on behalf of his entire family. "We greatly appreciate your efforts, but we have enjoyed an excellent meal and are full. Nevertheless, many thanks for your offer."

I could not help but look distraught and deflated since their unexpected response was like a slap in the face. I headed for the bakery where our executive chef Anil and the baker were blending the ingredients for the special desserts, and put the piece of paper with the order on the table in front of them. Since this book must remain devoid of profanity, I am not allowed to quote the curses which they uttered at the sight of my order form.

Upon my return to the restaurant I was met by the sight of two empty tables. The gaggle of guests were just heading for the exit, led by a man wearing a turban.

After I had quickly cleaned the station, grabbed a bite to eat in the canteen, and ignored my colleague's malicious question whether I had chosen an Indian meal, I went to room service to assist there for two hours. It wasn't as bad as I had anticipated since I only had to show up for the second breakfast sitting the next morning.

There was a lot to do in the meantime. Guests from the first breakfast who had not eaten anything for three hours called to order a sandwich, a salad or chicken nuggets so they would have enough energy for the various excursions on the next day.

Almost done, I thought. *Another 10 minutes – then you'll be finished with work and can finally go to bed!*
1:45 am – only 15 more minutes. I was already packing my bags and arranging the menus for the next day, when the phone rang. A voice with a distinct Indian accent which I immediately recognized assailed my ear; I could already feel beads of sweat forming on my forehead. "Good evening, this is Mr. Rakesh Nanda speaking, May I please order some desserts? After dinner we were too full, but now we would like to have desserts for 11 persons. Our waiter and executive chef Anil have already prepared something for us, haven't they?"
That can't be happening, I thought while listening to the order. "Three portions of *rasmalai,* five portions of *halva* and three portions of *gulabjamun,* please! Can you bring? Ah, and also some nutmeg tea for 11 persons, can you bring?" "Yes, of course!" I shouted into the earpiece. "I bring, I bring, he he, I bring." "Ingmar!" I yelled at our night shift baker. "Hurry up and bring *halma, goulash ummune* and – he he — *rasmarmalade,* we'll bring it to the cabins in the middle of the night. That will be a fun thing to do, don't you think, ha ha!"
The baker stared at me with bloodshot eyes. Thank God he had been previously instructed by Anil to keep the unordered desserts in the fridge.
He interrupted his work to retrieve the requested desserts.
Half an hour later we were equipped with the desserts – properly and lovingly arranged as we had been taught – and placed them in front of the first of the four cabins. *An Indian dessert party in the middle of the night must be quite amusing,* I thought. Looking forward to a generous tip which is the usual reward for all room service staff around the world – particularly with such a large order – I firmly knocked at the cabin door three times as per the regulations.
Five minutes later the door of a dark cabin was slowly opened. One of the mothers, looking at me with a finger on her lips, appeared at the threshold. "Be quiet," she instructed. "Most of us are already sleeping. I'll only take a bit of *gulabjamun* and a cup of tea. Many thanks! Bring the rest to our neighboring cabins; maybe some of

them are still awake," she recommended and silently closed the door.

Great! I thought. *Bring, bring – and I still have two full serving carts of desserts!* Okay, go ahead, he he, *junk, junk, halma halma* or *halva*, who cares?! Knock, knock, knock at the next door. The door opened and I recognized the friendly face of the Indian who had previously worn a turban. He looked peculiar without the turban since he didn't have much hair, but was wearing large glasses instead. "The desserts are very late," he whispered. "Yes," I admitted. "But it takes longer to prepare these special desserts," I explained.

"Okay," he whispered. "Bring one of the carts into my cabin and the other one to my neighbor." I agreed to bring it in and pushed the serving cart into the dark cabin. My guest briefly nodded his head to express his thanks before he closed the door.

Five minutes later I pushed the second cart into another dark cabin, ignoring the comments of a bearded man who had opened the door. Having closed the door in next to no time I hurried downstairs to room service. All I wanted at that moment was sleep. As already mentioned, I only had to show up for the second breakfast sitting, thank God. By this point I was dog-tired, took a quick shower and fell into a short, but very deep sleep. Mahatma Gandhi appeared in my dream, showed me around the Taj Mahal and extolled the beauties of his country. Just as he was inviting me to join him in a cup of tea, my alarm clock unfortunately starting ringing.

It was 8:00 am; the second sitting started at 8.30 am. After a quick shower, getting dressed and eating breakfast I was again at one of the tables in my station serving some American and Irish guests who were in good spirits while discussing a planned joint excursion.

I was also in a good mood as well, considering the late meal from the previous evening, although my mood was short-lived, since I didn't expected to see my Indian guests until lunch time. "Of course they will have breakfast," my station neighbor assumed who had noticed my fatigue and frustration. "Here they get whatever they want. Imagine this gang going to a restaurant in Mexico and ordering *junk mahal* and *goulash-immune* with *mirchi mirchi*! The Mexicans would totally dismiss their order and go away after

106

leaving a bowl with rice and chili peppers and a bottle of Corona on the table. And can you imagine being on holiday in Mumbai with a group of German-speaking tourists, for example, and going to a restaurant with total disregard of the waiter's menu choices? I wonder how an order like this would go over: "As appetizers we'd like four portions of corn salad with bacon, five portions of steamed quail eggs with sauce Mornay and three portions of tarte flambé with extra crème fraiche, please. For the main course we'd like knuckle of pork with dumplings, marinated horse beef with spaetzle and, unless it is too inconvenient, sweetbread in truffle stock. Don't use too much marjoram, but more tarragon instead." "Indeed," I agreed, "we should try it sometime and, when the waiter asks why we're ordering such food in India, reply with: "Why not?" The Indians also always request their local food no matter in which country they stay. You've heard this before: "Come on, hurry up and prepare the meals we ordered and quickly bring bring. We are hungry!"

All of a sudden we were startled out of our little scenario. The head waiter was just closing the doors, when a man in a turban appeared on the threshold. "Namaste," he said politely. "We would like to have breakfast. Not all of us have arrived yet, but will be here very soon. Is our waiter on duty? He is perfect at his job."

"Yes, he is," the head waiter answered. "Look, he's over there, the waiter with the deathly pale face."

Dear reader, I will stop recounting the story at this point, because anyone could imagine the waiter's condition when he went into the galley where the staff was busy cleaning and preparing lunch. To make matters worse, the waiter, instead of putting in a customary breakfast order for scrambled eggs with bacon, porridge or cornflakes submitted the following order form: three portions of *jdiyappar* with *kadala curry*, three portions of *uthappam wada curry*, two portions of *iddly killumulaga sambar*, some *thairsadam urugai*... The galley brigade could hardly believe their luck.

A similar order was placed for lunch, including the Indian's instruction for the waiter to "bring bring quickly!"

"Well, by that time the waiter's patience had reached its limit. He again tried to serve dinner to the best of his ability, but after the third command to "bring bring" he lost his head – as you can see.

107

The nice doctor has given him some valium. A more experienced waiter will take his place for the rest of the week. Don't worry, he is okay, but he has not had the pleasure of taking care of a large group of Indian guests since. After some chill pills he will be his old self again."

"We are pleased to hear that," the guests at the neighboring tables said. They clinked glasses. "Let's toast to the waiter. We hope that he will soon be himself again. And another toast for our exotic and friendly Indians: '*MIRCHI MIRCHI BRING BRING*!!'"

Chapter 13:   Pickpockets, Theater and More

Let's carry on with the excursion tour... Ninety percent of all guests eagerly look forward to the shows presented in the theater hall in the evening after dinner.

It must be such a great feeling to get up from the table without having to lift a finger. You don't have to clear the table or even do the dishes. All that's expected of you is to politely say goodbye to the waiter and immediately head for the theatre – either staggering or in an upright position, depending on your previous alcohol intake.

The evening shows are really excellent. Artists from all parts of the world entertain the guests with eclectic performances and often receive standing ovations for shows which are usually only seen on TV, in Las Vegas, on Broadway or in Atlantic City. A different program is offered every evening. Sometimes first-class dancers present parts of popular musicals and even sing live on stage; on other evenings professional magicians perform magical tricks on board our cruise liner. You can also enjoy comedians whose anecdotes and jokes guarantee to make you erupt with laughter. There is always a variety of singers who not only cover well-known songs by famous artists, but sometimes closely resemble the original singers and even have a similar voice. Impersonators I especially like include a gentleman from Great Britain who looks startlingly similar to Sir Elton John and performs his songs in every detail; the critically acclaimed band, Beatlemaniacs, who fascinate all age groups with the British cult band's top hits and – last but not least – a member of the former band, "Foreigner". He is a virtuoso who always creates a sensational performance with his accompanying band .

There have been other performers that made a huge impression on me. I will never forget a performance of a Russian musician who played fiery gypsy music on an ordinary violin. After the first song, he put his violin away and unpacked another one which was considerably smaller. With this violin on his shoulder, he enchanted the audience with the same fascinating music. As soon as this song had ended, the violin disappeared in its case. The next instrument came to light, a violin as large as a male hand. It was unbelievable that he even managed to coax sounds out of such a tiny instrument. After every performance he received thunderous applause from the audience who were totally surprised and enrapt by his considerable talent. Waving his hand, he asked them to stop applauding and rummaged again in his bag. A little box in the size of a glasses case appeared. Having carefully opened it, he held a violin in his hand which was as tiny as the smallest mobile phones on the market today. Everybody refused to believe it when the master of this mini-instrument positioned it in the crook of his neck and raised the violin bow.

"He must be kidding," a guest standing next to me commented. "I bet he'll only be able to play 'Chopsticks'." However, he and everyone else in the theater were proved wrong. Once again original gypsy music rang out from the stage, and the musician was accompanied by the rhythmical clapping of the audience. I will never forget the applause for this man. The listeners did not want him to leave the stage. His music provided the same sensation as though I were attending the Bayreuth Festival.

Another artist who always considerably impresses me is an acrobat from Argentina whose performance is out of this world. This incredible artist does a slightly different version of a headstand which is death-defying. He starts his show by doing a headstand on a soccer ball which is balancing on a wine-bottle. It is clearly visible that the ball doesn't want to rest on the bottleneck; it's wobbling tremendously in its actual position. Don't forget that this performance is very often shown on a high sea which the ball obviously doesn't like at all. With his head resting on the football, the artist balances his body, stretches his arms and legs and grasps a pack of cigarettes and a bottle of beer. As if he had all the time in the world, he takes a cigarette out of the package, puts it in his mouth and lights it. Afterwards he seizes the bottle of beer and starts smoking and drinking. He then puts the bottle down, drapes his arms and legs with colorful hoops and rotates them as quickly as a windmill. As I said before, he does this while balancing his head on a soccer ball which is resting on a regular wine-bottle!

Up to this moment it may be only remotely possible to conceive of these acrobatic stunts, but in the next step he not only executes the

111

spectacular headstand, but also a finger stand. Before I describe the acrobat's act, let me point out that there are musclemen like me who, if they are fit and healthy, can only manage to do five push-ups before collapsing, gasping and totally exhausted. By comparison, there are musclemen like Rocky Balboa who practice one arm push-ups, and others with astonishing strength and agility such as Bruce Lee who can easily do a hundred push-ups with only one thumb.

But this Argentine enters the stage, puts a candlestick on the table of a swaying cruise ship, inserts his middle finger, then supports himself on the table with his left hand and does a finger stand with only his middle finger resting in the candlestick. Balancing his body weight of 72 kilograms on his middle finger, he is precariously positioned on the table aboard a ship on the high seas - and smiling! Unbelievable!

I've often talked to him and asked him which muscle he uses to carry his total body weight with only one finger. "I use just one muscle," he replied, tapping his head. "If you start persuading your brain early enough to be able to do something impossible, it will one day become possible"

On another occasion, I even woke up with a jolt after recalling an especially entertaining show by a juggler. Once he had swirled the usual pins and balls, hoops and bottles in the air, he put them in a corner, shortly disappeared behind the curtain and returned with two chain saws. Without making a noise, he threw them into the air - and caught them. After he had put them down on the floor to shake out his arms, he again picked up one of the saws. Seizing the starter rope with his fingers, he looked around. "Shall I continue?" he shouted provokingly. Despite the high level of anxiety spreading in the hall the curiosity of the audience prevailed. A chorus of "yeeees" and the nodding of numerous spectators answered his question. The deafening noise of two saws echoed in the theater and captivated the crowd. This was the first time that many of the guests, myself included, had ever watched two whining chain saws swirling in the air. One carelessness moment or lapse of attention could have meant serious injuries for the artist. The audience breathed a collective sigh of relief when the saws finally fell silent and the master left the stage with a smile on his face.

The funniest and greatest performance I have ever seen during my work on the ship and about which I repeatedly tell my friends and guests even today was presented by a so-called 'professional pickpocket'.

This fellow, a chubby, white-haired man at the tender age of about 65 years, entered the stage. Before he did anything, he first selected seven or eight male guests from the audience and asked them to join him in the bright lights.

He shook hands with each of them in a friendly manner and helped them line up next to each other. Afterwards, he walked in front of and around them, teasing them. He asked one guest whether he could lend him his handkerchief. Imagine the guest's bewilderment when he handed the artist a used, reddish tissue. Holding it between his fingertips, the artist contemptuously scrutinized it.

"Oh my God!" he called out at the man. "If this is your handkerchief, I surely wouldn't want to see your underwear!"

The audience burst into laughter, while the owner of the tissue blushed furiously.

Once again the artist, muttering idly, walked around the group, while the men on the stage and the audience were still trying to figure out what kind of show he was presenting. Suddenly he stopped directly at the stage wall, grinned at the audience, turned his head towards his victims behind him and shouted: "Gentlemen, are you perchance missing anything?" The men shook their heads with a questioning look as they did not know the meaning of this question.

Why would they be missing anything?

"Well then," he continued, "let's have a look at the things you had in your possession until a moment ago."

Opening his jacket, he reached into his trouser pockets. Handkerchiefs, ties, wallets, watches and many other things which had been in the possession of his victims shortly beforehand came to light.

The gentlemen gaped in disbelief at all the objects in the performer's hands and started feverishly rummaging in their pockets - without success! Everything was gone! Stolen right from under their noses!

Murmurs were heard in the hall. This nimble-fingered artist had

113

managed to steal from eight men without the audience or the victims themselves having been the wiser.

The artist received thunderous applause when he returned the valuables to the hapless victims and sent them back to their seats in the audience.

"It's all nonsense, everything is faked!" I heard one of my guests commenting on this show during dinner the next day. "These men belong to the pickpocket's own team and pretend to be unaware of the theft." "I don't think so!" I butted in. "Our company would never pay eight men for entering the stage twice a week, looking a proper Charlie and allowing themselves to be robbed. I am sure that the artist and his show are genuine."

Taken aback by such an outlandish accusation, I mustered up my courage and verbally confronted him. "If you believe that this show is a fake, why don't you come forward the next time? I've heard the 'artist-thief' will perform again in the farewell show."

"Deal," he replied, much to my surprise.

"I'll buy a bottle of Dom Perignon for the whole table, if the guy manages to steal even one item from my pockets." "Wow!", all guests at the table called out. "We're sure looking forward to the champagne." "Not going to happen, Nobody will steal from me!" the doubting Thomas announced.

The evening of this event was fast approaching and I made preparations. I explained to my guest that he had to be fair towards the pickpocket. That is, he would not be allowed to enter the stage half-naked and in shackles like Houdini so that he would not have anything on his person that could be stolen.

"Don't worry," he said. "I'll be dressed appropriately for a formal evening. I'll wear a suit with all accessories. No more, no less."

Eventually the moment had come which almost every guest had eagerly anticipated. The news that this daring and flamboyant pickpocket would enter the stage once again had circulated very quickly.

Prior to the performance I paid a visit to the pickpocket in his cabin to draw his attention to my impertinent guest. I did not intend to tattle, rather, I wanted to make sure that the master would be especially attentive to this disbeliever, and he laughingly complied.

After the artist had accomplished his usual astonishing feat of stealing unbeknownst to his victims, for example an expensive Rolex watch from my guest as well as various objects from the other gentlemen he had selected during this performance, the audience witnessed something very peculiar. The guests were starting to leave after the master had returned his victims' valuables when at that moment it was glaringly obvious that the disbeliever's trousers were at half-mast. In other words, his trousers had slipped down to his knees. Can you guess how that happened? Right! The foolish man had worn suspenders instead of a belt. As they were no longer attached to his trousers, but now dangled from the thief's wrist, his suit pants had gradually slipped down. The audience was very amused to notice two ugly legs and even uglier underwear. The poor guy was evidently very embarrassed, desperately and angrily trying to cover his nakedness by pulling up his trousers. "I am awfully sorry!" the thief smirked. "Come on, I'll help you put on your trousers." The victim was really annoyed to have to accept his help because, as you know, it is far easier to attach suspenders with the assistance of a second person.

"Okay, my dear fellow," the thief continued, "done! Godspeed!" "The hell with that!" the victim replied so that the audience started laughing again while he returned to his seat. "By the way," the master shouted from the stage, "don't you need your watch and your wallet anymore?"

The audience couldn't stop laughing because there was no doubt that the thief had again stolen the watch and wallet from his victim while he helped him get dressed. My dear guest looked crestfallen when he went back to the stage dragging his feet to collect his valuables. Amidst the increasing applause he sneaked off. Totally fed up by the evening and its antics, he left the theater hall.

The next evening, the promised bottle of Dom Perignon packed in ice had been placed next to his dinner table. A fact his table neighbors noticed with malicious pleasure. He was very cordially welcomed when he gave me a sign to open the bottle upon his arrival in the dining room.

"Unbelievable!" he remarked. "I still cannot believe I never noticed or felt anything. The guy was terrific! In the future I will be more careful about commenting on performers. After all, I can't exactly afford champagne in this price range every day."

115

After the show I paid a visit to the master in his cabin to congratulate him on his fantastic performance. I also wanted to know how long it had taken to perfect his skills. "Fifteen years," was his reply, which did not surprise me at all.

The brilliant thief continued to perform this magnificent, crowd-pleasing show for only another two years before he died, much to my regret. I have attended several similar shows since, but none of them was as good as his exceptional performance.

Apropos pickpockets... Dear Readers, keep an eye on your belongings during your shore excursions at all times! The pickpockets hanging around in the ports to rob naïve tourists are becoming increasingly audacious and resourceful. And these thieves are the genuine article! Nowadays the pilferers do not even wait until a tourist is momentarily distracted to quickly and skillfully remove a wallet from a back trouser pocket. No, these days they approach you in a friendly, unsuspecting manner, and before you realize it, your wallet has been stolen. Also beware of pretty ladies who welcome you in the respective country and offer you a beautiful rose. Of course you will respond to such a hospitable gesture why not? After all, what's the harm in being greeted by two cute young women who give you a lovely flower? You honor the kindness shown by admiring its wonderful scent, have a laugh with the nice ladies, and if you have a command of the native language, you might even briefly make small-talk with them before moving along, smiling about their generosity and charm. Minutes later you want to buy a souvenir, but then you make the awful realization that your wallet is gone, stolen by the girlfriend of the friendly rose-offering woman who took advantage of your carelessness, walked behind you and grabbed your wallet.

Also be advised of the 'pregnant woman-trick' which is employed by young pickpocket couples. This is how the scenario usually plays out. As a tourist is out walking, he suddenly bumps into a woman who seems to have appeared out of nowhere and is in an advanced stage of pregnancy. She then immediately groans and convulses in severe pain. In complete shock of the prospect of having hurt the lady and her baby, you unsuspectingly bend forward to apologize. The young husband has waited for exactly this moment to pick the tourist's wallet out of his trouser pocket. The

116

young woman must be careful not to lose the cushion which she uses to feign pregnancy. A word to the wise; please beware of pregnant women who appear rather clumsy!

The gangs of thimble riggers who are up to no good throughout the world can also be categorized as audacious. Almost every tourist remembers the small tables on which either cards, nutshells or little hats are skillfully mixed to cheat innocent takers who are supposed to remember certain cards or an object hidden under the shells. This always goes wrong, ensuring the tourist consequently loses his hard-earned money. Ladies and Gentlemen, always bear in mind that the guys who seem to win these games are not random tourists but belong to the gang so that the money always stays in the family. Upon mastering this thimblerig, I couldn't resist the temptation to try my hand at this popular shell game in Barcelona. During the first round I played dumb and moaned after I had lost 50 DM. But afterwards it was my turn, I bet on the right card three times in a row and won 150 DM.

I had not gone far when three of the guys appeared in front of me, all wielding knives, and politely asked me to return their money. As I had already expected this to happen, I forked out the money and – thank God – escaped unscathed, hearing the words, "You are one of us!" This was the first and last time I had taken on these idlers. Let me give you a good piece of advice: always stay far away from the thimbleriggers.

And now you've had an insider's view on not only the goings-on aboard a cruise ship, the spectacular evening shows, as well as situations to avoid. Anyone who would like to combine a pleasant trip to the most beautiful places of the world, experience fantastic food and a touch of Las Vegas will never be disappointed.

I am often asked whether I have already had the pleasure to have celebrities among my guests, which was the case, even several times. Let me share some of my more stellar experiences…

For example, I had the privilege of serving the most famous wine experts throughout the world, Mr. Philippe Rothschild and Mr. Mondavi, who introduced us to the popular wine, Opus One.

Members of ruling families from Saudi Arabia, Kuwait and Qatar have also been guests on our cruise ship on numerous occasions. They evidently enjoyed forgetting about government affairs for a few days and mingling with the other regular guests without being encumbered by their official attire. They were not at all conspicuous and ate and drank like everyone else. They were also thrilled by my magic tricks and couldn't seem to get enough of them.

You have likely already heard about the enormous tips bestowed by sheiks which are likewise given away to all waiters and assistants without exception. At the end of the cruise, a few hundred dollars are handed out to everybody, which is a pleasant surprise for the waiters who were likely not even aware that royals had been on board. It is, however, less surreal for those who have served the sheiks during the entire week and who have expected to be in a position to retire upon receipt of their tip.

I experienced another very enjoyable and especially memorable moment when I was playing the grand piano - a fixture on most cruise ships - at the restaurant. A friendly older gentleman sat down next to me. He indicated I should continue, whereupon we played a lovely duet. The melodic sound was hardly surprising as I was accompanied by the popular composer, Bernie Wayne, who wrote world hits such as "Blue Velvet." We played, made mistakes, laughed, and had a lot of fun. I still have his address although he died long ago.

Once I had the opportunity to welcome the rapper Coolio and the super-rapper and actor Ice-T at my station. While Coolio was very tight-lipped and reserved, Ice T was very candid. He let me know where he got his ideas for his songs and how scenes in a film are shot. He told me about the many aspects of being a actor and how action scenes sometimes need to be shot repeatedly until they are acceptable. What a nice guy! On another occasion I served the acclaimed actress Whoopi Goldberg, whom I also had the pleasure of dancing with at the disco. I also met legendary comedian Jerry Lewis and teen idol Macaulay Culkin. He showed up with his friends on board our ship shortly after the shooting of Home Alone and enjoyed bantering with us.

One day as I was sitting at the captain's table preparing the bookings, actor Corey Feldman approached me. He asked for a table for two as he wanted to eat without being disturbed. We were pleased to fulfill this wish. He enjoyed talking about his great

118

successes with films such as Stand by Me, Lost Boys and License to Drive with Corey Haim, as well as discussing his dream of becoming a producer.

Singer Gloria Estefan is a very lovely woman who enchanted everyone with her charisma and candor. Even today, the waiters talk about the cruise with her, and they all hold the opinion that she is the most ordinary superstar in the world.

The family of basketball legend Magic Johnson was also very impressive. He joined a group of devoutly religious persons aboard our ship with the intent of enjoying the cruise atmosphere with us to the fullest. They were all unassuming and unpretentious, and the children, although very young at that time, were likewise well-behaved and polite.

In addition to singers and actors, numerous other stars from radio and TV as well as voice actors and newscasters were among my guests, and I only have good things to say about all of them. The guest who meant most to me even to this day was the daughter of the once-in-a-century comedian, Stan Laurel. I hve been in close contact with Louise Laurel for many years. While we were spending a few hours together, she told me about the life of her famous father. My own film collection includes 96 Laurel & Hardy movies. Louise Laurel was amused and laughed when I re-enacted a few popular scenes from some of the movies. I've enjoyed mimicking Stanley's facial expressions and gestures for years, especially when he'd exasperated his partner, Olli. I made Louise a lifelong promise to encourage and remind fellow Laurel & Hardy fans to buy their movies and to watch them on special occasions. The legends Laurel & Hardy must not be forgotten, and I will do my utmost to resurrect their memory as well enjoy watching the films with friends and family and inevitably exploding from laughter.

But now let's refer again to the interesting aspects of a cruise and activities to while away the time between meals. It's no secret that gyms have long been very popular, and it's no different on a cruise ship. Our guests regularly go to fitness centers, regardless of their level of fitness, as they do not want to spend all time on board only exercising their mandible muscles, but also want keep their entire body in shape. While the fitness equipment was quite unpretentious twenty years ago, nowadays the most sophisticated, cutting-edge equipment is directly delivered from fitness industry gurus to our cruise liners.

In the 21sr century, however, gym equipment for the modern woman is far more advanced. There are machines that shape the body, relax muscles, knead feet, scratch backs, varnish toenails, perform electrolysis, display the latest cooking recipes on a screen and can even rock a baby to sleep while Mommy works out.

Fitness equipment for men today isn't anything to sneeze at, either. There are mechanisms to help build up muscles, shape buttocks, massage a potbelly, remove nose hairs, polish a bald pate, and even inform of the latest losses at the stock exchange via high-tech headphones.

Perhaps I've exaggerated slightly, but it is really incredible to what extent modern technology can keep the body and brain fit. However, pushing, pulling, running and stepping is too exhausting and strenuous for females and males alike. Instead, they prefer relaxing in our wellness areas which nowadays are also most exquisite. In addition to the usual facilities such as outdoor and indoor swimming pools – often designed in the most beautiful Roman style reminiscent of the time of Julius Caesar – guests looking for wellness or aesthetic facilities have a myriad of options at their disposal: Turkish baths and eyewash facilities, saunas, massage studios, mud baths, manicurists, pedicurists as well as our hair salons which are predominantly managed by first-class British hair stylists.

The wellness program is completed by an acupuncture station which is increasingly consulted for the treatment of minor aches and pains. For many people, myself including, a visit to the doctor is something to be avoided at all costs. Moreover the acupuncture practitioners do not only treat health problems, they also care for your well-being as a whole and inform guests of other ancient treatment methods using extremely fine needles.

Dear Ladies and Gentlemen, anyone who is still fearful of this cure can be assured of the following fact: the fine art of acupuncture has nothing to do with the stereotypical little Chinese person wearing a white coat and horn-rimmed spectacles who takes pleasure in jabbing needles into the victim's skin while grinning sadistically as the unsuspecting patient loses consciousness. Acupuncture is a serious alternative to more conventional methods and gives your body a treat. It is true that my guests who have previously been afflicted with headaches and migraines feel much better thanks to the relaxing cruise and a few acupuncture treatments. In general, a cruise on board our ship combined with the wellness treatment specials offered daily is a balm for the soul.

Other facilities such as climbing walls and mini-golf courses are also exciting diversions which are located in the rear of our ships. They are popular with all age groups who would like to show off their skill or physical strength. Many guests get enthusiastic about climbing steep rock faces and are of course protected against falls by a safety rope around their waist. The expert climber manages to scale the wall which is more than six meters high in next to no time. Having reached the top he may enjoy a magnificent view over the sea or the port. Untrained summiteers, by contrast, often misjudge the degree of difficulty involved in climbing the wall. They make quite a spectacle as they slip down and frequently dangle from the rope like Spiderman who has just eaten something amiss. Even worse, they don't know which side is up. Luckily, minutes before they plummet to their demise, they will be rescued from their precarious situation and brought down to the floor by use of a rope. After such a strenuous experience they will undoubtedly have sore muscles and their aching limbs will need to be treated at the wellness facilities.

The bright green golf course is another truly enjoyable facility. It is slightly different from the usual mini-golf course where the ball has to overcome obstacles before it is putted into a hole. With the exception of the first long drive, our golf course is similar to a regular golf course. Typical, non-artificial obstacles such as deep ditches filled with water, sand pits and ground waves need to be overcome to hole the ball with as few drives as possible – a rather difficult task which nevertheless enthuses every golf fan and keeps him busy in the open air.

The golf course is often open until late at night, allowing you the pleasure of wreaking havoc with the little ball under floodlights. Nearly every night you can watch tipsy guests who take a short break from the activities in the disco and play golf in order to

121

become sober. This, however, is not hazard-free, since the ball is rather frequently duffed, meaning that the unfortunate person standing too close to the clumsy amateur golfer invariably ends up getting hit on the shinbone by a golf club.

Chapter 14: Minigolf and Ice-Skating on the High Seas

It was an evening I'll never forget... I was walking past our small hospital after work late at night and noticed three individuals with various bandaged limbs sitting in the well-lit waiting-room. They were in a foul mood, groaning with pain and quarrelling with each other.

As is proper for a good waiter who cares for the well-being of his guests, I politely asked what had happened and whether I could be of assistance.

"It's impossible to tell," one of the two gentlemen replied. "We had a bit too much to drink in the disco and wanted to play golf to relax and sober up." He pointed to his neighbor, "This idiot was too inept to hit the ball so the club crashed into my hand instead with full force and broke my little finger. I was so angry that I smacked his ugly face in. He ended up with a laceration that needed stitches."

"That's terrible, really terrible," I said, "and what happened to this guy here?" "Well, he unfortunately ran into some bad luck. After I'd slapped my silly friend, he crashed backward into our third man. He in turn also fell, got his foot stuck in a seat and ended up with a twisted ankle!"

I tried to take the situation seriously, but I almost burst out laughing. The sight of the three patients who were sitting there with a bandaged hand, a bandaged head and a bandaged ankle – simply because they had attempted to play mini-golf – was more reminiscent of a Laurel and Hardy movie than of a sport involving three adult passengers. But that's the way they are – our young and hot-headed British guys!

At this point you will perhaps wonder whether there are even more facilities on board for whiling away the time. The answer is: yes, of course there are!

There are few cruise ship passengers who would expect an ice skating rink on board. Dear reader, it's the truth! Our latest cruise ships offer a small ice skating rink which everybody is allowed to use. You can start right away, that is, once you've changed into warmer clothes and have donned a pair of skates. The rink's area comprises approx. 500 m², offering sufficient space for beginners and advanced skaters alike.The first ice skating rink on a cruise ship all over the world was inaugurated by our German ice princess Katarina Witt who was thrilled about the possibility to revive her performance onboard a cruise liner.

Would you perhaps like to know whether entertainment is offered at the skating rink? Of course it is! Once or twice a week we invite you you to an abbreviated version of Holiday on Ice where former stars often demonstrate they are still able to perform complicated maneuvers. It's a wonderful cavalcade of talent which nobody would expect to see on a cruise. Sometimes even the crew is allowed to showcase their skating prowess, which results in sly, knowing smiles the next morning. The sight of some of the waiters hobbling and contorting with pain at work the following day immediately reveals that they were perhaps not as skillful on the ice as they had imagined the evening before. A bandage here, a scratch there, and sometimes even a missing tooth are evidence of attempting a feat such as the triple axel which ended in a crash into the advertisement board.

Have you now been completely apprised of all entertainment facilities on board? No, not at all! Even the surfers among you will get your money's worth on our modern cruise ships. At this moment I imagine you asking, "What? Surfing on a cruise ship? Impossible!" Well, you're wrong! Nowadays beginners and advanced surfers have the chance to demonstrate their skills on a surfboard in an ultra-modern facility which I call Little Hawaii. You can perform your stunts while balancing on a wave which can be set to different heights. There is no danger of being swept away by a tsunami or washed overboard. Little Hawaii is great fun for professionals, beginners, as well as children.

On that note, you may be surprised to learn that there are indeed entertainment facilities that cater to children on a cruise ship.

First of all I would like to assure all parents who have never thought of taking a cruise because they assume their offspring would get bored, or fear that a cruise with children might be extremely stressful and consequently impossible. Believe me when I claim that you will be lucky if you see your children more than twice a day. Also be assured that the little ones will be perfectly cared for and kept busy almost around the clock.

Special activities and events for all age groups are on the agenda:

sporting activities, all types of competitions, a disco, a craft corner, video arcade, karaoke and of course, the swimming pools. These are only a few examples of entertainment your children can look forward to, no matter whether they are toddlers or teenagers. Activities are created and supervised by specially trained caretakers who not only consider the supervision of children an important occupation, but also a pleasant job. Their primary aim is to get their charges so hyped about being on a cruise that they will beg their parents to take another holiday on the high seas. In most cases the parents will be pleased to fulfill this wish since they are also looking forward to more incredible adventures in the panoramic atmosphere on board a cruise ship. Parents welcome the luxury of enjoying a break while qualified staff takes care of their offspring during their stay. What's more, they needn't worry about their children's whereabouts, what they are doing and with whom. While relaxing at the pool, don't be surprised if your little sweethearts suddenly approach you and announce they are going to play golf or play in a table tennis tournament or even boast that they were taught how to dance on skates. And don't be alarmed if you're suddenly accosted by a crowd of strange children dressed as pirates and happily brandishing their plastic swords while you are dining alone. Their caretaker, dressed up as chief pirate, gathers the little pirates of the Caribbean around the microphone and shouts, "Hi everyone, the ship has just been boarded by pirates. Are you frightened?" The guests of course reply with a loud "Yeeeeeess!" before the chief pirate again rises to speak. "Hi pirates, do you see the captain sitting over there?" The children shout, "Hi Captain, we are capturing your ship!" "And where's the captain's wife?" the chief pirate wants to know. The children reply, "She's on a shopping tour on the island!" "And where's the captain's grandma?" "She's playing binnnnnngoooo!"

Everyone cheers as the little pirates leave the dining room as quickly as they'd barged in and then proceed to the swimming pool for more pirate games, accompanied by thunderous applause.

Entertainment on board a ship doesn't necessarily entail going to the theater to watch performances by professionals. You can expect amusing entertainment anywhere and at any time. During my year-long work in the restaurant I not only watched numerous funny

126

waiters' performances while serving meals, but also participated in them.

Our guests attach great importance to their private, ceremonial occasions. No matter whether they celebrate a birthday, a wedding, honeymoon, or university graduation, there is always an occasion for enjoying a good wine or a delectable dessert.

I was told that on the inaugural cruise of our ships the shipping company was impetuous enough to promise a free cake and a bottle of champagne to all guests celebrating a birthday during the cruise. On the first evening on board, exactly 180 guests showed interest in celebrating their great day at the company's expense. On the second day, another 120 dear persons prevailed on the food and beverage manager's generosity: he was obliged to provide 300 bottles of champagne and 300 cakes to the passengers – free of charge – and seemed to have aged at least twenty years after the fact. However, the impudence of one young couple trumped everything up to that point. One evening they beckoned the head waiter over to let him know that they had a reason to celebrate the next day. They were very mysterious and only wanted to divulge the reason once the cake and champagne had been served, and when all table neighbors as well as the waiters, assistant waiters and head waiters would be present to raise their glasses in a toast to the announced reason and sing an appropriate song.

The following evening numerous employees had gathered around the table when the head waiter – balancing the cake in his right hand and the champagne bottle in his left hand – approached the couple's table to help celebrate their great day. As the head waiter had not yet been advised of the reason for this celebration until that moment, he crouched next to the man and asked him to whisper the reason for celebrating into his ear. When he learned what the couple had to celebrate, his face reddened with anger. Nevertheless he put on a brave face and went through with the ceremony.

"Ladies and Gentlemen, may I please have your attention," the head waiter requested. "These lovely people have booked a cruise to celebrate an important event. They have come on board our ship to toast their successful divorce two weeks ago. Let's raise our glasses and hope that both of them will be happy forevermore!" He turned to the waiters and table neighbors: "Ladies and Gentlemen, I kindly

127

ask you to sing the appropriate song for this occasion, but with a small change in wording: We will simply replace the word 'birthday' with 'divorce'."

Shortly thereafter, dinner guests who were standing around the table, visibly distraught yet amused, loudly sang out the revised song, "Happy divorce to you! Happy divorce to you!" while the head waiter filled the glasses with champagne.

The company's patience was understandably exhausted by this strange celebration of a divorce. The generous offer to grandly celebrate private occasions was abruptly cancelled irrespective of the protests and imprecations of other guests who had also contrived a reason worth celebrating.

Families whose members of all ages had birthdays during this particular week and who had already expected to receive as many as five bottles of champagne free of charge went away empty-handed.

This type of avarice-inspired scheming was also the undoing of George, one of my roommates. He wanted to demonstrate his ingeniousness and on each cruise he informed his guests that he was celebrating his birthday that particular week. This strategy worked to his benefit for quite a while. The kind, well-wishing clients paid their tip and even included extra cash in an envelope with the note Happy birthday, George!

One day, however, the wise guy had to serve a particularly large station when a waiter fell ill and was unable to work. As George was very busy looking after his guests and informing them it was his birthday, he did not bother to commit any of the guests' faces or names to memory. Consequently, he did not realize that one of the customers, a very quiet but resolute widow had not only been on a previous cruise but had also dined in his section. She patiently listened to the 'birthday fairy tale' for the second time and decided to take action. She wrote an indignant letter to the shipping company and exposed George's methods of capitalizing on the guests' good faith in order to make extra money. As a consequence of his misbehavior, waiter George was downgraded to an assistant waiter. He was informed that he would not lose his job, but could never expect to be upgraded to a waiter or head waiter. A few weeks later George quit and tried his luck with another shipping

128

company. We don't know whether he still celebrates his birthday every week or whether he changed his tune and now celebrates his saint's day.

130

Chapter 15:   Whales, Chinese and Bread Pudding

It was always a highlight and a welcome change for our guests to be entertained by the crew during a meal. Such entertainment is still customary nowadays, but is carried out in moderation.

Back then, the waiters started playing some very popular tricks on the guests at lunch time. For example: a guest ordered banana ice cream for dessert and was duly horrified when an unpeeled banana garnished with a few ice cubes and a mound of whipped cream was served to him on a plate. "What is this supposed to be?",the confused customer asked the waiter. "What this is supposed to be?" the waiter countered. "You ordered banana ice cream, didn't you? Look at your plate! I brought you exactly what you ordered." The waiter once again specified the ingredients and pointed at the banana for emphasis. "Enjoy the meal," was all he said as he left the table to watch the guest's reaction among the other waiters. The staff was of course well aware of the guests they could banter with and that they'd avoid getting into trouble. However, the reaction of some guests was indeed rather surprising. You likely assume that most of the guests realized the so-called banana ice cream was a joke, but this was not the case. A fair number of our dear customers really believed that the dessert was legitimate. Why wouldn't sweet delicacies be presented differently on a Caribbean cruise than the desserts back home? In any case I felt a bit sorry for any clueless customer who dutifully peeled the banana, cut it into small pieces, dipped it into the whipped cream and ate it as-is. The only difficulty was in disposing of the ice cubes which were usually poured into a glass of water or iced tea once the 'banana ice cream' was eaten.

Another very popular meal was the bread and butter pudding which is known as Arme Ritter in Germany. It usually consists of stale bread (day-old rolls as a rule) which is first soaked in milk to soften it, then dipped in the egg and milk mixture and pan-fried until it is golden brown. The last step is a garnish of either vanilla, chocolate or fruit sauce and a few raisins, and voilà you have a delicious dessert. Older ladies in particular who had been eagerly anticipating the dish they recalled from their childhood, looked very surprised when the waiter placed his variation of bread and butter pudding in front of them. The waiter had brought an old, rock-hard roll, made a hole in it with his thumb and then put three little packets of butter on it. This specialty was topped off by a huge dollop of whipped cream which the baker, who always liked to participate in our jokes, had artfully arranged around the roll.

"Bread and butter pudding, Ma'am. Just as you ordered!" the waiter said when he put down the strange dish in front of his guest. In most instances this disgusting dessert was revealed as a lighthearted joke, and the chosen guest would laugh along with the waiter. But there is always an exception to every rule.

"What did you order?" an older lady wanted to know while she scrutinized her friend's dessert. "Bread and butter pudding," she replied. "But I am not sure whether it is exactly the way I remember it from home." "Well, to each to his own," the older lady commented. "I'm glad I didn't order it."

The unwitting victim then started to open the packet of butter and looked at the old bread more closely and tentatively before tasting the 'dessert'. She was very relieved when the waiter suddenly appeared at her side with the correct version of the pudding shortly thereafter and served it to her with a smile.

Our little pranks did not exclusively involve food, rather, they were generally intended to test the credulity of the customers in a fun way. Once a week, usually on a day on the high seas and during lunchtime in the fully occupied restaurant, the following scenario would play out: a waiter would suddenly shout, "Whaaale, whaaaale!" while standing at the window. Four or five more waiters would jump up, go to the window and join in the chorus announcing the whale that had just been spotted on the ocean.

None of the guests wanted to miss this spectacle as most of them had never caught sight of a whale. Similar to mass hysteria, the guests who had sat down for their meal on the other side of the dining room abruptly left their places to get a seat at the window on the 'whale' side as quickly as possible in the hope of observing these colossal mammals at close range. Overturned tables and broken chairs were a common sight as a result of the frenzied panic. Some guests even suffered from bruises and sprained ankles after the crowds of people tried to squeeze onto one side of the restaurant.

Five hundred guests stood at the window in a tiny space, pressing their noses against the window so as not to miss such a phenomenal sight.

They kept looking and gaping out the window while excitedly talking among themselves, yet they couldn't discern anything that resembled the mammal. No surprise, since there was no whale to begin with!

Suddenly another waiter showed up in the middle of the dining room. He held up a large cardboard cutout of a large, laughing whale painted in blue ink which impishly grinned at the bamboozled guests.

After the fact, most of our dear guests were alternately outraged and amused by our antic and returned to their seats.

This trick worked quite effectively until a lady weighing around 150 kilograms broke two toes during her attempt to get through to the "whale" side. She took legal action, and the cardboard whale which had caused amusement for many years was subsequently burnt and disposed of in a celebratory ceremony.

Shows performed by the waiters are also part of the entertainment and offer an enjoyable diversion. These shows have a two-fold purpose: to amuse guests and provide a temporary change in routine from their evening meal. These performances are an integral part of our service even today and you must also bear in mind that the management of our ships is American, which automatically means that anytime is show time!

These shows are usually presented as follows: at a preordained time during dinner, a signal such as a loud melody rings out over the loudspeaker, whereupon all the waiters disappear. Upon the signal the waiters and assistant waiters gather at the entry of the galley where they await further instructions.

The orders are given by the head waiters while the other staff stand in line and march into the dining room against the backdrop of the guests' applause and to the beat of a popular piece of music. The show is followed by a speech in several languages which is customarily given by the head waiter before a song is squeaked and sung out of tune by the waiter brigade to the best of their collective ability. The song O Sole Mio is very popular. Thank God the legendary Mr. Pavarotti has never been a guest on board one of our ships. If he had listened to the unofficial Italian national anthem performed by 150 waiters from at least 30 different countries, his appetite would have been spoiled for at least a month. Our guests, however, enjoy the vocal stylings of the not-so-musical staff. During every performance their thunderous applause changes to rhythmic clapping which accompanies the waiter brigade while they leave the restaurant.

The waiters, however, do especially enjoy this type of singing. One of their favorite performances, however, is the weekly bullfight. On one occasion two assistant waiters masqueraded as a bull ran in stooped position in front of a head waiter. He in turn wore the uniform of a matador and elegantly waved a red cloth. I usually played the role of the matador and looked ridiculous. The fact that I am fair-haired, do not sport a mustache or the facial expression typical of a Spanish torero notwithstanding, I did my best to make the bull sweat. I was always given a round of applause when I held the red cloth in front of the service station so that the bull would crash into it at full force and collapse. Of course we had rehearsed this stunt in advance so that none of my colleagues were hurt.

This performance worked quite effectively until it was my Spanish colleague Pablo's turn to portray the matador. He wanted to demonstrate to everybody what an authentic bullfight should look like. The bull was running, puffing and blowing and tried its utmost to obey the matador's commands. The show came to an abrupt end, however, when Pablo – in the heat of the moment – let the bull crash into the wrong service station where ten bottles of expensive Dom Perignon champagne had been stored for VIP guests at the captain's table that evening. With a loud bang all of the champagne bottles successively fell to the floor where they either spilled or lay in fragments. In consideration of this substantial damage the head waiter immediately put a halt to this kind of entertainment in the restaurant.

The Chinese show was another very amusing show. On the evening in which Asian cuisine was served, some of the waiters and assistants politely excused themselves from their guests for a few minutes to prepare a surprise. Behind the curtains they changed out of their uniforms, put on red shiny silk suits, then stood in line in the restaurant. Two of the Chinese men in the group were particularly conspicuous due to their Jamaican origin. After they had procured a large gong typically seen in Asian movies, the show started. The dining room was dimmed, music one would expect at a traditional Asian restaurant rang out and the peculiar procession slowly started moving. The waiters solemnly walked past the guests, step by step. While each one concentrated on marching on step, the colleague carrying the gong had an additional mission to fulfill. Without moving his head, he scoped out a victim among the guests, one who was no longer wide awake either due to the delicious food or a strenuous shore excursion that day. There was almost always one of the guests on the verge of dozing off at the table, thus providing the perfect sitting duck for our waiter with the gong.

At the very moment in which the unsuspecting guest's head started sinking to his chest, the 'Chinese' man slowly raised his arm with the gigantic mallet. As soon as it was at eye level with the inattentive guest on the verge of a post-dinner nap, it happened: The mallet slammed down on the large gong and a tinny clap of thunder echoed through the dining room. The guests who had watched the odd procession with interest and a knowing smile saw the stroke of the gong coming and covered their ears in anticipation. The poor sleepy victim, however, awoke with a start and looked as if wrested out of his slumber by the trumpets of Jericho. Some of the drowsy guests wildly gesticulated and cried out, "What's the matter, what's going on? Is the ship sinking? Is it in distress?"

Laughter and words of consolation from neighboring dining guests brought the hapless victim – who by then must have suffered a nightmare – back to reality, and explained what had happened. This gag was carried out until a guest vehemently complained to the shipping company and threatened to take legal action after the gong had purportedly caused his hearing defect. This humorless guest's complaint put an end to the Asian rendition of a wake-up call.

The funniest and most extravagant show I have ever participated in was a dance known as the flaming babaloo, a biscuit cream cake with half an eggshell on top filled with high-proof rum. After the alcohol had been lit, the respective waiter balanced the cake with the small flame on his head. All the waiters crossed the dining room by dancing in rank and file to the rhythm of the festive music.

135

Although this sounds quite easy, it is virtually impossible to execute. First of all, none of the waiters were overly accurate with regard to half an eggshell and adding only a modest portion of rum because they all were eager to be recognized and enthusiastically spurred on by their guests. Consequently we – myself included – used three to four eggshells instead of one half, and as opposed to only a few drops of rum a quarter liter was generously poured over the cake. Suffice to say, it was a struggle to balance this flaming creation on our heads without dropping it. The bar waiters from the Caribbean were regarded with envy since they could effortlessly swing their hips to the beat of the music without missing a step. The other waiters used napkins which they put on their heads like a wreath to stabilize the cake. Nevertheless, we frequently had to hold the cake with both hands to prevent it from dropping. Of course even so the cakes fell down quite often, which was extremely amusing for the guests. Ray, a waiter from England, prepared very meticulously for every show and always led the way. He painstakingly measured the high-proof rum by pouring half a bottle on the cake and drinking the other half. The second half was combined with cola or another soft drink. "Fuelled by alcohol" was his catchphrase as he staggered to the door and awaited the music that was our starting signal for dancing into the dining room. Would he be in a position to balance the cake on the head as properly as the other bar waiters? Not at all! He was one of the most unskillful waiters and was always forced to firmly hold the flaming inferno in order to put one foot in front of the other. Nevertheless he stalwartly kept leading the procession. In this context I have to note that contrary to nowadays, back then it was possible to perform duties as a waiter in a semi-conscious and tipsy state. As long as nobody complained, the following rule was applicable: "Anything goes, as long as you don't get caught."

The guests always reacted with side-splitting laughter whenever the dessert dropped to the floor. The drunken Ray did his utmost to pick it up as quickly as possible and place it on his head again. It looked funny and ridiculous at the same time as he tried to imitate the local dancers from the Caribbean. They in turn would have liked most to throw this well-oiled idiot overboard as he ridiculed their dancing.

One day, however, our English firebug did not properly measure the alcohol and ended up drinking much more than what he poured on the cake. By the time he started dancing, he was squiffy. The guests welcomed his show with rapturous applause and were nearly in hysterics when the 'master' again and again lost the cake which was lying somewhere on the floor, still aflame. "Not enough eggshells, not enough rum!" Ray exclaimed with slurred speech as he was once again forced to pick up his cake and run back to the galley. In less to no time he positioned a dozen eggs on the cake and filled them with half a bottle of alcohol. Firmly holding the cake on his head with both hands, he hurried back into the dining room to join the procession which had already reached the middle of the restaurant. Forging ahead, he reached for his lighter.

All of us could foretell the accident that the hothead was about to unleash. In defiance of all warnings regarding the excessive amount of alcohol poured on the cake which had since spread onto Ray's upper body as a result of his frenetic activity, he proceeded to light the babaloo. At first nothing happened; the cake was still on top of Ray's head. This, however, changed within moments when he again removed it to check the height of the flame. Some of the rum dripped onto his head in the process and – stimulated by the heat of the fire – immediately started burning. As the remaining alcohol on his head and on his uniform also wanted to participate in the dancing party, more than just a few drops of rum were burning by that time. Only three seconds later our hero Ray was decorated by a crown of fire on his head and around his shoulders – while he remained completely oblivious! Due to his drunkenness he continued dancing amid the audience's thunderous applause. Interpreting their shouts as cheers of encouragement, he reveled in his fiery performance. The colleagues who had all been prepared for this moment put an abrupt end to his dangerous antics. Three or four buckets of iced water which are always on hand in every waiter station were used as fire extinguishers without further ado and emptied on his fine head.

There he was, the poor tipsy devil, looking baleful with his burnt hair, destroyed eyebrows and the charred cake in his hand.

By this point all of us were well aware this episode heralded the end of the babaloo procession, at least in this version. And we were right. Fire as a prop during the show was only permitted for dancers who hailed from the Caribbean or who were extremely talented. Most of these privileged dancers originated from Jamaica, the gorgeous and fascinating island with its famous reggae atmosphere.

Chapter 16:   Jamaica

The tropical island of Jamaica is one of the most beautiful islands of the Caribbean Sea. During our cruises we often anchor in the famous port of Ocho Rios.

Visiting this green island is a must in order to understand how the most popular Jamaican, Bob Marley, got inspiration for his worldwide hits. After having paid a visit to almost every island of the Caribbean Sea, I can tell you that many of them are very similar with regard to the landscape and the people. Jamaica, however, is entirely different.

As soon as you set foot on the island, two things will catch your eye straightaway: first, the nonchalant behavior of the islanders who are evidently not familiar with the term 'timid' and second, the tall, gazelle-like physique of most of the island's inhabitants. This will help you understand why so many world-class athletes originate from this relatively small island.

Expect to be enthusiastically welcomed in front of the cruise ship; everybody is keen to be your travel guide and offers his services. Those who have not booked an excursion on board the ship beforehand are pleased to be guided by a local. In return for a few dollars he will show his guests the town, the beaches and above all the famous Dunn's River Falls of Ocho Rios. Not only can you admire the beautiful falls, you can also climb them as this attraction is not a typical waterfall with thundering water waves but with a river gently winding downward. The river falls are usually climbed barefoot, which will help you not to lose contact with the small and large rocks and more important, prevent you from falling into the water. Of course one occasionally hears the yelps of a tourist who has lost his balance and ends up taking an involuntary bath in the cool water, but this is part of the attraction. In any case I can recommend this adventure. The good doctor on board the ship always has band-aids and dressings on hand to tend to any injuries sustained.

Being a great fan of reggae music, I had already asked the first available taxi driver on my first shore excursion whether it would be possible to see Bob Marley's town and the house where he was born. Of course I received the standard response to all questions in

Jamaica: "Yes, Mon" which means "Yes, Sir."
Nothing seems to be impossible for Jamaicans because the happy "Yes, Mon" is the accommodating reply to most questions every five seconds.

Shortly thereafter I made myself comfortable, that is, as much as it was possible, in a rickety taxi that transported me to Nine Miles. Off we went towards the house and village of the godfather of reggae music, Bob Marley. My God, what a trip! We passed roads which were more or less fit for traffic, trails which should more accurately be described as deluxe jungle paths and villages in which the people leisurely did their work (provided that they had something to do). We went past tropical gardens, waterfalls and sugarcane plantations until we finally reached our destination, Nine Miles. It was a small, inconspicuous town where I was cordially welcomed as was the case everywhere on this island. Everyone offered their services and tried to peddle goods such as homemade rum, spices or jewelry unique to the area.

Shortly thereafter I found and inspected the house where Bob Marley was born. It was very unspectacular, even rather miserable, as if to say: "Look, although the reggae genius has come from a humble background, he has become famous throughout the world!" Lost in thoughts, I walked around the house and imagined Mr. Marley living here and writing his legendary songs. Suddenly, I felt someone patting me on the back. It turned out to be my driver, who asked me whether I would like to see Bob Marley. I was dumbfounded and asked what he meant. "Get in my car," he answered, "the place where we're going is not within walking distance." After only ten minutes of again navigating the rough roads we stopped in front of a structure which looked rather bizarre from my perspective. "What is it?" I curiously asked my local driver. "A gravesite," he replied, "a so-called sepulcher. You do know what has been done with the famous Russian, white man Lenin after he had died, don't you?" "Of course," I said. "He was embalmed and can still be seen today." "You're right," the Jamaican continued, "we've done the same. However, we don't talk a lot about it because we want to avoid large crowds of curious individuals who would disturb the peace and order. Only few tourists are let in on this secret." We entered the small building and what I witnessed made me catch my breath.

There he was, laid out in a crypt with a small window as if he had died only yesterday. Next to him were his guitar and a football. Staring at the lifeless body of the famous musician, I had the feeling as if all melodies and words from his songs started to ring out in my head at the same time. I stayed in front of the small window for a long while until the elderly Jamaican again patted me on the back. He whispered to me that it was time to leave. When we were outside I shook his hand and thanked him for allowing me to be privy to this secret. I generously tipped him and his family, which he gratefully accepted.

I have only seldom mentioned this particular excursion, because whenever I did, I was laughed at and nobody believed me. But I know what I saw and will always be grateful to Jamaica and its inhabitants for granting me the privilege of seeing this site and affording me the opportunity to once again see this grandmaster of Caribbean music.

It is said that the Marley family tried to take his corpse to Ethiopia to fulfill his dying wish. According to Marley his last resting place should have been in the country of his ancestors. However, the Jamaican people did not agree. The elderly Jamaican, with whom I am still in contact today, claims that Marley's dead body has never left the island.

"Come on, Mon," my new friend said. "Now my wife would like to offer you a local specialty for lunch. You must try it!" Still lost in thoughts, I thankfully accepted this invitation. Not long afterwards we arrived at a little house in front of which a barbecue had been installed and noticed an old Jamaican who was happily waving large barbecue tongs. I could clearly determine that the meal being prepared would be savory from the mouth-watering aroma. "Try this, white man," he ordered, "this is the famous 'jerk chicken'. We first rub it with local spices and then roast it. It's very delicious." I was more than willing to tuck in because by that time I was ravenously hungry. The chicken was outstandingly tasty, spicy and smoky yet the perfect accompaniment to the local beer which I discovered was excellent as well.

After the meal I finally said good-bye before we headed for the ship along the back roads of Jamaica. I looked at my watch. Although it was rather late, I asked my driver whether it would be possible to go for a refreshing swim in the crystal-clear water of the Caribbean Sea. As usual, he replied with, "Yes, Mon." Moments later he stopped at a deserted bay which was ideal for swimming. I didn't need a towel since the sun was hot enough to dry me later. Fortunately I had already put on my swimming trunks so that I could jump into the warm water right away and watch the numerous colorful fish whose habitat is the Caribbean Sea.

"How about some good smoke?" my driver asked me when I returned from the water and offered me a joint. "'Good smoke', eh?" I smiled knowingly. "Yes, Mon," he answered. "Good smoke is a proper medicine for body and soul." "Sorry, my friend," I countered. "I can't even stand the taste of a normal cigarette. No marijuana, no good smoke for me, I'm afraid." Both of us laughed because we were well aware of the fact that 'good smoke' does not have a positive effect on a properly working human organism; on the contrary, it can do a lot of harm.

Jamaica is a beautiful island, but the interior of a prison is certainly not one of its tourist attractions. Would you perchance like to know whether any incidents involving our guests along those lines have ever occurred? Of course they have! Guests and crew members have repeatedly tried to smuggle some or even a great amount of the 'good smoke' on the respective cruises and consequently gambled with their liberty very carelessly. The future of a young couple in this regard looked very gloomy indeed. They had evidently booked the cruise for the purpose of buying 'good smoke' in Jamaica at a favorable price and then selling it at a profit in other countries as opposed to relaxing and having fun. It's hard not to laugh at their expense once you learn the story of these two people who were as gullible as can be.

It seemed as if these mules had likely already placed their order in their home country and subsequently received the goods in a dark room somewhere in the backwoods of Jamaica. If you think that the amount of drugs only consisted of a few joints, you are totally mistaken. The parcel, which our young couple lugged towards the ship in the hope of filling up their holiday piggy bank, weighed fifty pounds. Imagine how badly they had planned their action: it would have been wiser to board the ship at the very last minute among all

143

other passengers who wanted to enjoy the beauty of Jamaica to the fullest until the ship's foghorn sounded. In that case they would have only been subjected to a speedier security check without the parcel being found. The couple, however, arrived at our cruise ship at 11.00 a.m. and demanded entry. Eleven in the morning, the time at which nothing special is going on board the ship except for the galley where lunch is being prepared. The passengers and the crew are either still in town or on a shore excursion. Even the captain has disembarked the ship to play tennis. Thus, the bored security guards at the gangway have plenty of time to thoroughly check every person approaching the ship.

"What's that?" one of the guards asked. He of course guessed the contents of the various little packets, but was eager to know how the young couple would try to talk their way out of the predicament. "Tea!" the young husband unabashedly replied, his ashen face betraying his bravado. "Green tea which is particularly aromatic in Jamaica."

I'm sure it's not necessary to tell you what happened next … Half an hour later the local police had arrived on the ship and took the couple and its 'tea' into safe custody. Seven years of prison in Jamaica was their sentence, as we were advised two weeks later. This court decision gave rise to a lot of discussions and should be a warning for everybody.

Be assured that drugs in this quantity will inevitably be traced, either by the guards or by the detectors which immediately trigger an alarm.

Upon my return from Nine Miles I was deeply moved to have gotten familiar with such a beautiful island and to have been let in on one of the inhabitant's secrets. I have rarely spoken about it because the body language and reactions of all I had advised of my experience had always been very negative. In the years that followed I confined myself to engaging in a few interesting shore excursions and haunting the magnificent beaches of this island paradise with local food and beverages.

All told, I have only good things to say about Jamaica. It is an amazing, very lively island with loud, but proud and sportive people. Jamaicans are game for fun and always willing to help tourists to get to know the country and its people.

144

Even today I often remember the silly couple who tried to get past the ship's security guards with 25 kilograms of marijuana. I have often told my guests about it and have to admit that, as a rule, younger passengers who probably had the same intentions regarding 'good smoke' eyeballed me very nervously. I made it clear that anyone trying to get past our security guard with forbidden substances is already dancing too close to the fire and will ultimately get burned. According to my experience, a cruise ship is an impregnable fortress offering first-class security in all areas. I have been working on board ships for 26 years and as far as I know, nobody has ever succeeded in misusing our ships as a drug carrier or trafficking venue without being caught.

I remember a tragic incident involving a couple going to Alaska – who did succeed in boarding with a minor quantity of hard drugs for their own use – which ultimately resulted in the husband's loss of life.

By the same token, I can recount a single example of an employee who was an addict and smuggled a hard drug in small portions onto our ship. He did not intend to make money out of it, but only wanted to satisfy his addiction, which, however, also had disastrous consequences.

146

Chapter 17:   Chef Heinze and Waiter Theobald

Heinze was a man who had not lived a happy childhood. He had left school very early to earn money for the family without a father. His childless marriage had failed after a short time. In order to escape for a few hours from the reality of this cruel world, he started doing drugs. In the beginning the drugs were rather harmless; he seemed to cope quite well with a joint and pill now and then. These substances did not keep him from signing up on the ship and managing cooking duties. He was a good chef, and consequently the shipping company raised his hopes of a promotion within a short time. He would have easily managed to work his way up, had he not acquired harder drugs somewhere on the islands or in Miami. Slowly but surely they drove him insane. At the onset of his drug-fuelled descent he threw a fit at least once a day and acted foolishly. Negative tendencies were manifested for the first time when he pilfered a box of clay pigeons which were shot down from the ship as one of the entertainment activities at that time. He lugged the clay pigeons on deck, threw them overboard high into the air and tried to fire tomatoes at them. Although he didn't have a gun, we could hear him shouting from afar, "Fire!" Flinging a clay pigeon with his left hand, he threw a tomato towards it with his right hand. Whenever it missed the pigeon, he would rant and rave. Curious guests and employees who were all attracted by his behavior laughed uproariously at the crazy chef, until one of the security guards put an end to this performance, and Heinze was given a written warning. Nowadays he would have been fired immediately since it is strictly forbidden to throw anything overboard, regardless of the object. A word to the wise: no matter whether you are an employee or a guest, if you are caught, you will be forced to disembark the ship.

The second time it was evident there was something wrong with Heinze occurred in the galley during dinner. Heinze's stove didn't work properly and he was beside himself with rage. While he was crawling under the stove in search for the defect, a new assistant waiter appeared and bent over him to ask for some salad.

Within two seconds Heinze bolted from under the stove and planted himself in front of the terrified man. "You want some salad?

147

Salad?" he shouted at him. "You've got it. Just stay put!" Four seconds later he returned, carrying a huge portion of salad which he dropped into the assistant's hands without giving him a plate. "There it is, fresh salad, Sir!" he called out loudly. "Would you also like some dressing, Sir? I'll get for you immediately." He returned with a large ladle filled with sticky French dressing which he poured over the salad. The assistant was totally shocked, particularly as the dressing had not only sullied his hands and sleeves, but also the floor. "There you go, fresh salad!" Heinze continued shouting. "Now get off my back!"

It was completely silent in the galley. Nobody could believe what had just happened – least of all the assistant who was staring at the mess on his arm and was at a loss for words.

"The guy is on drugs," someone commented who had witnessed this scene. "This type of behavior has nothing to do with a violent temper." The man was right. However, at this point no measures were taken, since the management wasn't aware of Heinze's drug consumption. Moreover, it was not customary to accuse a person of being on drugs only because he had lost his temper. Heinze was given another written warning by the head chef with the comment that this would be his last warning and advised Heinze that he should control himself.

Two weeks had passed when I saw the executive chef and his sous-chef hurrying across the dining room towards the galley. Both of them were swearing and as they were talking about Heinze, there was no doubt that there had been another episode. Shortly thereafter we watched as a grinning Heinze was leaving the galley and heading for the hospital. He was accompanied by the executive chef, a security guard and a nurse. A wet cloth had been wrapped around his hand which was held by the nurse. I went to the galley and asked the second executive chef what had happened.

"Heinze!" was his succinct reply. "This guy is crazy. While standing at his station to help a junior chef, he probably accidentally put his hand on the edge of the boiling hot deep fryer. Then it happened! I don't know whether you realized it, but a few minutes ago the ship unexpectedly moved sideward. Heinze lost his balance and his hand slid into the deep fryer. Okay, this could have happened to anyone, but any other human being would have

148

screamed with pain. Heinze, however, did not! Looking at his hand which immediately turned blazing red, he laughed and wanted to continue working. He has just been taken to the emergency room. We can only hope that the skin on his hand will recover. Believe me, that man must be on something."

Since nobody had advised the responsible hospital personnel about Heinze and his strange behavior, they didn't analyze his blood or urine for forbidden substances. Consequently, his trip to the hospital was classified as an accident. A week later Heinze was fit for work again despite his severely injured hand.

Three weeks elapsed. Up to that point Heinze had snapped only once over trivial matters and had received a further written warning from the executive chef, In the meantime, he found it amusing to tease the new chefs. For example: Heinze asked a new junior chef to come to his office where he instructed him to go downstairs and collect a bacon extender from the butcher which would be required for preparing the breakfast. Of course the master butcher laughed at the poor guy since he suspected that such nonsense could only originate from Heinze. He advised the fledgling chef, "Don't let the idiot upstairs take the Mickey out of you!" The junior chef was then sent back to the main galley where he glared angrily at the guffawing Heinze.

Another newcomer was asked by Heinze to collect the rice splitter from the vegetables section which would be required to split and hollow the rice in order to remove the starch. This new colleague also returned after a short while and would have liked nothing more than to go for Heinze's throat after he had been ridiculed. During the following weeks we repeatedly saw new chefs hurrying across the ship in search of either a basket with water steam to stew the potatoes, butter powder to make the cake dough smoother or the stove extension which would enable him to roast whole pigs. One day Heinze summoned an inexperienced rookie to demonstrate to him how to properly season and test French fries. Beforehand, Heinze had put some clarified butter on three fingers of his right hand without the new chef's knowledge. Putting the French fries into the deep fryer with his left hand, he ordered the junior chef, "Pay attention! Now I'll show you how to test French fries to see whether they are cooked." Before the junior chef's eyes he

149

pretended to spice the fries in the deep fryer, immersed the three fingers protected by the applied clarified butter into the hot fat, took one of the fries and put it into his mouth. "Delicious." he said. "Now it's your turn! Show me what I just taught you and do the same!" The poor fool didn't hesitate to comply with this absurd request in order to avoid difficulties and actually raised his hand towards the deep fryer. At the very last minute Heinze rescued the hand from its fate and sneered as he let him in on the joke. Heinze, however, was the only one who could laugh about his gag; the poor guy who had almost severely burnt his hand did not see any humor in the prank. Bad luck for the joker Heinze, who finally got his comeuppance. On this particular occasion he was not only observed carrying out his nefarious deeds, but was also tattled on, which got him into trouble again.

But then the day came which spelled the end for Heinze. Up until that day the crew on board had only considered Heinze a nasty joker and choleric person who would someday pull himself together. This assessment proved to be wrong. The chefs who witnessed Heinze's next flight of fancy and I still discuss what happened on that special day. Heinze was busy roasting meat and paused for a moment to think about something. Seconds later, a peculiar burnt smell suddenly reached the nostrils of a chef who was working behind Heinze. Acting on instinct, the chef looked around the station without detecting anything suspicious. When he turned to Heinze, he was scared stiff at what he saw. Once again Heinze had supported himself with the hand injured in the deep fryer a few weeks before, only on this occasion he had put his hand on the grill that is normally used for preparing steaks. And once again Heinze evidently did not notice anything amiss. It was only when the shocked chef pulled him away and surveyed his hand, the bones of which were visible due to severe burns, that Heinze also looked at his hand. "Oooh!" he commented. "It looks rather bad. I think I should go to the hospital again."

Upon his arrival at the hospital his hand was initially tended to in the emergency room, after which Heinze was transferred to a specialist hospital. As Heinze still did not feel any pain, the doctor became suspicious and eventually conducted the drug test which had been long overdue, before the patient was taken to the other hospital. The diagnosis was extremely bad: Heinze was on PCP, also known as 'angel dust', which is probably the worst drug among all forbidden substances. It had destroyed everything: the chef's brain, which no longer functioned properly, and his already tarnished reputation after having been exposed as drug addict. Since his hand had become useless, he could no longer work as a chef. Needless to say, he was immediately dismissed and flown back to his home country Austria. We never heard from him again.

The story about Heinze the chef spread rapidly throughout the shipping company. The managers in Miami decided to intensify the fight against the soft drugs which reached the crew cabins despite all detectors and electronic devices. Everybody behaving suspiciously was to be examined more thoroughly from then on.

A young man among our waiters named Theobald suffered from extremely sweaty feet. Due to their very strong smell he always resided in a single cabin because no other colleague could cope with it. Although he persistently asserted he was doing something about the smell, the situation was regarded with suspicion; after all it is more desirable to be accommodated in a single cabin.

One day the ship was secretly searched for drugs. Officers of the coast guard who were accompanied by trained sheepdogs inspected our ship without tracing anything until they passed Theobald's cabin. One of the dogs started barking, yelped and scratched at the door. After our watch officer had opened it, the dog bounded into the cabin. Theobald sat on his bed in petrified horror and watched as the dog immediately ran to his closet. It continued rummaging until it had finally fished out a suspicious plastic parcel out of a dark corner. The gnarling dog put it in front of the officers, whereupon the parcel was slit open with a long knife. What happened next was very embarrassing: the parcel contained socks that stank to high heaven, not drugs, and the pungent odor nearly bowled over the attendees and even brought tears to the sheepdog's eyes. They continued searching while holding their breath, but did not find anything; the dog had indeed mistaken the socks for drugs.

Both the captain and the hotel manager invited Theobald to a serious talk and advised him to either care for his feet or look for another job in a more suitable place such as a garbage dump. Theobald was completely shocked and mortified by the event, but learned his lesson, did a 180 degree turn, and became one of the most well-groomed persons on board with whom everybody enjoyed sharing a cabin.

I now invite you to continue reading the next pages and learn what else can happen during a cruise and consider it an amusing warning. I will recount a trip I took part in shortly after my adventures in Jamaica. This time the powers that be were involved, which restored peace and order in the dining room.

Chapter 18:   Philipe, the Tip King

It was a cruise like any other. The employees were working; the guests relaxed and let themselves be waited on. In short, everything was as it should be – with one exception. A group of cheerful passengers had indicated at the time of embarkation and table booking that they were a vivacious bunch who would celebrate each day and be boisterous during most meals in the restaurant. For these reasons they asked to be accommodated in a corner of the restaurant so that they would disturb as few fellow passengers as possible.

It is not unusual to have small, alcohol-fuelled groups among our guests. Due to the fact that guests who enjoy laughing and drinking copiously are usually generous tippers, such groups are always warmly welcomed and all waiters enjoy serving them. However, we had not experienced the likes of such a rowdy gang. The head waiter realized within a short while that we would have to deal with a few very peculiar individuals. To be on the safe side, a table at the far end of the dining room was reserved for them, a table where none of the guests wanted to sit since it didn't offer a view to the rest of the restaurant, and they feared they might miss something interesting.

It didn't help a lot! These high-spirited passengers were always loud, raucously laughing, cackling and fooling around and acted as though they owned the place. Even though the dining room doors opened very early in the morning, they were always among the first to arrive, ordered everything off the menu, were boisterous, cracked jokes, and would laugh uproariously at every turn. They even drank champagne and red wine at breakfast – for digestive purposes, as their group leader explained to us. These fun-loving guests were never drunk, but their babbling never stopped. Various members of the noisy clan would leave the restaurant between meals to use the bathroom or go out for a cigarette only to return to their seats immediately afterwards and resume their incessant chatter.

The waiter who was responsible for their section went through hell. Even though his guests were friendly to him, they were demanding and didn't give him a moment's rest. According to their slogan, "If you take care of us, we will take care of you!" they fuelled his expectations of a gigantic tip and allowed him to be at their constant beck and call in the galley, the bakery and wine cellar. They did not care a fig about the weather conditions or whether they were on the high seas or at port. There was only one thing that mattered to them: idling all day long at their table while chatting and stuffing themselves with food. Every once in awhile they would play a short game of cards, look at photo albums, make speeches and sing songs. A French waiter at the restaurant, who usually worked the later shift and had not yet had the pleasure of serving such guests, was sent into the galley to prepare sandwiches. As a consequence he had to spend every afternoon standing at a table in a corner of the galley and making sandwiches, cursing all the while, while the other restaurant staff was either busy exploring the islands or taking a rest. "Hi, Philipe." the chefs who were on duty in the afternoon teased, "Why aren't you going to the beach? The weather is great." "Damn party-goers!" Philipe replied. "I hope they will adjust the tip to the sound level of their babbling. I really have to pull myself together and stop myself from throttling them!"

It was often nearly impossible to tolerate the gang's constant chatter. During meals the assistant waiter and head waiter had to admonish the group several times for being so disruptive and repeatedly asked them to be quieter. Disturbing guests with rambunctious behavior is absolutely unacceptable in the restaurant.

On the fourth evening of enduring the wild bunch, something happened which neither the guests dining in the restaurant nor the employees present will ever forget.

The group in question had only held court at its table that day until the early evening before they returned to their cabins to dress in the formal attire required for dinner

They indeed looked very elegant, the gentlemen in expensive tuxedos and the ladies in colorful designer ball gowns. The first-class clothes did not at all match the group's behavior. They apparently wanted to demonstrate their bulging wallets which they believed somehow justified their behavior in the restaurant. The gang's slogan was: "Look at us, we are filthy rich and can do whatever we want!"

Having loudly taken their seats, they were welcomed by the waiter Philipe who was still in an upright position in spite of being dog-

155

tired. Large quantities of food, wine and spirits were again ordered, and as per usual, they started babbling and driving us crazy. They did not talk loudly, since it was frowned upon at dinner, but they did chat – continuously.

"My God!" I exclaimed. This week I was responsible for a station next to Philipe and had already been repeatedly asked by my guests what the deal was with this strange gang. "Lord, please do something to stop this babbling, at least for a few minutes!" I wasn't the only one with this plea. I did get my wish, but in a truly bizarre fashion.

All of a sudden, two or three girders broke off from the ceiling and wall above, right next to the blatherskites. Tremendous floods of water cascaded over them and their table.

How did this happen? Somewhere and somehow, a few conduits piping the seawater from the swimming pool into the sea several decks above us had burst. As they passed the ceiling above the restaurant at one spot, the water could now easily penetrate the dining room and directly soak the gentlemen and ladies in their expensive evening ensembles.

After the initial and short-lived silence at the usually extremely loud table, the ladies' screeching and gentlemen's ranting could be heard. They couldn't believe what had just happened.

At the sight of the draining swimming pool a potato fell off the hotel manager's fork who was dining close to the table in question. He and the head waiter were the first to evacuate the guests from their favorite table and to calm them down. The waiters had at first been slightly worried and surprised, but now increasingly enjoyed the welcome change in entertainment caused by the temperamental swimming pool. This was something so extraordinary, so terrific, and above all, an event to joke about for a long time.

"Oh, have a look," one of the waiters said, "the gentlemen look like wet penguins and the ladies should have their hair done. It's really scandalizing to go for dinner in such a get-up!"

If you think that anybody in the dining room felt pity for the gang members, you are wrong. The other guests reacted with loud laughter and jeering at the gang's expense, a scene which reminded me of Porky Pig, the fat guest who had died the 'lobster death' at the table a few months prior.

Waiters and passengers alike considered this show as a welcome change from the usual performances on stage. Some of them even applauded, particularly the British, who found the debacle reminiscent of their heroes from the Monty Python cast.

The head waiter and the hotel manager ushered our wet chatterboxes out of the dining room to take care of any arising problems.

The captain who arrived at the restaurant a few minutes after this minor disaster to inspect the damage was the most worried individual on our cruise ship. While he was waddling and splashing about in the water on the carpet and being harangued by passengers, he consulted with his officers who had also been invited for the damage inspection, when an excited guest suddenly showed up in the restaurant. Obviously intending to find a victim whom he could hold responsible for his problem he made a beeline for the captain and shouted: "Hey you over there, are you in the driver's seat?" "You could say that," the captain calmly replied. "What can I do for you?" "Officer," the man continued, "something terrible happened on the sun deck at the swimming pool up there. My wife went swimming before dinner, and all of a sudden, the water was gone. Now she is sitting on the pool bottom, unable to get out of the pool. I was told that I could find the pool water in the restaurant, which I didn't believe. But now I see that it's true. Please take action, otherwise I will be forced to complain to the captain!" "All right," the captain complied. "I'll arrange for the necessary measures to help your wife get out of the swimming pool."

I absolutely have to see this for myself, I don't want to miss this bizarre rescue operation! I thought to myself at that moment, since fortunately there wasn't a lot to do. I immediately took an elevator to the sun deck to revel in the sight of a fat, ranting lady on the bottom of the swimming pool. Unfortunately I arrived too late as a few dauntless gentlemen had not waited for the officers' assistance, but immediately tried to rescue the female guest who reminded me of a beached whale, considering her body weight of at least 140 kilograms. The helpful gentlemen had reached out to her so that she managed to climb onto the first rung of the ladder and leave the swimming pool, groaning and moaning all the while.

There were a lot of funny comments by the guests about this

157

strange incident which circulated on the ship for a long time. Shipbuilders and technicians throughout the world were cautioned accordingly and took measures to avoid such damage ever recurring.

Would you like to know the end of the story? Well, the carpet in the dining room had to be replaced immediately as the seawater in the restaurant would have cause an unbearable stench after a few days. Only the soaked part of the carpet was removed and replaced until the end of the cruise so that the restaurant operations could continue. Upon our arrival at the home port in Miami three days later the new carpet was already available and lain within a short time. The damage amounted to roughly 50,000 Euro.

Perhaps you are also interested in knowing what became of the waiter Philipe and his little horror story gang? Nothing changed: the flash flood had no effect on their debauchery. The next morning his guests were again the first at the restaurant, waiting for the doors to open. In their usual laughing manner, they sat down at another table assigned to them and told all of us waiters about the management's efforts to apologize on behalf of the shipping company and about the compensation extended to all guests. A great sum of money had been paid to replace the unfortunate group's attire. What's more, every gang member had received a gift certificate for a future cruise for which they would only have to pay half of the usual price.

In consideration of this generosity it was of course a simple thing for the showered guests to forget the incident and enjoy the remaining cruise. To be more precise: they enjoyed it, while longsuffering waiter Philipe was forced to withstand this group for another two long days. Two days in which he could have put up a tent in the dining room, since he was not afforded so much as a minute's rest.

While other waiters sipped their Piña Colada or Mai Tai on the beach, he served exotic drinks in his station. When his colleagues relaxed in their cabins after the lunch service, he served coffee and cake. If a gang member recovered in the cabin from the strain of guzzling, gorging and sloth, Philipe was sent to him to offer a few snacks. While he placed the main dishes on the table during the dinner service, he politely answered his guests' question about the midnight buffet specialties. In other words: There was no possibility for Philipe to escape his bizarre group. After six days of continuous partying its members did not seem to be tired at all. Several times they comforted Philipe with the promising words: "We'll take care of you," meaning, "Be assured that you will be tipped generously" and indeed stayed the course of continuous partying until the 'Last Supper' on the seventh day of the cruise.

"Would you like to take time off next week?" the head waiter asked as he was of course well aware of the nerve-wracking and exhausting guests his employee had to cope with. Philipe stopped him with a dismissive wave. "I'll make it," he replied. "Many thanks for your offer, Boss, but I can't afford a week without tips." "You're really doing a great job!" the head waiter and all head waiters in the area praised Philipe.

Before I tell you the rest of the story about Philipe and his party gang and of course reveal the amount of tip for our tormented waiter, I will first deal with the topic of 'tips' in general.

Chapter 19:   Tip

Since money doesn't grow on trees for most of us, we have to work hard to be able to pay the numerous bills at the end of the month and, if possible, save some money for expenses such as an impending divorce. It is not difficult to imagine that most of the wives who are married to a waiter grow weary of being a ship widow after a few years and decide to run away. Therefore it is important to take precautionary measures and to work with a shipping company which allows its waiters to earn some extra dollars in addition to the fixed salary at the end of the cruise. What I am trying to point out are the greatly varying waiters' salaries within the shipping company. Let me explain it to you: First of all, there are companies which pay a good salary to their restaurant staff and also allow them to keep their tips. There is no doubt that this kind of remuneration is more than welcomed and most appreciated; unfortunately only very few shipping companies conduct business accordingly. Secondly there are companies which only pay a fixed salary to their waiters – nothing more. Thirdly, there are companies which pay a fixed salary and additionally pass on only a small percentage of all tips received to their waiters. Last, but not least there are the really lucky waiters on board – just like us – who are working according to the following slogan of the shipping company: "This is your station, a small restaurant of your own. Make the best of it! The better your work, the more you will earn." These waiters depend entirely on the tip since they are paid only a very small, rather symbolic salary. Dear reader, you may think, "So what?" and wonder if the service is any different. You can bet your life on it, Ladies and Gentlemen. Waiters who are only paid a fixed salary render the worst service. By contrast, service from waiters who may expect an extra dollar after having rendered a terrific personal service to his guests is the best-case scenario. In the latter case the guests willingly pay a tip to express their gratitude to the waiter. Using a few examples I will explain how differently waiters with and without fixed salary think and work. My dear Ladies and Gentlemen, if you find yourself sitting in the restaurant of a cruise ship and enjoying the waiter's services someday, you will easily notice the category your waiter belongs to.

The 'tip waiter' will dutifully introduce himself the first evening and recommend dishes which are the best in his opinion. Equally as important, he will encourage the passengers to let him know if a meal isn't to the guest's liking so that the galley's mistake can be smoothed out right away with the head waiter's assistance.

Examples:

Guest: "Waiter, my steak is tough!"
Tip waiter: "Please accept my apologies. One moment, I'll inform the chef and in two minutes you'll have the tender steak you requested."
Fixed salary waiter: "The meat is tough? I'll give you a sharper knife!"

Guest: "Waiter, my soup is cold!"
Tip waiter: "I am very sorry to hear that, Sir. I'll go and get another bowl of really hot soup for you right away."
Fixed salary waiter: "The soup is cold? Let's see whether the microwave is working again; this could be your lucky day, Ma'am!"

Guest: "Waiter, this tablecloth is still stained from today's breakfast service!"
Tip waiter: "I am sorry, Sir. I'll set up a different table for you."
Fixed salary waiter: "So? The stains are very small. Besides, wash day at the cleaner's is tomorrow!"

A guest arrives for dinner very late.
Tip waiter: "It's a pleasure to see you. Better late than never!"
Fixed salary waiter: Looks at his watch, visibly annoyed. You can just feel his excitement and enthusiasm in serving his guests so late into the evening; you can be assured of the best service.

After dinner:
Tip waiter (moves the chairs back so that the guests can get up from their seats): "It was a pleasure to be your waiter again today. I hope

161

you have a pleasant night and I look forward to being at your disposal again tomorrow!"

Fixed salary waiter (sipping his beer somewhere in a dark corner where he can watch his guests without being discovered): "I hope they'll hit the road soon! I want to clear the table and finally call it a day!"

Although I could give you numerous examples of the different types of waiter behavior, I will stop now and refer to the most interesting tips I have received from satisfied guests in the course of my career.

First let me tell you about one friendly gentleman whose generosity I remember very well. On the last evening when the envelopes containing the tips were handed over by all guests to my assistant waiter, my head waiter, and to me, one gentleman held up an envelope and sent for me. "Johannes," he said, "this envelope contains 50 dollars. Red or black?" "Red or black?" I repeated. "What does that mean?" "Quite simple," he replied. "I'll pay a visit to the casino now and put your money on a roulette game. You will either receive the 100 dollars as a reward for your excellent service or your efforts for the service rendered to me last week were in vain." His dining companions and I were wide-eyed, some of them even scowled at the very idea. Secretly, all of us, including my humble self, dismissed his actions farcical. Upon my reply he indeed left the restaurant towards the casino. Not long afterwards he returned, looking very sad. "Unfortunately I lost all of your tip!" he explained, his head lowered. He shook my hand, thanked me again for the perfect service and left the restaurant forever.

I soon realized that there had been no money at all in the envelope, because the casino manager to whom I told the story the next day started laughing. He confirmed that this guy had already gambled away most of his money in the casino so that he would not have had enough to distribute generous tips.

Another nice guy, a musician, approached me on the last evening before dinner. He explained to me that the amount of my tip would depend on the singing of the restaurant staff. 'Singing' was his description for the traditional procession of waiters who perform a well-known farewell song before the distribution of tips and the

162

final farewell to the guests.

It's a well-known fact that we are waiters, not singers. It's funny to sing, caw or mumble the song, but of course it's not at all professional. As usual, the guests applauded and laughed at our evening performance and everybody was exceptionally impressed by our attempt to imitate the Fischer choir. Except for our musician, who was sitting silently and staring into space.

With a facial expression which could only bode ill, he handed an envelope to me after the fact which contained a slip of paper with the comment: "Terrible singing, a poor show which wasn't worth a cent." Strangely enough he had already been carrying this envelope in his suit before the dinner and the show, which clearly indicates that he had planned his excuse for not tipping right from the beginning. This case was subsequently filed under the category, 'Inherent stinginess' in the cabin.

I was amused by the couple who shook my hand at the end of the cruise and exclaimed, "Johannes, thanks for your excellent service! Unfortunately we have spent too much money during the holiday, the bank machine is out of order, so there is no money left for tips. But don't worry, we'll send you the money." This was okay for me, but strangely enough these dear guests left the ship without having asked for my address or bank account. They must have been bad clairvoyants because I still haven't received the money.

I also remember a devout couple whose table manners didn't match the prayers they recited before meals. The prayer had been planned very carefully. They never would have said: "Come Lord Jesus and be our guest and let these gifts to us be blessed," as the Lord would have left starving if he was impressed by their pious behavior and had actually taken a seat at the couple's table. They had scarcely said "Amen" when they immediately ordered two or three starters, at least two main courses and three desserts for each of them. Huffing and puffing, they stuffed mountains of food into their potbellies while staring at the plates of their table companions as they were eager not to miss anything which might be worth ordering. They were the first at the buffet and their plates were loaded with so much food that it nearly required two waiters to bring them to their table. They put me through my paces at breakfast, lunch and dinner. As the icing on the cake they

163

encouraged all guests at their table to do the same. "Order anything you like!" they repeatedly said. "The Lord has blessed our planet with this beautiful food; we must prove ourselves grateful and sample everything."

On the last evening after dessert all of the guests, aside from this couple in question, handed over the envelopes with tips. They explained to me in a cool, matter-of-fact way that the tips should be distributed only after the very last meal, which to them meant after breakfast on the day of disembarkation. Nobody knows who had told them such nonsense. As always, they were the first in the restaurant the next morning and ordered everything offered by the galley and wine cellar.

Then it was their turn to hand over their tip envelope. The righteous lady was breathing heavily after devouring the large Spanish omelet with a double portion of bacon and fried potatoes, while her holy counterpart still had drops from the Eggs Benedict hollandaise sauce stuck in his beard. The hypocrite seized my hand and shook it cordially.

"Johannes," he said, looking earnest, "the Lord is living deep in your heart. When we are back at home, we will go to church every day and pray for you. This is all you need. God bless you, my son!"

And off they went. Naturally they did not forget to once again reach into the bowl of pastries to make sure they didn't starve on the long way from Deck 5 downstairs to the exit on Deck 1.

My colleagues who had witnessed everything raucously laughed at my expense, knowing very well that they also often had to cope with guests who avoided giving tips using the most bizarre excuses. This happens now and then to every waiter on almost every cruise. During my career I received the most generous tip from a crazy man living in Cologne who acted as 'Easter bunny' every evening.

The guest's antics had already begun after the first dinner when all guests bid us a good evening before going to the theater. As usual, I cleared up my station and checked my menus to see whether they were clean and complete. When I opened one of the menus, a 100-dollar bill fell out and fluttered onto the floor. As I was not certain why cash had been left in the menu I stopped short, but was nevertheless pleased with this little bonanza. The next evening the aforementioned guest from Cologne approached me and asked me

164

in a low voice and a wry smile whether I had found the money. Answering in the affirmative, I contentedly returned his smile as I now knew who had hidden the dough. After dinner the following evening I cleared up my station as usual. I was in the process of refilling the pepper grinder when another 100-dollar bill appeared instead of pepper. The expertly folded note seemed to smile at me. It was a great feeling as 100 dollars were a lot of money at that time, enough for two tanks of gas in Germany as opposed to only half a tank nowadays.

"Was the pepper sufficiently fiery?" my friend from Cologne asked me the next evening. Answering in the affirmative, I grinned sheepishly. As I said, up to that day I had never before earned so much money within only two days.

After the end of the third dinner, the satisfied guests left for the evening, whereupon I started searching. Maybe there was more money hidden somewhere! As of that particular evening I would always sent my assistant into the kitchen to work so that my search wouldn't be disturbed. My game plan paid off: once again I discovered money! This time it had been hidden under the molleton blanket. This type of blanket is made of cloth or plastic and placed on the table before the tablecloth is spread over it. It is used so that the guests don't have the sensation of eating on a wooden plate, and it helps to avoid unwelcome noises while serving and setting the table. My dear guest had slid the bill under the plastic cloth – nearly to the middle of the table – so that it only appeared when I thoroughly cleaned my tables and the molleton blanket. *I see,* I thought to myself, *every evening it will be more difficult to find the money.* This turned out to be true. When the guest in question scrutinized me before dinner, I signaled my successful search with thumbs up à la Julius Caesar. Nobody was privy to his little game – not even his wife.

On the fourth evening I started sweating because I only detected the note during my examination of the flower vase. Instead of water it contained another note which was stuck in between the flower stalks. It was a mystery to me how my generous guest had managed to empty the vase and fill it with money during dinner without being noticed.

On the fifth day I had to search for half an hour; I could not find the

165

note anywhere. Everything had already been cleaned when the housekeeper showed up in another part of the restaurant and started moving the chairs to do the vacuuming. I paused and pondered my next step, then started to give the lady a helping hand. Voilà – the fifth note had been folded to the size of a Euro coin and glued under the leg of my guest's chair with a drop of super-glue.

"Wow!" exclaimed my head waiter, who had suddenly shown up. "You really do a thorough cleaning – even under the chair legs. Top-notch work, Johannes." "Isn't it?" I proudly replied. "Sometimes extra work turns out to be quite lucrative." "You're right," the head waiter agreed. "If you go the extra mile, you will earn more money." He disappeared after wishing me a good night. On this particular evening I was the last one to leave the dining-room. I was whistling as I headed for the galley with the note in my pocket and an empty stomach. During my late meal only one thought crossed my mind: *What outlandish idea will my crazy guest conjure up tomorrow?*

The next evening he was again standing in front of me, turning his thumb down and up, waiting for my sign. I proudly gave him the positive signal and served him dinner with a big grin.

The sixth dinner was over. Searching again, it was soon apparent that it would be a very long evening. I couldn't find the note anywhere! My tired, yawning assistant had disappeared out of sight a long while ago. The light in the restaurant had already been dimmed when I once again carried out thorough inspection – in vain! It seemed that my guest had forgotten me this evening! I very nearly gave up out of frustration. Maybe my crazy guy had not found a sufficiently complicated hiding place this evening and therefore refrained from hiding a note. I was about to go to bed, but first had a cup of tea in the canteen to calm my nerves. I was emptying two small packets of sugar into my hot beverage when I stopped short. At the sight of the sugar packets another idea where I might find the money suddenly crossed my mind. "Can it be? Is it possible?" I wondered, hurrying upstairs to my station. A minute later, nearly 200 sugar packets were lying on the table in front of me, waiting to be examined with utmost scrutiny. I turned around each of the packets and – who would have thought? – one of the packets was slightly heavier than the others and placed among another 100 sugar packets on the bottom of the sugar bowl. "Bingo!" I removed the note with my fingertips and went to bed with a feeling of satisfaction. Six hundred dollars had already accumulated in my wallet and tomorrow evening I would additionally receive the other guests' tips. I was totally content as I fell asleep.

I'm glad to report there were no ordeals or mishaps on the last evening! Thanking me for my service, the guest from Cologne was the first guest to hand me an envelope despite his daily generous gesture, chuckling all the while. All the other guests followed his lead: in addition to earning a considerable amount of money, I was rewarded with five stars which would again grant me more leisure time. This cruise was really great, although I had been short of sleep due to the rigorous treasure hunt I embarked on every evening.

Now it's time to disclose the secret about the tip bestowed on waiter Philipe whom I trust you will remember.

On the last evening everybody waited with bated breath to find out how the guests would reward their waiter's 24-hour service who, by that time, was nothing short of a nervous wreck. Everybody was waiting for a friendly handshake, the handover of envelopes and the thank you speeches. However, nothing of the sort happened! The gang leader simply shook Philipe's hand and thanked him. "We'll take care of you," were the group's words of farewell as they left the restaurant.

This time there was no laughter, ridicule, or scorn. All of us were thunderstruck, surrounding our waiter colleague who had turned very pale. He was sitting at the table and struggling to regain his composure.

"This can't be true!" incredulous over the gang's behavior. "I can't believe it!"

There was dead silence in the dining room. The head waiter who had also witnessed the gang's farewell to their obliging waiter approached Philipe, patted him on the back and comforted him. He invited him to dine at the head waiter's table. After our poor French waiter had guzzled two bottles of wine, he staggered into his cabin. The boss had promised him that he only had to work at dinner the

167

next day.

The gang did not show up for breakfast. They were the first to leave the ship for the airport. On their way to the luxury sedans that would take them to the airport, their boorish actions incited the waiters' evil glances – which they blithely ignored. A few seconds later, the only sight of the miserly gang was the rear lights of the cars as they disappeared in the harbor site.

Several weeks elapsed in which the waiters' main topic of conversation was the unconscionable behavior of this bizarre group. They came to the conclusion that they refused to tip due to the involuntary shower caused by the swimming pool; they were unable to find any other explanation.

After almost three weeks the cruise ship harbored in the home port of Miami and we prepared to welcome the guests for the next cruise. The waiters were still busy thoroughly cleaning the restaurant when an announcement was made: "Waiter Philipe Beaudin, get in touch with the gangway, please!" "Damn!" he muttered. "What have I done now?"

A man in a snow-white work coat welcomed him and handed him a pencil, requesting, "Please sign there – under 'receipt acknowledged'!"

"I'm not going to sign anything," Philipe grumbled, "I haven't placed any orders." The man laughed and turned to a heavy truck where two more men were waiting for a hand signal. They were instructed by a "thumbs up" once again. At the push of a button the truck's ramp opened, creating a loud rumbling. At that moment most of the restaurant staff who had heard the announcement were already standing on one of the weather decks to witness which tip was about to roll down from the truck.

The black Corvette Stingray stopped directly in front of Philipe.

"There is a letter under the windshield wiper," the delivery man said. "Open it and decide whether you want to sign!" Philipe seized the envelope with slightly trembling fingers and opened it. His eyes were as wide as the proverbial flying saucers.

"Thanks for your service!" he read. "Have fun and don't speed too much! Best regards, the Webermann Family and friends. New York."

There was silence. Everybody stared at the expensive sports car

168

which was shining in the sun of Miami. "Yes, it's yours", the delivery man explained. "Do you like it?"

Without saying much, Philipe signed the paper and accepted the keys. Around 200 employees were standing outside the cruise ship, either looking enviously or congratulating their colleague who had meanwhile slid into the car to admire the cockpit.

The happy waiter got out of the car and addressed a very justified question to the man in the white work coat.

"Excuse me," he said, "what shall I do with my car now? In two hours I have to start working again on board the ship and can't leave the car here." The delivery man laughed. "Don't worry!" he said. "We've expected your concern. We will return the car to the company. When you are back in Miami next week, you can pay us a short visit and we'll see."

After Philipe had pondered all week what to do with the "tip," he decided to sell the car. This was no problem at all. After all of the costs had been deducted, $56.000 were still at the disposal of the lucky devil which he immediately transferred to his account in France. He was too frightened to either lose the car or get involved in an accident. "Well done!" everybody praised his decision. A fantastic car, but unfortunately a millstone around your neck, if you are working on board a ship in a foreign country!

These were just a few stories about tips which I still remember from my time as an assistant waiter.

Chapter 20:   Promotion by Jesus

A short while after the wonderful trip to Jamaica I was advised by the head waiter that my promotion from assistant waiter to waiter had been taken into consideration by the top management.

I was very glad to hear this news because working as waiter would not only entail far more responsibility, but also a substantially higher salary. Compared to back then it is now quite easy to get promoted since you can expect to have full support by all maître d's, the head waiter, the food and beverage manager and the training manager. At that time we were told the following: "We believe you are able to do the job of a waiter and to assume the respective responsibility. Find out how to acquire all the information you need and be familiar with the unwritten manual of waiter tricks. You must ensure the guests are satisfied, no matter how you do it." At the end of the cruise your rating needed to be 'excellent'at the bottom line of the rating form. In case of a worse rating you were not granted a second chance; instead you were immediately told to continue working as assistant-waiter and it took many months until you were considered a waiter candidate again.

I was barely able to keep my composure when the head waiter asked me to come to his office to answer his question: "Do you have what it takes to do this job?" After I had hesitated for five seconds, I replied to it with a loud and definite, "Yes." "Okay," the manager said, "get in touch with an experienced waiter within the next few days and gather as much advice as you can until the end of this cruise. Good luck!"

It wasn't difficult to find the most experienced waiter. His name was Jesus. Jesus Manuel Gonzales, a Spaniard who had been working with the shipping company for 14 years. Everyone told me he was the most experienced among our waiters and knew every trick in the book.

"Jesus," I greeted him that particular evening at the end of dinner. "Jesus, I start working as waiter at the beginning of the next cruise. Would you please help me and give me some valuable advice so that I won't be a total failure in the first week?"

"Darling," he replied in a very high, rather feminine voice, "your timing is very convenient. My assistant waiter is sick and I need a

171

helping hand. Come see me tomorrow morning and help me during breakfast, then I will teach you the ins and outs. There is good reason why I am called 'Jesus Ports-Off,'" he boasted "Jesus Ports-Off? What exactly does that mean?" I asked. "Well, Darling," he explained to me, "every week I get a five-star rating, because all the guests are 100% satisfied with my service. As you know, you are granted leisure time in the ports at lunch time if you are rated with five stars. As I am continuously away from work at lunch time, I am called 'Jesus Ports-Off.'"

He is the right one, I thought. *Thanks to his training I will also be in the habit of sunbathing at lunch time very soon instead of sweating in the dining room.*

The head waiter relieved me from the regular breakfast service for the next three days so that I, the so-called replacement waiter, could entirely focus on my forthcoming position as waiter.

I got up at dawn so I could be the first in the restaurant. Holding the coffee in one hand and the breakfast menu in the other, I read it very attentively so I'd know exactly which dishes were offered.

The first waiters arrived. Another 45 minutes until the glass doors of the restaurant would open. Some guests were already waiting in front of them so they could be served first. Another 35 minutes elapsed and most of the waiters were busy preparing their stations with the help of their assistant waiters. I panicked: there were only 25 minutes left until breakfast! "Benny," I asked an Austrian waiter, "where is Jesus? He should have arrived a long time ago. The table only has a tablecloth on it, nothing else. It hasn't even been set!" "Jesus?" Benny laughed. "If you are lucky, he might arrive at the same time as the guests, but sometimes they come here even earlier than he does! Try to put the most necessary items on the table so that it doesn't look too empty!"

It's not supposed to work this way! I thought to myself. *This guy is already sabotaging my new waiter job.*

I hurried to the office and asked for the phone number of his cabin. "Jesus," I shouted into the phone, "only 20 minutes left before breakfast, come here right away!"

"Calm down, Darling!" he chirped into the phone. "Haste makes waste. Get the coffee and pastries. I'll be with you in a minute. See you soon, my little waiter!"

I was in a frenzy as I hurried back to the station where a head waiter looked at me pitifully. "Is the lazybones late again? Good luck!", he said, then disappeared.

Gripped with terror at the threat of coming across as 'blithering waiter-idiot'on my first day, I took action and collected the cutlery, plates and cups and started to set the table as best as I could. Coffee, pastries, iced water and iced tea were ready at hand when waiter Jesus finally arrived. Imagine my horror at the appearance of a slovenly unshaven man with considerable bulk shuffling towards me. He must have weighed at least 100 kg, and wore dirty shoes with a stained shirt and trousers. And his fly was open. *I must be seeing things!* I thought, *Is this a joke? How can he dare to show up in such a get-up?*

"Good morning, little waiter!" he whispered. "How are you? Did you sleep well and have sweet dreams?"

"I think I *am* still dreaming," I replied, still in shock over his unkempt and unprofessional appearance. "I hope I wake up soon!"

Jesus did not understand the nuance of my reply and looked at the table on which I had hurriedly placed knives, forks and spoons. "What a nice table," he squealed. "You are already doing a great job. Later I'll show you how to take an order."

Is he kidding me? I thought. *The tables* are *a disaster!* "I don't get it." I wailed desperately, "all I did was put some cutlery and a few cups – some even without saucers – on the table."

"Which is more than enough," Jesus said while zipping up his fly. "Look, our guests are arriving. I'll show you how to deal with them."

At that very moment I was taught the first commandment for waiters which will make or break a restaurant, a commandment which is sadly disregarded in numerous restaurants although the staff do their utmost to work professionally: "Provide wholehearted service." That's the magic formula!

Brimming with friendliness and kindheartedness, Jesus cordially welcomed the hungry masses, helped them to their seats, pilfered napkins from the empty neighboring table and put them on the laps of his own guests. At the same time he had them engrossed in a conversation and held the breakfast menu in front of their noses so that they did not have a chance to complain about the unset table.

173

While the guests focused on the menu, Jesus put a table, knife and fork in front of each of them. The pleasant anticipation of the numerous appetizing dishes whet everybody's appetite. The guests smiled at Jesus' effeminate voice as he gave me his first instruction: "Darling, please be so kind and serve our customers pastries and coffee. It seems that a few of them are still half asleep." I heartily joined the guests' giggling while I followed the waiter's instruction. During breakfast I listened to Jesus as he chatted with the guests and asked them about their respective home countries. He then painted a glowing picture of the beautiful island where we would call at port the next day. It was easy to see his calm demeanor made the guests feel relaxed; my earlier fears and misgivings about Jesus' waitering style had entirely disappeared. I learned an invaluable lesson during these first ten minutes: the appearance of the table did not matter at all, as long as the guests were provided with some basic food such as bread, butter, coffee and some beverages, and were treated in a friendly and obliging manner.

I paid utmost attention to respecting the first unwritten law for providing perfect American-style service, which is: always ensure cups and glasses are full. Along with this rule I also learned to anticipate and fulfill my guests' expectations. Missing cutlery which would have thrown the manager of every European restaurant into a tizzy was a trivial matter. The items were placed on the table on request; minor complaints were returned with jokes and humorous remarks.

"Jesus," a guest remarked, "you brought me the wrong main course. I ordered scrambled eggs, but it was my wife who had asked for pancakes!" "Dear guest," Jesus riposted, "you are right. I only wanted to test you and your memory power. You passed!" Everybody was laughing while Jesus corrected his mistake.

"Jesus, my glass had cola in it, but you refilled it with iced tea. Although both beverages are the same color, this combination doesn't taste very good at all!" "Oh, excuse me!" Jesus answered. "Unfortunately I am not as clever as I look!" The guests and I nearly split our sides laughing at his quick retort. I became aware of how much easier it is for a waiter with a sense of humor to keep his guests happy.

We served only seven customers during this first early breakfast sitting. However, the guests stayed in the restaurant drinking coffee until only fifteen minutes were left until the second sitting. When they eventually got up to leave, I immediately began clearing the table and changing the table cloth in order to offer a professionally set table this time.

"Darling, what are you doing?" Jesus asked in bewilderment. "Changing the tablecloth and then ..." I replied. "Changing? No way! Take a doily to cover the stains so that nobody can see them!" I was lost for words as two doilies had been put on the table three seconds later to hide the egg stains.

"Hurry up, Darling!" Jesus whispered. "Get some cups and cutlery so that we can go for a smoke." "You want to go for a smoke *now*?" I asked incredulously. "The table looks even worse than it did for the first sitting – and all you care about is going for a smoke?!" "I need one," Jesus said as he disappeared.

The doors opened and two minutes later the guests for the second sitting were heading for our station. My head was spinning. The table didn't look presentable at all and there was neither hide nor hair of my dear Mr. Jesus! What would he have done in this situation? Mustering all my courage, I enthusiastically greeted the guests. "Good morning, nice to see you! Take a seat, please. The coffee is hot, fresh bread and tasty pastries are waiting for you, and the hens have been particularly diligent in supplying the raw material – the eggs – for your omelettes."

Following Jesus' example and having already learned my lesson regarding proper handling of guests, I helped the customers to their seats, held the menu under their nose and described the delicacies they could order for breakfast in full detail. Their content facial expressions revealed they were happy to be served by such a good-humored waiter.

Jesus shuffled into the station a short while later. Meeting him half way, I told him, "Your tried-and-true strategy works. Everybody is happy because I am also happy. Nobody even noticed the doilies on the tablecloth." "Of course my strategy works!" Jesus laughed. "It's very easy; just keep cool and be happy."

At the end of the second sitting four larger and two smaller stains had been left on the cloth by the customers who had greatly enjoyed their breakfast. As it was time to set the table for lunch, I seized the tablecloth with both hands and was about to change it, but once again my waiter intervened. "Why are you putting on a new tablecloth?" Jesus asked, "aren't there any doilies left?" "No," I said, hiding the doilies behind my back. "No doilies left!" "It doesn't matter," Jesus deflated my good intentions. "There are other methods. Look!" I didn't believe my eyes when he took the little milk jug filled with condensed milk for the coffee and poured a few drops on the stains. After he had carefully dabbed the condensed milk with his middle finger on the stains until they were covered, he announced, "it's fine now! Now it just has to dry!" "Jesus," I complained, "we can't leave the table in this state!" "Of course we can," he replied flatly. "We're all ready for lunch, Darling! I'll hit the hay for an hour. After lunch we'll get together and I will teach you the high art of being a waiter on a cruise ship. I'll explain what you need to be able to do, what you need to know and what you are allowed to do or vice versa." And off he went! I was standing there, unable to understand how it was possible that no head waiter had ever put an end to Jesus' behavior. But in those days the slogan was very simple: "Do whatever you want as long as the guests are satisfied. And if your rating at the end of the cruise is bad and you get less than two stars, you will have to fly home." Lunch was served. It was a good thing that I had thoroughly read the menu so I was able to reply to any of the guests' questions, because Master Jesus only deigned to show up after the guests had already sat down at their tables. Before they could notice any crumbs or the dried milk on the table, I had already handed the menu to them and recommended my favorite meals. Jesus appeared behind me and listened to my repartee. "He is a fantastic assistant waiter, isn't he?" he asked with a smile. "A real jewel, a superman! Someday he will be the best waiter in the dining room – besides me, of course!" The guests laughed and were pleased to see their waiter giving his assistant a chance to prove himself. He continued with his usual aplomb while taking orders and ensuring everything was running smoothly.

The first sitting was over. Returning from the galley with fresh water glasses, I realized immediately that there were even more crumbs on the table.

176

"Jesus," I said, "the time has come to change the tablecloth, don't you think? Your guests for the second sitting won't need to read the menu, they'll just have to look at the table and will know right away what's on the menu." "Why do you think it needs to be changed?" he replied. "To me it looks quite funny!"

I felt queasy. Thanks to his friendly tactics and helpfulness this guy managed to restrain his customers from either peeping under the crumbs or scratching at the dried milk stains to see what they were covering.

"We've made it, Darling!" he said. "Now we can set the tables for dinner. Please get another few..." "No way!" I interrupted him. "We won't subject our customers to a dinner table that looks more like an overturned garbage can. I'll clean up while you take a rest, and we will get together later for my lesson!"

After I had finished my work, the tables looked beautiful. I had gotten some sheets of paper to write down what I would learn from the waiter Jesus and sat down.

"Oh, somebody has been promoted to waiter!" I heard the familiar and scornful voice of busboy Harry, the troublemaker, behind me. "How is it that you are already being promoted? Although I have been working here longer, I've never been given a chance so far to work as a waiter and earn more money." Without looking at Harry, I replied, "No surprise When you consider all the stunts you've pulled on your colleagues!"

"You'll fail!" he explained to me. "You haven't been working here long enough to be promoted; the guests will get you down."

"All I can do is try my best," I replied. "If I fail, I will work again as assistant waiter." "That's not the way it works around here!" he spat in a voice oozing with jealousy. "You know that you will be dismissed if you make so much as a small misstep and the guests are not satisfied at the end of the cruise!"

Although Harry's remarks stung, I immediately pulled myself together and countered, "Jesus will explain everything to me. He assured to me that I won't fail." "We'll see about that," Harry replied with a smirk.

During the next two weeks I worked extremely hard, even until late at night, having lessons with Jesus in between shifts and putting my lessons into practice. I made great progress with all the tricks and

177

secrets of the waiter job I had been taught which I will pass down to the next waiter generation, if they are interested in learning these tricks of the trade.

I was dead beat and bone-tired at the end of the second cruise when a head waiter approached me to praise me to the heavens. "Well done!" he said. "We've been watching your efforts and are very impressed. You will work as waiter on the next cruise."

Everybody attended the big meeting during which the maître d' announced before the beginning of the first dinner sitting that one of the assistants had been promoted after only three months. As I was presented to the brigade, I was given a round of applause and felt proud of my achievement. Prior to being assigned to a small station consisting of a table for ten guests in the corner, I was advised I would be assisted by a very experienced busboy who, in case of an emergency, would be able to discreetly smooth out any "faux pas" by the waiter.

As I started setting the table I once again thought of everything I had been taught in the past two weeks. I then grabbed the menu, went to the galley and checked every starter, main course and dessert so that I would be able to describe all the meals in accurate detail.

When I returned to my station and realized who was polishing the glasses there, I broke out in a sweat and my heart started racing. "Namaste," the Indian Harry welcomed me, which is the Indian translation for "Hello!" Folding his hands on his chest, he took a bow in Indian style. "I am your loyal assistant and look forward to cooperating with you!"

"Harry," I said, "if you give me a hard time and don't help me, I will get back at you, make no mistake. As you've already mentioned, this is my one and only chance and I'm taking it."

"Don't worry, my friend!" he assured me in a tone which I did not like at all. "I am the best in the dining room!" "The thing is that nobody knows exactly *what* you're the best at." I mumbled and tried to focus on my work.

The doors opened, the guests rolled in and shortly thereafter my station was occupied. Friendly Americans from the southern States shook hands before they delved into the menu. "Good people," Harry whispered. "You are very lucky!"

178

They were "good" indeed: congenial and interested in the waiter and his busboy. They wanted to know where we were from, how long we'd been working with the shipping company and which meals and beverages we could recommend.

Jesus approached me, gave my guests a once-over, looked at me and showed his approval with a thumbs up. "Five stars!" he said. "All you have to do is remember what you have learned and focus on the things that matter!"

I then took a deep breath and started working.

Everything ran smoothly. The guests seemed to be totally satisfied with me and my busboy who, contrary to my expectations, did not cause any problems, but was actually a great help.

The dessert had been served, the aromatic smell of coffee was enticing and the guests enjoyed themselves. We made it! The first dinner went without a hitch!

I was really proud at the way dinner had turned out and patted Harry on the back as a gesture of gratitude. "Thanks!" I said. "Thanks for helping me make a good impression!" "No big deal," Harry replied, "all you need is a good memory." "A good memory? What do you mean?" "Oh, nothing special," he answered and left to do the dishes.

Mindless gibberish, I thought to myself. *Not a single day without that guy trying to bring me down.* Since I couldn't have guessed that he had planned to play a dirty trick – his last – on me all along with this gibberish, I had soon forgotten his nasty words. I was very content since I knew I had satisfied my dinner guests. After work I went to the crew bar where a toast was made to my success with my favorite drink, a nice whiskey sour.

The next day it was time to serve the second dinner sitting. Since water, wine, soups and salads had already been placed on the table, I left the station to get the next course from the galley.

Carrying 13 fully loaded trays on my shoulder, I returned to put down my little tower in the station.

Brandishing three main courses, I once again threw a glance at my order form to avoid any mistake before serving my guests. "Your fish, Ma'am!" I said to the first lady and placed the meal in front of her. "Unfortunately you are wrong!" I was advised. "I ordered the chicken."

"Shit", I thought loudly, but remained composed and served the proper chicken dish to the guest. Afterwards it was the second lady's turn. After all, "Ladies first!" as the saying goes... "Madam, the lamb is for you. I hope you enjoy the meal!" "I am sorry," she replied. "I ordered the roast duck!"

A few choice colorful words flashed through my mind at that moment. *Pull yourself together*, I scolded myself.

Another intense look at my order form and only one more main course left to serve! I nervously returned to the table. "The steak for lady number three, the steak for lady number three, the steak for lady number three," I repeated continuously, just to be on the safe side.

"A juicy steak for you, Madam. Enjoy!" "I would like to," she sighed, "but I ordered the fish!"

Everything went black. I was completely shocked and distressed as I stood at my station, holding the unwanted steak in my hand. I kept checking my order form but didn't see anything amiss. "Harry the Ugly" grinned malevolently at me and asked, "What's the matter? Have you lost your memory?"

This was exactly what I needed at that moment: my busboy's, inane, superfluous comments and his ugly, hammer nose face which seemed to gloat: "As you can see, I was right. You fail!" I was on the verge of doing something drastic when all of the guests burst into loud laughter. One of the gentlemen got up to put his arm around my shoulders.

"Just a little joke," he said, "don't worry, everything is okay with your memory. As instructed by your assistant, we changed our places, while you were in the galley. Have a close look, none of us are sitting where we had been sitting at the beginning of dinner. So it's no surprise that you mixed up the main courses! Please accept our apologies, but Harry's idea to play a trick on you was too tempting!"

This confession took a weight off my shoulders, and I joined in their laughter. Although I was beside myself, deep down I knew that the guests liked me and that I was well on my way to my first five star rating. All that remained was for Harry, who felt very clever and smug about his joke, to be taken to task before the cruise was over!

The next evening the guests had already sat down and were thoroughly engrossed in the menu. Harry had just gone to the galley to get water and iced tea for the station, when I suddenly appeared in front of my guests, grinning ear to ear, with two large buckets.

"Dear Ladies and Gentlemen," I said, "now we turn the tables. My busboy gave me a real scare yesterday, which cries out for revenge!" "OK!" the guests laughingly complied. "What do you intend to do and how can we help?" "Quite simple," I explained. "I'll put these buckets under the table and you, my dear Ladies and Gentlemen, will pretend to be extremely thirsty tonight. As soon as Harry has filled the water glasses and served iced tea, you will only take a sip and pour the contents of your glasses in the buckets under the table at a suitable moment. It is important that you look innocent. I will do the rest. Watch out, Harry is approaching with his pitchers of water and iced tea. Ladies and Gentlemen – cheers!!!"

"Harry," I said when he arrived at the station, huffing and puffing under the weight of the pitchers, "our customers' water glasses are empty. Haven't you prepared any iced water?"

"Of course I did," Harry replied. "You know that I always perfectly prepare my station. The guests are thirsty and I will refill their glasses right away."

So far, so good! The glasses of water and iced tea were again full according to the American service standard. On this particular evening we didn't sell much wine, which was okay with me on this occasion. My revenge on Harry was far more important. I had to put him in his place once and for all! .

After briefly checking his bread basket Harry prepared the bread service. While he explained the various types of breads to the guests, he realized that the glasses which he had just refilled were empty again. Visibly distraught, he served the bread and again grabbed his pitchers. "Very strange," he mumbled almost inaudibly, "I just refilled all the glasses only a second ago!"

"Harry," I advised my busboy, "I will go to the galley to get the appetizers. Take care of our guests and make sure to refill their glasses!" "You don't have to boss me around," Harry replied indignantly. "I know how to do my job!"

181

Afterwards my busboy poured the two pitchers of water and iced tea into the guests' glasses while I disappeared into the galley.

"Sir",I whispered to Harry in a harsh voice when I placed my tray filled with shrimp cocktails, quiche Lorraine and a few other dishes on the gueridon. "Our guests' glasses are empty – again!. Why haven't you refilled them?" Harry, who was busy polishing cutlery, looked at the table and couldn't believe his eyes. He was beside himself upon being given a dressing down by the head waiter and hurried to the galley with his pitchers to get them ready for the thirsty guests. After he had returned in record time, he again refilled their glasses.

He had just served guest number 20, when the guest numbers 1, 2, 3 and 4 raised their glasses and shouted: "Harry, have you forgotten about us? We are thirsty!"

Hammer Nose Harry gaped at the sight of the raised drinking vessels. "Just a moment, Ma'am," he said, evidently flustered. "I'll be right with you!"

"Damn it, Harry!" I scolded in an indignant tone. "It is not sufficient to only provide the guests at *one* table with drinks. Why haven't you refilled the glasses of our guests at the second table? Do your job properly, please!" "Don't talk to me that way!" Harry wanted to counter, but was interrupted by the slightly furious voice of a guest at the second table.

"Mr. Harry," a guest grumbled. "What's the matter? Why have our glasses been empty for so long? What's wrong with you? Did you give up on us or have you lost your memory?" The hapless busboy stared at the empty glasses, then at the angry facial expressions of the customers. Horror-stricken, he seized his empty pitchers and headed for the kitchen once again.

As fate would have it, the head waiter passed him whose harsh comment, "Harry, hurry up, most of your guests don't have anything to drink!" played perfectly into my dirty trick.

"Yes, I know," the distressed assistant gasped. "I'm on my way."

One of the guests sent for me and suggested, "Johannes, why don't you follow your busboy and try to find out what he is saying about us. It would be very interesting to know!"

"A great idea," I agreed with him and arrived at the galley within five seconds.

Soaked in sweat, Hammer Nose Harry panted like a dog on the verge of collapsing. "What's the matter with this pack?" he shouted. "Have they turned into horses overnight?"

"Cop out!" I jeered. "You're not as smart as you think!" "You bugger!" he shouted. "You are a dumb-ass! I have already refilled the glasses seven times," Harry tried in vain to defend himself. "*Seven times?*" I asked in bewilderment. "How can the glasses be empty *again*?!"

"I don't know!" he whimpered. "If it keeps on like this, I will order them to take a shower and get tanked up on the water there!"

Although I could hardly suppress my laughter when I watched my assistant, who appeared to be having a heart attack, lugging water, I remained serious. "Yes," I said, "that's a great idea. Go to the guests and suggest this brilliant solution to them for satisfying their thirst!"

Of course it was impossible for him to follow this recommendation. Instead he was smiling uncomfortably and carried two more pitchers of water to the tables. He looked as heavy-laden as a pack mule. Our customers continued cooperating in an excellent manner and pretended to have a normal consumption of water and iced tea.

All the guests were dying to know if Harry had gossiped or complained about them in the galley. I used the opportunity to inform them accordingly while Master Harry was in the kitchen getting some new water. Upon his return to the station Harry was very suspicious of the passengers' laughter and he looked at me imploringly.

"Why are you staring at me, Harry?" I asked him. "Look over there, one of our customers would like to talk to you. He is waving at you." Harry approached the guest who was smirking at him.

"Look, there is something under the table which I suspect is yours. Would you remove it, please. I find it disturbing!" "What could it possibly be?" Harry asked and could not believe his eyes at the sight that greeted him when he looked under the table: two large buckets filled to the brim with water and iced tea.

Harry pulled the buckets out from under the table and gaped at his guests who burst into uproarious laughter. "There you are," the gentleman said who had brought Harry's attention to the buckets. "Yesterday you played a nasty prank on our poor Johannes, and today he turned the tables. We were totally sold on this idea! Please take the buckets away and serve us some water afterwards. To be honest, we have hardly had anything to drink until now!"

Almost boiling over with rage, Harry looked at me. "Will you help me lug the buckets back to the galley?" he asked me. "No way," I replied, "my arms feel a bit weak this evening!"

The guests and the restaurant staff were quite surprised to see our busboy crossing the dining room with two full water buckets and did not know what to make of it.

I followed him into the galley and I could tell he would have liked nothing more than to go for my throat. "Hold on!" I said. "Now we will both stop playing dirty tricks on each other. I only wanted to demonstrate that I am no fool and will pay you back in your own coin. Now, let's make a truce and focus on our work!" Harry pondered for a while then shook my hand. "Well done, Johannes!" shouted three waiters who had suddenly appeared behind us and observed what had happened in our station. "Today Hammer Nose Harry got what he deserves because he has also been playing dirty tricks on us. We hope that he will stop now."

"Okay, okay," Harry begrudgingly agreed. "You win. As of today I won't get up to any more nonsense," he capitulated.

We shook hands again and in fact, as of this evening, Cunning Harry reverted to the normal assistant waiter known as Diligent and Hardworking Harry.

The cruise was a great success for all of us. While the generous tips were being handed over, we were pleased to hear the comment, "We've never had so much fun during a cruise!" which raised hopes for an excellent rating of our service.

Chapter 21: Luigi

The next evening the maître d' asked me to come to his office. As soon as I arrived he shook my hand. "Five stars, Johannes! Keep up the good work! We also know about the dirty trick you've played on Harry and were very amused. But please be careful in the future since some guests don't appreciate being involved in such antics. And once again – congratulations!" Since the maître d' was so friendly to me, I summoned up the courage to ask a question which had been on my mind for so long. Now the time had come to confront him. "Boss? Ever since we put Harry in his place to stop him from annoying us, I've been wondering if you ever encountered a waiter or busboy in your career that was crazier than Harry and had to be dismissed?" "I've met several of them," he replied. "But the biggest nutcase who has ever worked in my team was an Italian. He was ten times crazier than the Indian and was so bananas that I sent him home after two weeks. His name was Luigi. As son of a rich hotelier in Rome, his parents had probably sent him on board a cruise liner just to get rid of him for a while. It seemed as if he had been goofing off at home as well. Although he was able to work as a waiter, he had not completed an apprenticeship, and I suspect his certificates were counterfeited. Despite this fact he entered my office someday to be advised of his tasks. He immediately frowned when I asked a head waiter to bring him up to speed. Since he did not attend the first evening meeting of the cruise, we called him in his cabin to find out the reason for his absence in the restaurant. "Seasick" was the answer, although the ship was still tied at the dock.and had not yet left Miami. Because he was new, we gave him the benefit of the doubt and allowed him to stay in the cabin the first night. The second evening he showed up in the dining room and had the gall to ask me if he would be paid a bad weather compensation in case of turbulent seas. I would have liked nothing more than to give him a kick in the ass, but I kept my temper and thwarted his idea instead. Thank God he started to work and even did quite a good job. Obviously he had gathered some experience as a waiter in his parents' hotel. But on the third evening he made his first colossal blunder! Instead of his tray and his bread baskets, he held a red toy telephone in his hands which he had probably stolen from the daycare. When the guests had sat down and wanted to order their meals, he put this telephone on the table and said, "Dear guests! Now I will demonstrate to you how orders are placed in Italy, my home country. Notice the telephone I have just put on the table and listen to my instructions. So, if you would like to order a Coke, dial 1. If you would rather have a Fanta or Sprite, choose 2 and if you would like iced tea or coffee, you must dial 3. Capito?" After his informative demonstration he left the restaurant. The guests were laughing since they had never before been told such nonsense. In any case his idea was funny, albeit inappropriate. The waiter scowled because he was fully aware of the fact that Luigi would not serve any beverages to the guests which meant he had to do it himself despite his lack of time. Luigi eventually showed up again and was immediately asked why he had not served any beverages. "Haven't you ever placed orders by phone?" he inquired. "Of course!" the guests replied indignantly. "We've dialed our fingers to the bone!" "Very strange," Luigi answered. "No messages were left on the mailbox. Are you sure you correctly used the phone?" While the guests split their sides laughing, the waiter became more furious as he had hoped that the guests would complain about Luigi. Instead, they enjoyed being his co-conspirators; the joke with the phone was far too funny! Thanks to the enormous efforts of the waiter all guests were eventually served a complete dinner. Of course Luigi was properly told off by the waiter and the head waiter. The next day we were on the high seas. After the guests had had lunch and wanted to leave the dining room, they suddenly came face to face with a register in front of the restaurant where an assistant waiter was sitting to cash up. The waiter was in fact Luigi, the crazy guy, who had placed a small table with a tablecloth in front of the restaurant and put an old adding machine on it which he had found somewhere. The guests were totally confused as they assumed all meals in the restaurant were included in the cruise fare. Our dear guests were standing at the restaurant exit, staring at Luigi who was typing on his machine with a serious facial expression and asking the guests to pay for their restaurant visit. While some of the passengers realized straightaway that it was a joke and laughed as they walked past Luigi, other guests angrily opened their wallets, paid the requested

187

amount and promised Luigi they would complain to the travel agency. Luigi simply laughed off his little joke and followed these guests to return their money since he had never intended to keep it. Although most of the passengers were relieved, some of them were rather shocked and tattled on Luigi to the maître d' the next day. The management again summoned Luigi to the office where he had to sign his first written warning.

The next evening we were heading for Puerto Rico and the midnight buffet was to be served at the pool. All restaurant staff was busy preparing a really magnificent feast. The guests were informed that following the evening meal and live music there would also be a spectacular presentation: an ice artist who would demonstrate to all interested passengers how to create an ice sculpture with a hammer and chisel in only 15 minutes. Although Luigi was also assigned to the pool buffet, his job that evening was mainly to clean the tables – a task he couldn't possibly mess up. He listened to the cruise director who announced the ice carving and watched the crowd of curious guests who gradually gathered around the 300 kg block of ice awaiting the master from the Philippines who would transform it into a work of art. Since Luigi was a real prankster at heart, he promptly forgot all about his promises to be on good behavior. He put the cleaning cloth aside and decided to act while the iron was still hot – or ice cold, as it turned out. Ensuring the ice artist had not yet arrived, he approached the ice block and announced, "I'm on my way!" He was accompanied by the guests' applause who of course had no idea what the genuine artist looked like. Encouraged by the crowd's fanfare, he grinned from ear to ear as he seized the hammer and chisel. As nearly all of the spectators had already admired an ice figure at one time or another but had not actually witnessed its creation, they were now excitedly anticipating a swan, fish or a mermaid to magically materialize from the ice block within the next fifteen minutes. Luigi did in fact begin hammering on the ice block accompanied by the guests' rhythmic applause. None of the other colleagues noticed what was happening since Luigi was hidden by the numerous people around him. Moreover the waiters were not especially interested in it, because they all knew that during this ice-carving demonstration nothing particular was to be done by them. It was

188

only when an older Filipino gentleman came running towards the crowd after he had heard the noise of hammer and chisel from afar that the crew's curiosity was aroused and they joined the spectators. None of them could believe their eyes, especially the ice carver himself, when they realized that the lean Italian had hijacked the show. The artist couldn't do much to prevent it as the guests were clearly enjoying Luigi's demonstration. The Filipino artist only hoped that the man was a colleague from Italy who was also a skilled artist and could carve a magnificent ice sculpture. Peck – peck – peck – peck – peck – peck … While the ice block continuously became smaller, the genuine artist pulled an increasingly long face. In the meantime he had of course realized that the ice block was not treated in a skillful and proper manner. Peck – peck – peck – peck, the ice block had almost disappeared, and the Filipino artist pulled an even longer face. He would have liked to intervene, but was totally irritated by the spectators' enthusiasm. Peck – peck, the block that originally had had a weight of more than 250 kg now looked like a snowman which had melted in the sun. Although the hammering was no longer as forceful as in the beginning, they still hoped that a somewhat smaller yet wonderful statue would be fashioned from the originally sizeable ice block. However, quite the opposite was the case. Luigi again started hammering at the block like a madman until nothing but a large pile of crushed ice was left. "Snow!" Luigi announced triumphantly as he wiped the sweat from his brow. "Have a look, isn't it fascinating? We are cruising in the Caribbean Sea, yet there is snow. I now invite everybody to get closer and admire my work of art. Have a nice evening." He threw the hammer and the ice pick aside and disappeared. All spectators were gaping at the pile of ice not knowing what to think, until a few guests started giggling. Most of the spectators eventually joined in the laughter as none of them had expected such an "artistic" demonstration. Two individuals, however, did not feel like laughing: the Filipino artist and the food and beverage manager who wanted to ensure everything was in order and was furious that so many people were laughing uproariously. Also he could not help but laugh heartily. Nevertheless Luigi was asked to visit his office for another good scolding that night. He listened to it as cool as a cucumber, but did

189

not lose any sleep over the incident. The next day the ice carving demonstration was practically the only topic of conversation on board the cruise liner since no other show had ever annoyed and amused so many guests at the same time.

The recollection of this "show" once again appeared in the mind's eye of the maître d', which he obviously considerably enjoyed.

Let me point out that the midnight buffets are not offered very often these days as most of the guests are too full after the sumptuous dinner. Today the only buffets offered in the late evening during a cruise are the pool buffet which takes place at the swimming pool in good weather and a sensational chocolate buffet in the restaurant at midnight where ice artists and celebrity cooks showcase their masterpieces against a backdrop of dancing and entertainment. This lavish buffet is of such beauty that the guests often take photos of it before indulging. One of my duties is to give a detailed description of this magnificent buffet in at least four languages. I have to admit that only very few guests are actually listening to my spiel because they are all so mesmerized by the fantastic display. Part of my job during this buffet is to make the following announcement: "Dear Ladies and Gentlemen! I would like to relay a message to the gentleman who has lost his 18-carat Rolex with a diamond clock face on board our ship. Let me repeat: this is a message to the gentleman who has lost his 18-carat Rolex with a diamond clock face on board our ship." This announcement is invariably met with dead silence. All guests are scouring the floor – with dollar signs in their eyes – hoping to find the valuable watch. Then I speak up again: "Please be advised that it is now 20 minutes past midnight, Sir!!!" The passengers burst into loud laughter and smile at me in amusement before they once again gaze at the buffet in fascination.

This unique, superbly presented culinary highlight has so far always been a great success. Yet despite its splendor I am compelled to recount an unpleasant episode. A hot-tempered male guest had overlooked the description "chocolate buffet" and queued up with a large plate in his hand expecting the usual selection of food. As the buffet was particularly marvelous that evening, the guests had to wait for about half an hour before they could indulge in the delicious sweets and pastries.

The gentleman in question was annoyed of having to wait in line. Upon his arrival at the buffet he noticed that no hot food was being served and was politely informed that it was a chocolate buffet, not a pizza stand. He was so enraged that he hurled his plate with full force towards one of the marble tables on which an ornate glass figurine had been positioned. Everybody watched the sharp splinters of glass spreading across the entire buffet like sparks of fire, which put a premature end to this magnificent spectacle. The troublemaker who failed to own up to his bad behavior and kept on ranting was immediately surrounded by the security personnel, then frog marched off the premises by three strong guards.

The nearly 200 guests in the queue were visibly distressed at the spectacle and subsequently returned their plates to the buffet table since they were well aware that there would be nothing offered that night, and that even the smallest splinters of glass as a result of the guest's outburst could pose great danger if ingested.

Now allow me to again refer to Luigi. The maître d' continued his anecdote:

"Anybody who believed that Luigi would finally stop getting up to no good was quickly disabused of this notion the next evening after our stay in Puerto Rico. The restaurant doors were opened for dinner, but Luigi was not seen anywhere. The guests started giggling because they were sure that the busboy would either not show up at all or turn up at the restaurant shortly with a silly excuse. They were right. He was sweating and gasping because the surfboard he was lugging was rather cumbersome. Everybody was gaping at him since the sight of a waiter in uniform with a surfboard in a restaurant was quite extraordinary. He happily arrived at the station with his burden and presented the board by boasting: "Hi guys! Look! I left the liner today and met a hot chick who fancied Italians. First she invited me to go to the beach with her and took me home afterwards, Then, after I had my way with her, I made off with her surfboard. Have a look – isn't it beautiful? It certainly was a very profitable day for me."

He disappeared again and did not return to the restaurant. The poor waiter had to find out the hard way what it would be like to manage the work without his busboy who – no surprise! – had to visit the office once again to sign his last written warning. Luigi was advised that the management's patience was beginning to wear thin and that in the instance of further misconduct he would be dismissed immediately.

We didn't have to wait very long for the inevitable. During the first evening of the next cruise everything ran smoothly in the beginning until the waiter returned from the galley with his main courses. When he put down his tray in the station, he didn't dare believe his eyes: there was no space left on the tables whatsoever. What then, you may wonder, were the tables entirely covered with? You would never guess: soldiers, tanks, cannons and military vehicles had been spread all over them! Luigi was running around the tables describing a famous battle from one of the two world wars. While his male guests had been promoted to a general, lieutenant and corporal, all female guests had to render medical services. Wildly gesticulating, he hurried across the station, imitated cannons and gun shots before eventually dropping dead on the floor. The head waiter and waiters rolled their eyes and stayed in the background, struggling not to lose their temper.

"I wish I were at war, because he would make perfect cannon fodder!" the head waiter swore. He then turned to the frustrated waiter who could not serve his main dishes which had meanwhile become cold and inedible as a result. He helped him return the piles of food to the galley where he begged the cooks for new main courses. After they had returned to the station a while later, the head waiter noticed the "dead" Luigi who was still lying on the floor without making a move to get up. Perhaps he clung to the hope of being tended to by the youngest nurse, which, however, did not happen. The maître d' strode towards him and violently wrested Luigi to his feet. The superior scarcely uttered a word since the spectators enthusiastically applauded this clown. The maître d' was thus forced to once again exercise the patience of job on the matter and even praised Luigi for his performance and for not annoying the passengers.

The waiter's good mood continuously faded as he did not know how to get his station ready for the second sitting. As requested by the maître d', a few nearby waiters assisted him at the last minute. After all the waiter had to keep his composure to ensure the dining

192

room would open on time, regardless of whether the preparatory work in the station was finished or not.

"Out he goes!" the hotel manager exclaimed after he had been informed of Luigi's escapades. "I don't want to see him ever again – neither on board our liner during the next cruise nor on board any other ship in our fleet. I hope I have made myself clear!"

Although Luigi's dismissal was a foregone conclusion, he was allowed to work on the last day of the cruise as the management was foolish enough to believe that he wouldn't cause trouble again.

Luigi, however, had yet another trick up his sleeve on his final day. Fully aware of his persona non grata status, Luigi was nevertheless anxious for one last opportunity to misbehave – and he was given this opportunity by an elderly lady. She was rather demanding and sent Luigi to the galley to fetch food for her far too often - at least in his opinion. While the waiter was serving the dessert, she waved Luigi to her table once again and said: "Instead of the dessert I would like a bowl of egg drop soup. Could you please take care of it?" Smirking and looking at her lewdly, Luigi put his hand between his legs – perfectly imitating one of Michael Jackson's moves – wiggled his genitals a few times and shamelessly answered, "Hey, Grandma, here it is – your egg drop soup – freshly prepared. Come and get it!" The lady was agog with horror and tried to regain her sense of decorum, but a head waiter who had witnessed everything immediately hurried over to comfort her and banished Luigi out of the dining room.

This was the last performance of our Luigi. The next day he had to leave the cruise liner, which, however, did not faze him at all. His dad was rich and life would somehow go on. But the waiter whom he had annoyed with his nonsense the previous evening ranted and threw a shoe at Luigi as he was walked down the gangway. He had to be held back by two colleagues to prevent him from following Luigi and beating him up. It took several days until he had recovered from the stresses and strains caused by the shenanigans unleashed by this odd duck. Thanks to the valium prescribed by the doctor he could again sleep at night.

"Well, I hope to have answered your question with my anecdotes," the maître d' concluded his story. "Now go back to work and do your best. Be careful not to get into trouble with your addiction to humor."

Assuring him I would do my best, I thanked him for this funny and detailed story featuring Luigi. I promised him that my jokes with the guests would neither become excessive or offensive nor give him the impression my service was in any way diminished by my shows and magical tricks. On my way to my cabin numerous thoughts crossed my mind. Once again I realized that the job of a waiter on an international level and interacting with a large number of guests required utmost sensitivity and tactfulness. You always have to recognize that the line between entertaining the guests and the moment of annoying them with exaggerated nonsense is very fine. Please read in the next chapter how you can nevertheless get into trouble, if you try to take utmost care of your guests and to provide perfect service.

Chapter 22:   Little Grandpa

A first-class tragedy occurred during my sixth or seventh cruise as a waiter. However, I didn't command the starring role this time, rather, it was a cabin steward called Sterling living on the same floor that took center stage, although reluctantly. This stout man from Central America had been working with the shipping company for a few years. We knew each other quite well and shared the same passion: playing cards after an exhausting day.

The week had been very tough as the weather was a catastrophe during the entire cruise. Our ship was surprised by a hurricane which gave us a good shaking on six of the seven days. During the severe weather we were able to drop anchor in Jamaica for a short time, but had to leave soon thereafter as the storm had already caught up with us. Our captain had to navigate a timely and safe arrival at our home port despite the heavy seas.

The third day was the worst I had experienced in 26 years. The waves were crashing the windows of the restaurant on the 4th floor. Crew members and guests alike were sick; everyone regretted they had embarked on this cruise. The cabin steward Sterling was one of those who had been hit extremely hard. On the fourth day of the cruise he told the following bizarre story.

"I have the feeling I will be dismissed at the end of this cruise," our rather drunken Sterling announced one evening when he welcomed his friends who were not seasick – among the lucky of which I was one – with a bottle of whiskey in his cabin.

"What's the matter, old chap?" we wanted to know. "You are really out of sorts!" "Yes, I am," Sterling slurred his words. "Such bullshit can only happen to me!"

"Come on, tell us what's wrong!" we cajoled him in chorus while sipping on our whiskey.

At our prompting Sterling started to recount his tale. "A family is staying in one of the cabins for which I am responsible. As they boarded the ship in Miami like all the other guests, they carried a medium-sized jug along with their luggage. I had never seen such a vessel before, and thought it was a bit curious that they placed it on the windowsill. They were very quiet – contrary to the usually quite talkative guests who were looking forward to their cruise and cordially welcomed the cabin steward as a rule. I was not surprised that they opened the door only ajar when I introduced myself to them. Sometimes customers don't feel in a particularly sociable mood and don't want any close contact to the staff. These are passengers who only think of us as servants.

I can cope with these types of guests and was happy to be allowed entry to the cabin later on in order to deliver their luggage. They had already taken the jug in question into the cabin on their own without telling me what it was. I didn't ask for any explanation, but realized that the head of the family – the father – was in a hurry to get rid of me and immediately closed the door behind me as soon as I had brought the suitcases.

"And then what happened?" we asked. "At that point the storm was approaching," Sterling replied truthfully. "Yes, we know," we agreed. "We had problems as well, but something must have gone completely haywire with you. So, what happened next?" we were eager to learn.

Sterling continued. "I was busy in the corridor near my cabins and ready to clean them, while the guests, including the family I've just mentioned, were in the restaurant. All of us will recall that one of the waves was so high when it hit the ship that it made us jump." "You're right," we acknowledged. "Everywhere we went we were asked whether the liner was okay. But such a ship is able to withstand quite a lot of wear and tear. What happened then?"

"Then," Sterling continued his anecdote, "I heard a loud clattering in my strange family's cabin. Since I am such an attentive worker, I opened the door to see whether everything was okay." "And...?" we asked. "The cabin was a disaster," Sterling told us. "Broken fragments as well as dust and dirt were spread all over the cabin. Since it is my duty as a proper cabin steward to keep my area clean, I immediately started to tidy up the cabin. Soon the broken pieces had been put in the garbage can, the slightly dusty bedspreads were changed in less than no time, and then I brought out the vacuum cleaner."

Sterling swallowed and sipped at his glass. "So far, so good, right?" we commented. "You did everything properly, didn't you?" "No," he sheepishly replied. "All of a sudden the wife of the family showed up at the door. First she looked at the empty windowsill and

197

at the floor, then at the vacuum cleaner and glared at me. "What happened?" she shouted hysterically. "Where is the urn?" "*Urn*?" I asked. "That was an *urn*?! I had no idea!" The lady turned pale as chalk, let out another yell and fainted. I managed to catch her as she lost consciousness. Of course I called the doctor immediately who wasn't really needed, however, since the lady came back to her senses after a minute and was sitting and crying on one of the beds. Her shouting attracted numerous curious people who had gathered in front of the cabin, but were sent away by the doctor and the father who had meanwhile arrived.

They immediately suspected what had happened and gave me the evil eye. "Where are the ashes?" the head of the family sternly asked. "Don't tell me they're in the vacuum- cleaner!" "Yes, unfortunately that's where they are," I explained. "I thought it was dust." The father looked at me contemptuously, as though he were ready to kill. At that point I was sent away. Damn it, how was I supposed to know that they had cremated their grandfather the week before and were obeying his dying wish to be on a cruise for the last time – even if was in an urn on the windowsill? I have to admit that I had only heard of urns, but had never actually seen one. Now the whole family is furious with me because I didn't realize what was in that big jug by the window. In my distress to resolve the situation, I opened the vacuum cleaner to salvage what I could. But I didn't manage to distinguish the grandfather's ashes from all the dust and bread crumbs. Poor grandpa!"

At that point of his story we all tried to remain serious and keep our composure, but due to the bizarre outcome of this story coupled with the alcohol in our blood, the atmosphere of sorrow and sadness dissolved into thin air very quickly and we broke into peals of laughter. Even Sterling, who had looked like a picture of misery the whole the time, joined in our laughter.

"Let's drink a toast to little grandpa!" we shouted while raising and clinking our whiskey-glasses. "May he rest in peace – in the vacuum cleaner!"

There were no repercussions for Sterling as a result of this incident . The family was accused of not having properly advised the cabin steward beforehand regarding the large jug and its contents.

Moreover, nobody can be held responsible for an accident which was caused by heavy seas.

The cabin steward's boss handed the dust bag including its contents to the family who emptied it into the sea during a private night-time ceremony with the help of a priest who had been engaged by the hotel director.

Chapter 23:   Isso Isso, the Brazilians are coming

At the end of my tenth or eleventh cruise my head waiter approached me to announce that a larger group of German guests was expected on the next cruise and that I was expected to give a helping hand during the check-in. In addition to being advised of place and time for this mission, I was told to be early for the influx of guests since the guests' first impression of the management was the most important.

Punctuality means the world in our business. If you are late for work, the management's cards are stacked against you and you are considered a failure. During my career as a waiter I was only late for work on one occasion, but I was so late that it made a sufficient impression on the rest of my career with our shipping company.

Only once did I ever wrongly set my alarm clock and it took the head waiter's thundering voice which shattered my eardrums over the phone to rouse me out of my sleep. He asked me whether I intended to come to the restaurant or whether I would prefer that the guests be sent into my cabin for breakfast there.
After I had given myself a severe scolding for my misstep, I arrived in a completely drowsy state at my station in the restaurant a few minutes later. Exactly 20 guests were already sitting at the tables on which the tablecloths had not yet been placed. My assistant looked at me in a panic-stricken manner. As he had already prepared the cutlery and dishes, we at least were in a position to immediately provide a service, albeit meager.
"Good morning, Johannes!" the dear passengers welcomed me who of course were well aware of my ultra-late arrival. At that moment I would have liked nothing more than to launch them into outer space. "What exquisite culinary dishes may we look forward to this morning?" they asked me in a slightly amused, yet sarcastic tone.
The lovely, unshaven face of waiter Jesus appeared in my mind's eye and calmed me. I remembered every detail I had been taught with regard to dealing with guests. I behaved in exactly the same manner as he would have in my precarious situation.

"Let me have a look," I replied, rather sleepily. "I think the specialty for this morning is to jointly set the table and hope that the galley has not yet closed!"

Everyone was quite astonished when I thrust the tablecloths into the hands of two of the guests, while all the others had to carry cutlery and dishes. None of them had expected such cheekiness from their waiter, but as we had become fond of each other during the cruise, my behavior did not cause any problems. Everybody laughed and lent a hand. My fellow waiters watched us from their stations. They were all curious to see how I would get myself out of this situation. Even my head waiter was flabbergasted when he noticed that the table was completely set seven minutes later and the coffee ready to be served.

"Dear Ladies and Gentlemen," I happily announced. "Many thanks for your collaboration. To recompense you for your help I've asked the head cook to prepare an extraordinary, nourishing and delicious entree for you!" "Great!" the guests answered. "Which one?" they were curious to know, especially after my unconventional behavior and service under the circumstances. "Scrambled eggs with bacon!" I smirked.

They laughed at my breakfast choice because they all understood that this was the best and simplest meal for guests who were in a hurry. I sold sixteen servings of scrambled eggs and four servings of pancakes which can be prepared and served as quickly as scrambled eggs. My busboy offered heaps of cookies and numerous liters of coffee until all guests were contentedly stuffed. After such a close shave, I sent three quick prayers up to heaven. My head waiter who of course immediately informed the maître d' of the morning's episode, however, could not pass up the chance to comment on it again! "In case of a bad rating or complaint about substandard service this morning you will have to pack your bags," I was told by the maître d' Ernest. "I hope you get my point"

"Oh yes, I get it," I answered. "But I still expect that five stars will show up on my rating form again tonight and if they do, I promise to treat you to a whiskey!"

This is the end of a short additional scenario about the only time I was late for work.

Now I would like to recount the incident of the previously mentioned reservation by the German guests which I will never forget.

"Report for duty at the entrance of the restaurant at 10:30 a.m. tomorrow!" I was instructed by my head waiter. "The maître d' will be assisted by two additional head waiters to welcome the new guests and allocate their tables for dinner. You will learn how to deal with the bookings. In case of communication difficulties with the German group you may need to translate. This is an important task, and we are counting on you."

I was proud to be of assistance and feverishly looked forward to the next day when I would be allowed to look behind the scenes.

I showed up right on time and was given the once-over by the maître d'. He checked my uniform and shook my hand to warmly welcome me.

"Maybe you will be the boss someday," he said. "Now you'll get your first lesson regarding reservations and problem-solving. There is no single day on which all guests are satisfied with their tables so be prepared to be constantly confronted with nagging and complaints. It depends on these next hours and our behavior towards the customers whether they will feel comfortable right from the beginning and whether they will show up for dinner smiling or in a foul mood. Most important, keep your eyes peeled! You have to know what's going on at all times. If translation problems arise, we will ask you for help because neither I nor any of my head waiters speak German."

He then sat down at one of the three tables which had been set up in front of the dining room and studied the seating plans.

"Oh no!" one of the head waiter suddenly shouted who was also dealing with some documents for the reservations. "Boss, have a look to see who's going to be on our ship in addition to the German group!" The boss took the papers, put on his glasses and then froze. "Two hundred and eighty Brazilians," he mumbled. "How on earth can *280* Brazilians just spring up like this? Nobody advised me of their arrival yesterday. Good gracious, what a nice afternoon this turned out to be! Can I have a glass of water and a chill pill?"

What an initiation to my new duties! As soon as the guests had been assigned their reserved tables, they approached us with their requests and concerns. For example, they wanted to know why they didn't get a window seat or a table for two, why they and their children had been seated at different tables and so on and so on...

The boss patiently listened to all concerns, silently discussed them with his head waiters and always managed to find a solution for the problems. It was only when guests acted up because of a so-called "bad table" that he lost his patience.

I witnessed a restaurant manager going ballistic on a beautiful first Sunday during Advent. We were busy with the reservations when a guest approached the table, threw a 100-dollar-bill on the maître d's writing pad and commanded: "A table for two!!" Such ill behavior towards the boss and the head waiters was totally unacceptable. "None available!" the boss replied without even throwing so much as a glance at the rude guest and put the note aside. "Next, please!" "Hey, you!" the guest hollered. "Hey, you!", the guest bleated out. "I guess you haven't got a table for two!" Seizing the note, he threw it on the table in front of the boss. "None available!" the maitre d' calmly repeated and threw the note on the floor in front of the honorable guest. "Next, please!" he called out once again and tried to beckon to the next waiting passenger. The impudent customer started ranting and posturing: "So, you puny little waiter, don't you get it? I need a table for two! Can't you speak English?" This comment was too much for our boss who was beside himself with rage. Without further ado he climbed onto the reservation table, looked down at the raging guest and shouted: "Go to hell! Go to hell where they are already waiting for you! Do you understood my English *now*, you silly jerk, or shall I repeat it once again for you? *Get lost*!!"

The guest was totally discombobulated not only because of the maître d's reaction, but also because of the other guests who were waiting in line behind him. They had evidently witnessed the churlish behavior of this "savage" – which is what they called him behind his back – and now started applauding and taunting him.

He stole off sheepishly and was never seen again. The staff at the reception desk where he had complained and requested a cancellation of his cruise informed him that he could indeed leave the cruise liner because the table reservation did not meet his requirements – but only at his own expense since it wasn't considered an emergency.

Losing his temper once again, the guy ranted, raved, cursed, and even threatened legal action against the shipping company, but to no avail! Since he wasn't at all willing to pay for a hotel and return flight to his home country out of his own pocket, he petulantly disappeared into his cabin and rarely emerged. He even enjoyed his meals there – at his own table for two!

The funniest part about all of this was his female companion – a tarted-up blonde whom he seemed to have hired for the occasion. She did not speak English, and evidently had not witnessed his hissy fits and was walking around alone on the ship slightly confused. During the entire cruise we watched the lady sitting contemplatively at the pool or in the bar. She obviously did not understand why the originally generous gentleman had suddenly locked himself in the cabin without explaining the reason for his behavior to her. She quite likely had another notion of what was meant by a cruise for two!

Regardless of the nasty scene, we continued making the reservations, the guests were coming and going, and everybody was in a good mood. The German passengers did not show up at all. Aside from two questions about the location of two particular tables in the restaurant, none of the Germans seemed to have a problem with the reservations. This was a good thing, because a few minutes later the management's patience was utterly taxed.

The reservation time frame had almost elapsed, and the boss and his head waiters happily realized that all Brazilians were evidently satisfied with their reservations. At that moment the elevator door opened and about ten chatty people stepped out. "Oh," I said, "I know this language, they are Portuguese." "No," one head waiter wailed, "they are Brazilians, not Portuguese! As you know, they also speak Portuguese, but with a slightly different accent."

The elevator arrived again and again; an increasing number of Brazilians who were all members of this group approached the reservation table. "They all seem very cute and friendly," I commented. "Dream on," the head waiter whispered. "The trouble is just beginning. Heaven help us!"

"*Boa tarde* (which means "hello")," the first Brazilian cried. "We would like to reserve a table for tonight."

"For two?", asked the head waiter, who was holding a pencil in his hand, while studying the reservation documents.

"*Isso* (which means "exactly, right!")", the Brazilian said.

Allow me to quote the verbal exchange I remember even today that took place between the head waiter who had jotted down a table number and the Brazilian guest.

Waiter: "Table 132, Sir. A beautiful table at the window for two."

Braz: "Fine, but the children are still upstairs in the cabin!"

Waiter: "What children? You asked for a table for two!"

Braz: "Yes, we need two chairs, but the children have to sit at the table as well."

Waiter: "Of course, how many children?"

Braz (looking at his wife): "Let me count, one, two, three, four ..."

Waiter: "Wait a second, so many children?"

Braz: "Yes, we are also taking care of my sister's children. She is sick and couldn't join us on the cruise."

Waiter: "I see... If I understand you correctly, this means: two grown-ups and four children. Right?"

Braz: "Isso!"

Waiter: "Look, table no. 18 for six persons – in the middle of the restaurant, close to the piano."

Braz: "Piano? No, the grandparents don't want to sit there, they do not like loud music."

Waiter: "Grandparents? What grandparents? Are they on our ship as well?"

Braz: "Isso, somebody has to take care of the children if my wife and I want to be on our own."

Waiter: "Where are the grandparents?"

Braz: "At the bar, they like to have a cocktail before dinner."

Waiter: "Now what? You, the children and the grandchildren – a total of eight persons. Right?"

Braz: "Isso, please choose a table next to our family! We are a very large family and you will certainly understand that we all want to sit together."

Waiter: "I don't understand anything right now. Where is the rest of the family?"

Braz: "I don't know. I'll call them now."

206

After rummaging in his bag, the Brazilian took out his mobile phone and dialed a number, while the queue of waiting guests behind the head waiter and the maître d', who were also busy with a group of Brazilians and evidently trying to solve the same type of problems, became longer and longer.

Braz: "*Oi* ("Hi" in Brazil), where are you? We are just reserving the tables. Okay, isso, yes, isso, see you in the restaurant, isso!"

The waiter (visibly exasperated): "May I please ask you to give me the correct number of your family members now so that we can serve dinner on time tonight."

Braz: "We are a group of about 26 family members and friends. Do you have a table for 26 persons?"

Waiter: "No, we don't! Please give me the names and cabin numbers of the whole family so that I can arrange three tables side by side."

Braz: "Isso."

The Braz then dialed another number on his mobile phone.

Braz: "Oi, what's your family name? The maître needs to know. Yes? Yes? Spell it, please! Oi, Oi, Isso. *Obrigado* ("Thanks")."

Waiter: "I don't mean to be so curious, but why don't you know the names of your own family?"

Braz: "We met today for the first time. We got to meet six of them at the airport, another five at the cruise liner and the rest of the family at the bar aboard the ship."

Waiter: "And you are a family now??"

Braz: "Isso."

Waiter: "How lovely for you! We are very pleased to welcome you aboard! Is your dog or little crocodile perchance on this cruise, too? We would need to know in advance in order to grant sufficient space for the animals between the tables."

The Brazilian guest and the head waiter started giggling, although our waiter didn't feel like laughing at all.

"Table numbers 12, 13 and 14. There you are. Enjoy your meal!"

I looked at the head waiter who was close to tears because even more guests with different problems and questions had queued up behind this family.

We somehow managed to get through the complicated seating arrangements; all the Brazilians had been allocated to tables.

Although they did not always comply with the desired size and location, everybody was satisfied.

As a testimony to the lack of originality typical of Brazilian family names, making of reservations for them is a cakewalk. In fact there seem to be only two different family names in this very large South American country, which doesn't faze the people at all. Their family name is either Silva or Santos. But as usual, there are exceptions to the rule. Other families are called Da Silva and Dos Santos to stand out from the crowd. The very similar or identical names aren't a problem for the waiters. But it's quite funny to call for a guest with the family name Santos or Silva at the front desk. Five minutes later no less than 75 people elbow their way through the hotel foyer to ask why they have been summoned., It's actually really amusing!

After dinner was over, the maître d' and head waiters wiped the sweat off their brows and thanked the guests for their collaboration in solving the seating problem.

However, if you believe that the evening's table arrangement had solved all our problems, you are totally wrong. Although everyone had been seated, all the guests still had to be served, which wasn't always an easy job. The waiters who were responsible for the Brazilian group moaned because they knew all too well what was in store for them.

Let me point out that Brazilians are very genial, funny customers and are easy to please. They eat far less than American or European guests and do not suffer from diabetes or allergies. But you have to be very patient with them, otherwise you will go crazy.

Cruise ships based only in Brazil also offer two dinner sittings: the first at 8:30 p.m. and the second at 10:30 p.m. While these times are entirely unimaginable in Europe and America, they are quite normal in South America, particularly in Brazil.

Nevertheless the session at 8:30 pm is neither much-loved nor met without ranting and clamoring, since 90% of the lovely customers prefer having dinner at a later time..

When I worked on cruise liners in Brazil for a few years, I was quite often greatly amused. We had reserved tables for as many guests as possible for the second sitting and punctually opened the restaurant door at 10:30 p.m. to welcome them, Except that nobody was waiting in the restaurant, not a single guest! As I looked at my stone-faced colleagues, I couldn't help but wisecrack: "Well, Ladies and Gentlemen, it's too early, but don't lose heart, everything will be okay!"

Half an hour later – at about 11:00 p.m. – a Brazilian came shuffling in and asked the first waiter who approached him where he was allowed to sit. Anxious to provide excellent service, the friendly steward accompanied him to his table and offered him a chair. "Oh," the man said, "I realize that my family has not yet arrived. One moment please, I will call the others," then left the restaurant.

A few children – still wide awake at this late hour – arrived from the other side. Knowing quite well in which corner of the restaurant the family would be seated, they hurried to the table and shouted to the waiter: "*Oi Mozo* (the Brazilian term for "waiter"), psst, psst!" Every waiter in any other country would either ignore this noise or look angrily at the guest. In Brazil, however, this behavior is quite common and not considered impolite. "Have you seen our dad?" "Yes, I have," the waiter replied in a slightly irritated voice. "He has just left the restaurant to look for you."

"Never mind!" they answered. "We'll start with dinner, then. Can you give us the menu, please?"

The waiter obliged and took the order shortly thereafter then went to the galley to get the desired meals.

Upon his return to the station he noticed empty water glasses, crumbs on the tablecloths and a toppled chair – but no guests. "Where are they?" he asked his busboy. "They just left to search for the parents and grandparents."

A few minutes later the older ones appeared, said "Good evening" and wanted to know where the children were. Unfortunately the waiter couldn't reply to this question, but he managed to convince the grown-ups to sit down and place their orders.

By the time the food and beverages had been put on the table, the children who had worried about the grown-ups gradually showed up again in the restaurant.

While a steady stream of Brazilian guests were coming and going throughout the whole evening, some of the guests were still enjoying their appetizers or main courses, while others had already asked for dessert. The waiters, busboys and head waiters were all very mindful not to get lost in the chaos and simultaneously satisfy all guests.

At the end of dinner they told us that they were already looking forward to the next evening, for which we were grateful – not to mention, relieved.

Similar to most of the guests, they then either went to the theater or the discotheque to conclude the evening there or were sitting in the bar to schmooze with the bar staff.

Occasionally a family would approach a head waiter extremely late in the evening to ask him whether it was too late for a meal. "No, quite the contrary," the waiter calmly replied, "you are too early." Since the guests did not understand this answer at first, they looked at the head waiter in bewilderment. "Too early for dinner?" they asked incredulously. "No, for *breakfast*," he answered drily.

"I am sorry, Ladies and Gentlemen," they were informed. "The restaurant closed three hours ago. Have a nice evening." "Already closed?" the head of the family shouted indignantly. "This can't be true. My children are hungry. We'll go to the restaurant!" "Go ahead," the head waiter commented who had meanwhile arrived had meanwhile, "Enjoy your meal!"

When they arrived at the dining room, they were surprised to be met by darkness. Nevertheless they walked around to make sure no buffet had been set up in a corner.

This type of incident occurred on a daily basis. While the guests from other countries adhered to the meal times, the Brazilians always had open-ended sittings, which tried the staff's patience.

Nevertheless everybody was happy at the end of the cruise. While the guests from the country renowned for the samba embraced and kissed the cruise staff to thank them for their hard work and perfect service, the waiters thankfully received their tips. According to their travel contracts all Brazilians were obliged to pay the tips when they booked the cruise.

Nowadays Brazil holds the sixth place throughout the world with regard to their enthusiasm for cruises. Since the beginning of 2000, a huge market has been opened by the shipping companies, which consequently leads to a continuously increasing number of cruise liners in Brazil.

It is also quite entertaining to watch guests from all other parts of the world aboard the cruise ships who have not been properly advised by their travel agents concerning the Brazilian culture and mentality.

Questions such as, "What do you mean, the first dinner sitting only starts at 8:30 p.m. and the second one at 10:30 p.m.? I'm already asleep by that time," are common. The staff always gives the same answer: "You're in Brazil, Ma'am. Have you not been informed about the meal times?" "No," the guest replies with surprise. "No, nobody told me. Just you wait, my friend in the travel agency is going to get a chewing out when the cruise is over."

Another typical question: "Why do they all come for dinner wearing shirts, Bermuda shorts and sandals? Don't they have manners?" an older lady remarked at the restaurant. "They do have manners, Ma'am," the waiter calmly replies. "Don't forget that you're in Brazil. Since it is hot and humid here, it doesn't make sense to pack pants, socks, vests or ties."

The staff would have liked most to recommend that these tourists contact their travel agency and ask for a refund, but the insufficiently informed guests frequently come up with the idea on their own. We have actually watched them standing and ranting at the ship's rail while they were on the phone with their travel agent somewhere in the world.

However, if you do your research on Brazil and study the local customs and culture, you will understand that what happens during a cruise there will be quite different from what is usually expected on board a ship. With this perspective in mind, you will have a lot of fun and will want to book another cruise someday since you know you are in for a good time and can look forward to enjoying the casual and familiar atmosphere. If you, my dear reader, are single and searching for a wife, I would like to provide the following recommendation: book a cruise in Brazil and go to the pool after the first breakfast on the first day! You will no doubt realize that the Brazilian beauties will knock your socks off. Take a chance! It isn't difficult to make contact with these gorgeous women since they tend to be more straightforward than American or European ladies. Moreover many of them speak English, if your knowledge of Portuguese isn't up to speed.

212

Chapter 24:   The Ghost in the Closet

A lot of guests are eager to know whether I have ever gotten into trouble during my career on cruise ships because of the lovely ladies I encounter. "Naturellement!" I always reply. Is there any quite attractive and red-blooded waiter who has *not* been caught in a beautiful woman's clutches at least once during the ancient cruise times and who has consequently almost lost his job? I would have twice fared very badly, had I not come up with an idea to save my skin.

It was a usual cruise like many others except for the fact that an extraordinary female guest was sitting in my station and we couldn't get enough of each other. At the beginning we exchanged harmless banter, then I invited her to a romantic lunch on one of the islands and eventually we decided to meet in her cabin after the end of my shift. We both knew that I would be sent home if I were caught red-handed. Moreover one of our guards had an eagle eye. This particular guard was from the Philippines, where they had specialized in zeroing in on crew members who had dates with female guests in their cabins which was contrary to the valid rules on board our ship. Was he successful? Not really, his success was rather modest since waiters are a very clever species! They know how to fool the security guard. Since the "mad dog" was egged on by his mediocre success, he was running across the ship day and night, lurking around the cabins which had been booked by single ladies. He never gave up his hope of catching a crew member in a compromising position, so to speak.

While I bought the champagne and chilled the glasses, I tried to calm down in light of my illicit intentions by recalling a joke about a gentleman who enters a bar and notices a lonely woman sitting at the counter; I had to do *something* to get over my nervousness. As the joke goes, the man in question approaches the lady and asks, "May I buy you a drink, Miss?" "No, thank you," the lady replies. "Alcohol is not good for my legs." "I am sorry to hear that," the man answers. "What happens if you drink alcohol? Do your legs swell up?" "No," the lady explains, "they spread apart!"

After I wrapped the ice-cold champagne and the glasses in a bag, I tiptoed into the cabin of my sweetheart who immediately welcomed me with a passionate kiss.

The champagne bottle was emptied in less than no time and our clothes had automatically fallen off our bodies, when suddenly there was a loud knock on the door. "Security!" a voice bellowed. "Open the door, please!"

"Oh shit!" I said. "I don't know what makes the guard think that I am here, but if he finds me I will lose my job. Damn!"

"Hide in the closet!" my lady friend whispered to me. "Maybe he won't think of looking there."

I could see my life flash before my eye as I entered the closet without a stitch of clothing in the hopes of averting the inevitable disaster.

While my new girlfriend opened the door with half-closed eyes and asked the guard if anything was the matter, I was sure from the bottom of my heart that he would thoroughly search the cabin as he was authorized to do. I had to come up with an idea right away.

According to the proverb. "Necessity is the mother of invention," I did, in fact, come up with a brilliant idea. My hands started rummaging in the closet until they eventually found what they had been searching for. Five seconds later I unfolded a large bed sheet and put it over my entire body. The security guard didn't waste any time with pleasantries and was on the verge of entering the cabin, when the closet door suddenly flew open. A white figure jumped out, pushed the flabbergasted and dumbfounded gentleman in uniform aside, crossed the corridor accompanied by loud shouts of "Boooooo, booooo!" and finally disappeared behind one of the numerous doors.

"Who was *that*?" the person in uniform shouted. "Was it a guest or a crew member? Come on, tell me! Now!"

The lady was no fool. She looked at him pitifully and sighed. "Oh well, who might it have been? I believe it must have been a ghost. A ghost in my closet. Unfortunately I cannot tell you anything else, because – as you know – ghosts don't have a face. It's really a shame. I have never flirted with a ghost before and now you've chased it away. Would you please let me go to bed now? I am very tired."

Gaping at the female guest, the guard didn't know what to do. It neither made sense to follow me as I was already miles away nor was it reasonable to continue questioning the lady. No ghost, no accusation!

He slunk away, gnashing his teeth without another word. It took a long time for him to get over this defeat.

The second time I was convinced I would be sent to the captain for the last breakfast due to my affection-ridden antics also involved a lovely lady. Right from the beginning she was unabashedly checking me out before displaying her beautiful legs for my benefit and later, since she was not wearing a bra during dinner, her magnificent bosom. By the fourth evening I was no longer able to withstand her temptations and agreed to meet her in her cabin. Once again I smuggled champagne and ice into her room. At midnight we raised our glasses and took off our clothes. It was a wonderful and amorous tête-à-tête and we had a lot of fun until dawn. Then my heart started racing again at the prospect of leaving the cabin without being seen. Before venturing out, I asked my girlfriend to check the premises for security staff while she set a few dirty glasses in the corridor for room service to collect. She confirmed that the coast was clear by nodding at me. But then we made a big mistake. Instead of quickly leaving the cabin and taking to my heels, we resumed the previous evening's amorous activities. "I've got to go," I whispered, left the cabin and then ... found myself looking right into the face of the security boss, the boss of the entire security department (as opposed to an ordinary guard). He seemed to appear out of nowhere and was suddenly standing in the corridor – just like me. Shit! Once again my whole life passed before me in a few seconds as is often the experience of a person on the verge of death who remembers the good and bad moments of his/her life in a bizarre and horrifying kaleidoscope. A moment later I did a double-take. Could that be who I think it is? I hesitated, but pulled myself together in less than no time as I suddenly looked at the situation from a quite different perspective. At that very moment the highly esteemed boss left the neighboring cabin holding something – or more precisely – some*body* with his outstretched arm. Being the daring and courageous soul that I am, I took a step forward to find out whose hand he was holding. My assumption proved to be correct: it was a beautiful – and braless – stranger who wasn't wearing anything but tight panties. She smiled at me uneasily. I returned the smile with relief and brazenly said to the safety officer, "I wish you a wonderful good morning!" "Thanks, the same to you," he quickly replied before we both left. He walked down the corridor on the right side, and I on the left. We met again later in the "I 94," the main corridor for the staff and cordially welcomed each other. Until this day I have never spoken about this incident with anybody. As far as I know, the safety officer remained silent as well; it was a gentlemen's agreement.

Do you wonder whether a colleague has actually ever been dismissed after being been caught in flagrante delicto with one of our female guests? Oh yes, of course!

Waiter Steve from Ireland was determined to escape unscathed from a dalliance with a female passenger and was convinced he had found the perfect hiding place for a wild adventure. But when one of our safety guards did his round on the weather decks and in the very early morning, he noticed that one of the lifeboats was heavily shaking despite the smooth sea. He carefully lifted the tarp which covered the boat and immediately caught sight of a naked bottom moving up and down and the smiling face of a blonde. She immediately patted her lover on the back to draw his attention to the unexpected and unwanted spectator.

Five minutes later a safety officer accompanied Steve to the bridge where he was greeted with laughter. Nevertheless he had to see the hotel director who signed the letter of dismissal. Laws are laws, after all, and need to be respected.

Chapter 25:   Flying Sugar

The cruise passed by without any further incidents. Europeans, Americans, Brazilians and the guests from the other parts of the world were on very good terms with each other. Everybody gathered new experiences with regard to culture, customs and table manners in the countries of this world.

I was again responsible for the well-being of the guests from all over the world. They sheepishly sat down at the table on the first evening, but were soon overwhelmed by the friendliness of the Americans. It was always interesting to see how guests from the U.S. welcomed the rest of the world and they all formed a bond of table fellowship in the course of the cruise. They got along well with each other and had a lot of fun during dinner and the other meals.

Of course there are silent moments now and then during a meal when the guests do not know what to talk about. This is often my lucky chance to perform my magical tricks to a captive audience . I love these moments in which I describe the various desserts – then nonchalantly pour some coffee cream into my fist where it disappears, then taunt the guests. "Are you sure you don't care about dessert?!" I inevitably get an onslaught of comments by the astonished guests. "Where the hell is the coffee cream? It's impossible! Show me your hand!" I then unclench my fist, but there is no cream! It's gone! The guests are gaping in disbelief, unless there are well-informed magicians among them. They of course know very well what has happened, but they don't say anything and are happy to have found a like-minded person. "Ladies and Gentlemen," I continue, "although the cream was nothing but an illusion, these sugar packets are genuine. They, however, face a problem because due to their Oriental origin they believe they are related to flying carpets and behave in a very strange manner. Have a look!" All guests are staring at the blue sugar pack which is lying on my palm and suddenly starts hovering between my fingers. After about 20 seconds I grab the packet in the air and throw it to a lady in front of her cup. "There you are, Ma'am, sweeten your coffee so that it will be especially tasty." The chosen woman unfortunately doesn't have a chance to use the sugar as it is grabbed by the other

218

guests for a thorough inspection. Although they excitedly discuss why and how these sugar packets are able to fly, they can't find an explanation.

One morning when I was preparing my station, a little girl who was about six years old approached me. Eyeballing me from head to toe, she asked: "Are you a magician? I saw what you did yesterday." "You are right, honey," I replied and noticed that the girl was rather excited, even a bit nervous. "Shall I perform a magic trick now?" I asked as I smiled at her question. "Yes," she pouted petulantly, "can you make my grandma disappear?" I stared down at the child who was obviously vexed at her strict grandmother and pondering the prospect of her disappearance. "Listen to me!" I replied. "Of course I am able to whisk your grandma away into the spirit world, but I can never bring her back to you. Have breakfast now and tell me afterwards what to do with your grandma!"

Poor little girl! She was sitting at the breakfast table with her family, but couldn't eat anything. She was picking at her food, looking at her grandmother, staring at her eggs, once again gaping at the grandma who had annoyed her for some reason. About an hour later she approached me again, sadly looked up at me and whiningly announced: "Thanks anyway, my dear magician, but I think it's better to have grandma with us. I'll give her another chance. But if she bothers me again, I will come to see you and then she'll really be in trouble. Can you please perform the trick with the flying sugar again? I liked it so much." I fulfilled her wish and off she went.

Every time I perform this trick I remember one of my former guests. He was a typical Italian who couldn't manage to keep his emotions under control. After I had performed the trick with the flying sugar, he leapt to his feet and was next to me two seconds later. "How does this trick work?" he cried out. "I have to know! Mama Mia, sugar isn't supposed to fly!"

Stopping him in his tracks with a wave of my hand, I explained to him that magic tricks are only exchanged between magicians. Hoping for his understanding, I expected no further questions from him in this regard. But it was not to be! The Italian sat down again and rubbed the sugar packet between his hands to generate static electricity, which he considered to be the trick's proper explanation.

219

He was no longer interested in his dessert. Unfortunately, nothing happened. While I saw his baleful expression, I couldn't help rubbing it in by advising him that the trick would not be based on friction. After all, paper and wood don't react on electricity or magnetism. This was far too much for the already angry guy. While his fellow table guests burst into laughter, he kneeled down in front of me begging to let him in the secret. Sizing me up with great interest, the guests at the other tables tried to find out why the whiny European had knelt at his waiter's feet and was insistently talking at him. I managed to serve dessert only with great difficulties as the poor man was so persistent.

Nevertheless, the guests enjoyed the show and left the dining room smiling. However, they did not forget to ask me which trick I would perform the next day that was sure to drive the dear Italian crazy.

Signore Stefano – the Italian – looked utterly downtrodden. He glared at me then stubbornly announced in the manner of a little child: "I'm staying here until I know the secret of this trick. I must demonstrate it to my children!"

He refused to accept my explanation that magic is not easy and requires a lot of practice. "Wait!" he suddenly ordered. "I'll be back in a minute!"

Shortly thereafter – I was busy setting the tables for breakfast – he returned and put a wad of banknotes in my hand. "There you are," he said with a flourish, "1000 dollars! Do hurry up and show me how to make the sugar packets fly!"

I smiled at him as I returned his money and agreed to let him in on the secret that same evening over a glass of wine.

He arrived on time at our meeting point and was visibly pleased to finally learn how to make the impossible possible.

The lesson was a disaster. Although the poor guy did his utmost to replicate my little stunt, he could only raise the sugar packet a tiny bit and it kept slipping from his hand to the floor. He retrieved the ill-fated packet at least twenty times, but he still couldn't make any sense of my instructions. I pointed out that it had taken many days to learn this trick, and that it would be improbable to make sweeping progress after only one lesson. But he didn't listen to me. Using all his physical strength, he twisted his arms and hands, tried to keep balance while standing on one leg and looked pleadingly at me. I demonstrated the trick to him once again. Of course it looked easy, since I had so much practice. My pupil, however, who was on the verge of going insane, never did succeed in performing the trick.

"That's it for today!" I declared. "Face it: this just isn't working and I have to get up very early tomorrow morning. I promise to keep in touch with you by e-mail so that I can give you further instructions." Although the hapless guy was totally at the end of his rope, he only left me alone after I promised him I would keep replying to his e-mails until he was able to perform the trick.

To my surprise, his first e-mail was long in coming. When it eventually arrived, I replied to it by meticulously describing all the details the trick required. After that, I never heard from him ever again.

Even today I combine the cozy ambience in the dining room with short performances for guests who are fond of magic. The vast majority of all passengers like to be entertained after a delicious meal. The restaurant is my stage, and every week new curious spectators attend my show. They greatly appreciate amusing and interesting performances in the dining room apart from the customary eating, drinking and chatting. If I am not in the mood for performing magic, I imitate Rowan Atkinson alias Mr. Bean as a waiter or perform the role of Stan Laurel who tries to pour a bottle of wine without disaster. On most occasions, the guests laugh until they cry. During those moments the thought of someday earning my money on the stage occasionally crosses my mind.

222

Chapter 26:   Health

The week had almost passed when our maître d' announced during a meeting that the inspectors of the local health authority would be waiting for us in the home port of Miami. All waiters, busboys and head waiters groaned as they all knew what to expect.

We started cleaning and polishing very early in the morning and finished only late at night. In between we of course had to take care of our dear guests as the usual quality of service had to be maintained despite our efforts to be fastidiously neat and tidy.

Let me point out that all our ships are extremely clean to the extent that you could eat off the floor. Nevertheless it was of utmost importance to avoid any mistakes during this particular inspection. As human failure with regard to hygiene had to be excluded, we practiced extremely hard and checked our work very thoroughly that week. I have to note that cruise liners operated by US-American shipping companies in particular are subject to the strictest food inspections you can imagine. It is very challenging for the managers and their departments – whether it pertains to the food & beverage operation, the galley, the commission department or the laboratory – to leave a perfect impression during the very irregular inspections. "Zero tolerance" – that's the slogan with regard to storing, preparing, heating and serving of food. The health of our guests and naturally, of the crew, is given top priority. Only ships which have been given the blessing of the U.S.P.H. inspectors (United States Public Health authority) are used for cruises on the high seas that are attended by the maximum number of passengers. A shipping company has to anticipate disastrous consequences within a short time if even one of its ships does not reach the minimum score (85 of 100 points). The ship will have already been condemned as filthy in the newspapers and travel magazines by the next morning, which will lead to cancellations of booked cruises. Moreover, the ship may not be allowed to leave the harbor until the shortcomings have been remedied and a second inspection has been successfully passed.

Let me briefly describe the procedure of such an inspection:

The rating of every ship is based on 100 points. Every fault/shortcoming revealed by the inspectors is penalized by a deduction of points. Depending on the degree of the inspector's fault-finding, either a very small, average or substantial number of points will be deducted. For example: even a trace of lipstick on a single glass among a row of clean drinking vessels on a shelf will lead to a deduction of one or two points. If the inspector catches a waiter who either picks his nose, runs his fingers through his hair and or puts a dirty plate in the sink without washing his hands afterwards, the waiter in question will be given a written warning and is responsible for a deduction of two to three points. If an employee – no matter whether he works as cook or waiter – touches food or ice cubes with bare fingers, the inspectors show no mercy and subsequently deduct five points. Should the respective employee continue breaking the rules despite endless meetings and explanations, he will be dismissed immediately.

The galley management gets into severe trouble if the cooling temperature is insufficient in the refrigerators or if hot food is not hot enough to kill germs.

If the inspectors have complaints about the water in the swimming pools and Jacuzzis, if small holes are visible in the galley tiles in which dirt can accumulate or if a waiter carries dirty and clean dishes on a tray at the same time, more points will be deducted from the original 100 points.

The inspectors use special tools to dismantle coffee machines, juicers, cooking stoves and large cooking pots and spare no effort in looking behind the scenes. There dare not be any smidgen of old dirt or hint of rust, otherwise points will consequently be deducted and both the head cook and F&B manager will pale with mortification.

A mere inspection of every department doesn't suffice for the inspectors: they also interview waiters, cooks and even stewards to check their knowledge of the regulations devised by the health authority.

For example, inspectors ask about the correct temperature in the fridge or of various hot meals, how long cooked food may be offered on a buffet and which rules are to be observed for the disinfection of the various service stations. The inspectors also test the knowledge of chemicals, that is, which chemicals are used, where they are to be stored and the proper setting of dishwashing machines to guarantee pristine cleaning.

The staff will be familiarized immediately with these and many additional rules. Afterwards they will be monitored while they work to see whether they are able to maintain a clean ship.

In this context you may wonder whether any cruise liners have actually been prohibited from leaving the harbor for hygienic reasons. Of course this has happened - but many years ago! I want to emphasize that it never happened on our ships. All shipping companies that had not taken the health authority seriously in the 70s and 80s were given a wake-up call when they suddenly had to explain to their passengers at the terminal that the ship was not allowed to leave the harbor due to insufficient hygiene. Since that time the cleanliness of ships has been given top priority. Nobody should be cavalier about it!

I would also like to dispel the prejudice that health problems on board cruise liners are caused by the crew's misconduct. I am sure all of my dear readers have seen pictures of ships on TV which suffered from a virus on board and were denounced as a "plague-ridden ship" or even "ship of death."

Headlines such as "Hundreds of passengers become violently ill on board!" or "Hundreds of cruise line passengers suffering from norovirus!" scream out on the first page of numerous newspapers and terrify travelers throughout the world. This is why I recommend taking an objective perspective in the face of such articles, dear readers! Whenever luxury liners have come into the press's line of fire, the articles almost exclusively deal with passengers who have fallen ill, yet there are scarcely any reports about a sick cruise as a whole. What's the reason behind it? Having worked on board cruise liners for 25 years, it's easy for me to reply to this question: Sometimes our dear guests bring viruses and bacteria on board and allow them to breed by severe wrongdoing. One example involves passengers who buy food from street vendors during a shore excursion since it is so cheaply and readily available. This food, however, is not subject to any strict hygiene or temperature rules... Consequently, the guests become sick within a short time and the disease can literally be carried on board. To make matters worse, the guests often refrain from calling a doctor at the first signs of illness because they want to save money. Although they are sick, they drag themselves into the restaurant so as not to miss a meal which is included in the cruise price and thus spread the virus by shaking hands with other passengers, touching salt and pepper shakers or using napkins which are to be disposed of by the waiters afterwards. I have often witnessed travelers ignoring their supreme duty of washing their hands as often as possible and particularly after a visit to the bathroom. More than once I have caught guests red-handed in this regard and had to explain to them the consequences of poor hygiene. This has sometimes led to arguments with the stubborn passengers who of course tried to talk their way out of the situation. In these instances, the entire shipping company supports the employee who was courageous enough to draw such guests' attention to their grossly negligent behavior. I have also had many negative experiences with sea-sick or drunken passengers who had stolen away after having thrown up in a corner. Vomit is the worst substance for spreading viruses. If somebody throws up near a staff member, he has to immediately evacuate all guests within a radius of ten meters and advise the bridge accordingly. In less than five minutes cleaning specialists are on the scene to settle the problem by using special equipment.

I remember a waiter who was serving next to me and all of a sudden approached a head waiter like a scalded cat. Waving his arms about, he asked his superior to follow him to his station. As I did not have a lot of work at that moment, I joined them to see what had happened. I couldn't believe it! Without having been noticed by his fellow dinner guests, a passenger had thrown up next to his table. Instead of heading for the toilet, he had covered the vomit with a napkin and continued eating! Upon the advice of the head waiter a doctor, a nurse and the safety guards rushed to his side five minutes later. They removed him from his chair and hurriedly accompanied him outside. We were all shocked at the careless reaction of some people who don't behave sensibly in the face of such bizarre behavior.

Although the man was not severely ill, he was not allowed to enter the dining room again. His meals were served in his cabin.

Let me summarize that nowhere on earth is it safer to enjoy meals than on cruise liners which are inspected by the American Health

Authority. The officers and the entire crew are routinely checked, vaccinated and trained to fight against viruses and other diseases in order to always have any situation under control.

At this juncture I have to add an amusing story regarding the unexpected arrival of inspectors. Since the management of course always calculates the period of time between the last and upcoming inspection, it has a rough estimate of when the esteemed inspectors are expected to pay their next visit to the ship. If the gentlemen announce themselves at the gangway, the hotel director nowadays is the first to be informed and then immediately advises the various department managers accordingly.

In the past, a peculiar announcement which the entire staff had agreed upon beforehand was made on the ship. For example an announcement such as "Head waiter, please call 900!" or "Food and beverage manager, please call the hospital!" echoed throughout the cruise liner. These announcements were used to inform the entire staff that the health authority inspectors had arrived on board and could show up at any moment to do their job.

I will never forget a time when the inspectors were anticipated on board our ship... I passed the gangway with a box of new pepper grinders and heard the following announcement: "The captain is requested to go to the casino!"

Immediately after the announcement I heard a voice behind me which sounded slightly annoyed. Two gentlemen in white work coats were just entering the liner. One of them barked at the safety officers and suggested the management should kindly come up with something better than such stupid announcements to advise the staff of the inspectors' imminent arrival. "Do you really think that we're not wise to this nonsense?" he ranted. "Do you actually believe that we don't know the meaning of these inane announcements? Tell your boss that this will lead to a point deduction next time!"

I disappeared into a dark corner as soon as possible to prevent myself from laughing out loud in front of the gentlemen in the white coats. The facial expression of the poor safety officer who had to listen to the inspectors' harsh words was too funny. All officers and even the captain were strongly advised to refrain from these types of announcements.

At the end of the inspection they all were in good humor again. The captain, the hotel manager, the head cook and some of the officers enjoyed lunch with the inspectors and were informed that our ship had passed the inspection with nearly 100 points. There were only a few minor issues that had to be corrected. All employees sighed with relief. Every department celebrated this success with bottles of wine in the hope of passing the next inspection as successfully as this one!

Chapter 27:   The Parrot and the Magician

What would this book be without my favorite tale about sea voyages? I would now like to share a whimsical story with you in order to distract you from the occasionally more serious topics:

A magician with mediocre success in his performances had great difficulties captivating the audience on one of the cruise liners in the lower price range because his tricks were too easy to see through. To make matters worse, he kept struggling with the ramshackle, dilapidated stage as well as a certain parrot who was a real chatterbox. This bird took residence in a cage on the wall next to the stage and belonged to the captain. Nobody was allowed to approach the parrot too closely or make disparaging remarks about it. It was part of the decor – and that was that!

Since the bird unfortunately was highly intelligent, it was the first to be wise to the magician's illusions. As soon a trick had almost succeeded in baffling the audience, it already started cawing: "I know, I know! The rabbit is under the table and the cylinder has a hole!" The spectators burst out laughing, while the magician gave the bird a dirty look! Just when it seemed as if the next trick would work; the loud voice of the bird was heard again: "I know, I know! The rose is hidden in the sleeve; the rose is hidden in the sleeve! I know, I know!" Malicious laughter echoed in the theatre once again and the magician who was almost reduced to tears by that point would have liked nothing more than to wring the damned parrot's neck.

Weeks passed until the disastrous day when a huge wave hit the ship and swallowed it. Nobody survived the shipwreck except for the magician who, by a twist of fate, was able to seek refuge on a buoyant wooden door from the wreckage and clung to it with the last of his strength. Floating in the ocean for three days, he never abandoned the hope that by some miracle he would be rescued. All of a sudden, he heard the flap of wings and noticed the captain's parrot sitting down on the door with a smug smile on its face.

"What do you want, you flying trash can?" the totally enervated magician asked. Despite his contempt for the beast, he hoped that the parrot might be able to help him.

The bird, however, stared at him from a safe distance and cawed in a serious voice: "Okay magician, touché! I give up! Now tell me where you have hidden the damn ship!"

Chapter 28:   Shipwrecks and Refugees

I am often asked the rather inane question of whether we ever had stowaways on board. My answer is short and unambiguous: No! The reason this has never occurred is that it is impossible to embark our ships without being spotted by the cameras and the security guards.

However, we have saved shipwrecked victims – several times. On three occasions I witnessed such rescue operations, including a very unsettling encounter with a large group of incredibly ungrateful individuals.

The first rescue operation took place exactly two months after I had been promoted to a waiter. The captain's stern voice sounded over the loudspeakers to announce persons in trouble. He used a code word to mobilize the crew members who had been specially trained for such situations. Although the officers did their utmost to keep the unendangered guests away from the forthcoming rescue operation, their attempts backfired – as is usually the case in these situations. There is always at least one guest on board who knows the meaning of the international code words and who will invariably alert his friends who in turn waste no time in spilling the beans to their friends. As a consequence several hundred curiously gaping guests will gather at the ship's rail shortly thereafter.

In the first case it was a medium-sized sailing yacht. Its rather shocked owner reported the ship had been hit by an enormous wave and had capsized before the mayday signal could be triggered. The crew consisting of four men and four women clung to the hull as they did not manage to climb their way to safety due to the plastic being too slippery.

The shipwrecked crew was lucky: the position of the fateful vessel had been detected by the modern equipment on our ship before they lost their fight for survival. A speedboat headed for them within a few minutes to take them on board on our way to Miami.

The second rescue operation I witnessed concerned a fishing boat in distress which had gotten into severe trouble due to the crew's carelessness.

We were just serving dinner when our ship was strongly hit from the side. Both the guests and the staff nervously looked around. As is the typical reaction to such startling situations, a group of anxious passengers shrieked as if it were the end of the world. A few high-ranking officers who had been enjoying dinner immediately ran off to find out what had happened. We all hurried outside and watched a rather large boat floating in the waves. Unfortunately there was no trace of a crew calling for help. The search beacons were directed to the boat from our bridge to shed some light on the matter, although initially it seemed as though there was nothing to see. Two speedboats were launched: the first was occupied by the first officer, the chief engineer and some safety officers from our liner who had started to inspect damages to the fishing boat, and in the second speedboat our staff captain, the doctors and some hefty guards from the gangway approached the floating boat to check whether everything was in order. We watched them as they used torches and loudspeakers to make contact with the crew. A few minutes later two men became visible on the fishing boat's deck who were staggering, flailing their arms and waving to our officers. None of our crew members entered the boat – after all they did not know what to expect.

The guests and crew continued waiting at the rail for a while, but there was nothing else to see. When they returned to the dining room they speculated over what might have happened. Guests sitting at the window on the side of the shipwreck watched as the fishing boat crew were having a discussion with our officers.

A short while later the captain announced to everyone aboard that the now incapacitated fishing boat (100 tons!) was floating on the sea after it had butted against our cruise liner (70.000 tons!) for unknown reasons. The coast guard had already been informed. Help was on its way to tow the fishing boat and take care of its crew members who, according to the rescue team, were safe and sound.

When I met the staff captain the next morning, I couldn't help but ask his opinion regarding the previous evening's event. Shaking his head in disbelief, he told me that the fishing boat crew had gotten plastered and then dozed off. "They will be sent to prison," the staff captain assumed. "They acted with gross negligence, which will not be tolerated. The coast guard is sure to give them hell!"

We never heard anything about the fishing boat and its crew again. The collision with our liner evidently was not sufficiently spectacular to be dealt with in great detail by the press.

The third rescue operation was about a boat, or to be more frank, a swimming pile of junk overflowing with refugees who likely tried to emigrate from Cuba to the United States. The ill-fated boat's motor gave up the ghost soon after beginning its dubious journey, and had been floating for days on the open sea.

Once again the signal sounded from our bridge, whereupon the captain positioned our ship close to the persons in distress whose shouts could be heard from far away. One of our speedboats was again immediately launched so that the crew members trained for such emergency situations could check to see whether everything was in order. Some refugees obviously could not wait for the arrival of our rescue team and jumped into the sea and swam towards our speedboat. Such precipitous action was not appreciated at all and they were requested by the first officer via the loudspeakers to immediately return to their boat, otherwise our support would be withheld. Although they only very reluctantly followed the instructions, all the refugees had eventually returned to their broken nutshell of a boat and started a loud discussion with our officers who had meanwhile stopped the speedboat a few meters away from the wreckage.

We weren't able to follow the discussion, but our crew was on board again an hour later to keep us apprised.

After the hotel director had been informed about the refugees' situation in an emergency meeting, management staff from the various departments were advised soon after in terms of the scope of support that was to be granted.

The maître d' summoned the head waiters and gave instructions. Since we had to provide food and beverages to relieve the refugees' distress, the waiters and busboys had gathered around a large table and prepared a simple yet delicious meal of sandwiches. The wine stewards poured water and juice into big containers, while the head waiters packed milk cartons and sweets. Various types of food had piled up at the gangway within a short time, along with clothes and medicine, before it was loaded on one of our lifeboats which can accommodate up to 150 passengers.

Nobody who was present at the following scene will ever forget what happened next. After our rescue team had reached the refugees' boat, we could watch the relief supplies being lifted on board by use of a small special crane. This work had just been executed when very loud voices could be heard. Wildly waving their hands around, some of the refugees started talking insistently to the team. More and more of the persons in distress participated in this heated discussion until most of the refugees seemed to have entirely lost their minds. When some of them again jumped into the water to approach the lifeboat, the first officer gave a signal to the coxswain to start our boat's motor and leave the uproarious scene. Being in close proximity to the refugees' boat, none of us expected what happened next! A fight broke out on the cutter's deck and after a few minutes the upset crowd had thrown all of the relief supplies back into the sea.

We couldn't believe it. The so-called "persons in distress" went entirely nuts, refused our support, and, as already mentioned, threw all the food and beverages into the sea, waved their clenched fists towards our cruise liner and proceeded to loudly curse in Spanish and English.

The officers disappeared into a conference room to consult with the captain and the hotel director. The guests and the crew speculated about the refugees' bizarre behavior, but had to wait for an hour until the captain made a statement via the loudspeakers. He did not say much and only informed us of the refugees' request to be taken on board and then disembark our liner in the port of Miami. Of course the management could not fulfill this wish, which the would-be emigrants, however, did not understand. They refused to accept that it was impossible to use a cruise liner as a ferry to illegally emigrate into another country.

We had no choice but to ask for assistance and continue our cruise. A few days later our officers learned how long the refugees had to survive without food and potable water. Neither the guests nor the crew wasted much thought on these people who had requested something impossible – not to mention, illegal – from the cruise ship's captain and reacted so maliciously upon the rejection. To be sure, the next ship or its crew – most likely a coast guard boat or a boat of the refugees' country – was unlikely to provide such delicious food and beverages. I supposed that a buffet of water, bread and handcuffs was more their style!

Chapter 29:   Flying Fish in Barbados

We have frequently sailed down to Barbados, a Caribbean island which is not very far away from the South-American continent or more precisely, from Venezuela. Barbados was also our next destination during the cruise in question. While on deck one day staring at the smooth deep-blue sea, I suddenly noticed an enormous dragonfly flitting over the waves. It was strange to realize that the animal flew into the water then seemed to completely disappear. I was totally dumbfounded when more of these creatures passed our hull a few seconds later. They covered an expanse of ten to twenty or even almost fifty meters in the air, until they disappeared into the sea. "Is there anything interesting to see out here?" a voice beside me asked. "Dolphins or perhaps even whales?" An English-speaking guest with an accent I had never heard before joined me and now also looked into the blue sea. "I haven't seen any dolphins or whales," I replied. "But oddly enough there seem to be some silvery creatures flying around that I've never seen before." "No wonder!" the sudden visitor exclaimed. He then elaborated, "you are talking about flying fish. If they are terrified by a ship or another larger fish, they are able to escape the sea for a few meters by quickly flapping their fins and flying into the air where it's safe. Sometimes they also fly just for the fun of it." Since his last words sounded more like a joke, I told the passenger that I doubted the validity of his information. But he assured me that these were in fact flying fish which make the seas their habitat throughout the world. I asked him where he was from. "I am Scottish," he proudly replied. "Have you ever been to Scotland?" "No," I said, "the only thing I know about the Scots is the fact that we owe the Grand Canyon to them." My discussion partner gaped at me. "What do you mean? What possible connection could there be between Scotsmen and the Grand Canyon?" "You honestly don't know how the Grand Canyon came into existence?" I asked, smirking. "No, I don't," he replied, slightly agitated. "But I am pretty sure you will explain it to me." "There is actually a very easy explanation," I answered with a grin. "Five million years ago a Scotsman lost a penny somewhere in Arizona and started searching for it!"

Thank God I was already talented at reading people in those early days and could feel in my bones that it was safe to tell this joke. My instincts proved correct: I hit the mark with this Scottish guy. He split his sides laughing, slapped my shoulder and said: "Very funny, I like you!" After chuckling at the vision of the frantically digging Scotsman, we again focused on the sea and the silvery fish which were flying overhead. "By the way, my name is Steven," he continued by way of introduction. "Do you know that flying fish – either grilled or steamed – are the specialty of Barbados and outstandingly tasty? They are served with certain sauces which are typical of the island, have nearly no bones whatsoever and are very delicious. The most famous sauce served with the fish and with all other dishes is what is known as the "Barbados Pepper Sauce." This yellow pepper sauce is really pungent and should only be eaten with utmost care. It is in fact very delicious, but I suspect it originates from the devil's fiery kitchen since it is so extremely hot and spicy. By the way, the insiders' tip regarding the tasty fish does not originate from Barbados, but from another Caribbean island called Aruba, referred to as "the island of gourmets." We spent our honeymoon there. Passengers with deep pockets who like to eat in grand style during a shore excursion of a Caribbean cruise can select between at least ten starred restaurants on the island. A multitude of restaurants open their doors to these well-heeled customers for lunch and dinner."

"Great!" I replied. "I never knew such animals existed. But when you mentioned grilled flying fish, I realized I was getting hungry. By the way, my name is Johannes." Shaking hands, I continued. "As already mentioned, I had no idea about these fish. All I've read is that the beaches of Barbados rank among the most beautiful of the Caribbean." "They are even among the most marvelous beaches of the whole world," he explained, "and I know the most beautiful one that's not mentioned in any brochures. You wonder how I know about this best-kept secret? The crew told me, of course; they always know exactly which locations and beaches to visit on the respective islands. Will you be on the island of Barbados for the first time?" he asked. I answered in the affirmative. "The island is magnificent," I continued. "I also like its inhabitants very much. They are very proud and well organized people with a very

239

distinctive sense of order and a bureaucracy that is common in several European countries. No wonder – it's a British island! We will pay it a visit tomorrow. If you like, you are welcome to join us." I accepted this invitation on the spot and we made arrangements to meet the next day.

Due to the midnight buffet I had been assigned to that evening, the rest of the night was rather short. However, looking forward to a fantastic beach and sampling grilled fish with spicy sauce banished any feelings of tiredness after the breakfast service the next morning. By 9:00 a.m. the Scottish couple, a friend of theirs and my humble self were sitting in a taxi. First we went to the capital, Bridgetown, where we had to make a brief stop since Steven's wife had to buy some sunscreen which she had forgotten on the ship. The stop was very convenient for me as well because I remembered that I had used up all my aftershave lotion in the cabin and figured I could find more here. As soon as I got out of the taxi, the beauty of the town caught my eye. I was confronted by the combination of Caribbean beauty and European orderliness in Bridgetown amidst well-dressed islanders who conducted their business against a backdrop of impressive buildings. I went into a small shop which offered cosmetics, perfumes and aftershave lotions in addition to the famous sauce and clothes unique to the island. Having found what I was looking for straightaway, I handed a bottle of ordinary aftershave lotion to a pretty young lady behind the counter. She seriously looked at the bottle which contained the fragrance before turning it around to find the price which she then jotted down on a notepad. Afterwards she tore the paper off the pad and handed her note and the aftershave lotion to another, slightly older lady who was sitting at a table in the back of the shop. She put on her glasses to scrutinize the bottle once again from top to bottom and then put it on the table. The data from the aftershave lotion were entered in a computer which was less sophisticated at that time and a large piece of paper was printed out after a short while. The older lady had thus completed her part of the accounting, got up and handed the papers to the first lady who received them with thanks. I thought the transaction was over and I would be allowed to leave the shop with my aftershave lotion, but a gesture by the lady indicated I was to remain patient. The document the young lady had in her hand consisted of two pages – the original and the copy – which were now detached. The original was taken into another room where the manager was quite likely situated and as a final step, had to approve the sale. Shortly afterwards he stamped the paper after checking it and attentively nodded to the young lady. At this point I assumed that the purchase would no longer be delayed. A few minutes later I had the copy of the copied copy in my hand to check it for correctness and completeness. The aftershave lotion was only handed over to me after I had duly signed all three papers. I finally received the bottle which seemed to have caused a great fuss and was very pleased to be able to leave the shop before sunset. The price of the aftershave lotion was only $2.12 and I didn't even receive a discount for paying cash!

The taxi occupied by my Scottish friends was waiting in front of the shop door. "Let me guess! Purchasing your aftershave lotion was as onerous as the purchase of my sunscreen," the Scotswoman remarked. "It also took quite awhile for me to buy it, but now we can finally go. Driver, please take us to the Crane Beach Resort!"

"Crane Beach," I repeated. "THAT Crane... ...?" "You will be overwhelmed," Steven replied. "If I had enough money, I would buy a holiday home near that beach, but the prices are far too high for my blood."

Our journey by taxi took 45 minutes, during which we traversed the interior of Barbados in bright sunshine and passed small villages as well as gigantic sugar cane plantations and fields with other agricultural products before the air was eventually filled with the marvelous smell of the sea.

We stopped in front of a small yet elegant hotel called Crane Beach Resort, paid the $5.00 admission and entered the hotel complex. After passing the main building, we arrived at a Roman-style swimming pool where affluent guests were bathing in the sun. We were politely advised that only hotel guests were allowed to use the swimming pool.

"Forget the pool!" Steven smiled. "Look what's in store for you now! You won't believe your eyes!"

We had a bird's-eye view from the terrace, where we could thoroughly enjoy the vista. "Incredible!" I marveled. "I have never seen such a beautiful sight!"

I realized that the Crane Beach Resort had been built on a high cliff and towered above a romantic bay – a bay with a snow-white beach where turquoise waves were breaking. I was completely bedazzled by the sunshine as I took in the breathtaking surroundings. We were standing on a terrace with white tables and chairs where a few guests had sat down to enjoy colorful cocktails. "We will have lunch here later," Steven promised. "Apart from the most beautiful beach in the world the restaurant features the same flying fish on their menu that we observed on board yesterday; they're incredible. But now let's go down to the beach!"

Climbing down to the beach was rather adventurous as there was no convenient pathway. The locals had carved a set of makeshift stairs into the rock and we gingerly put one foot in front of the other to avoid stumbling. Ten minutes later we had arrived at the beach. On that day we were the only travelers who had found one of the most picturesque spots on earth and were now looking for a shady place by the rocks to make ourselves comfortable.

"Have a close look!" Steven raved. "The beach looks white only from far away. What do you think is its true color?" Bending down to study the sand more intently, I was totally surprised. "It's *pink*, unbelievable!" I replied. "You're right," Steven affirmed before continuing, "This is another famous feature of Barbados. Its pink beaches are unique, and as you can well imagine, the contrast to the turquoise water is a popular subject for poets."

Steven then summoned a friendly local who was standing nearby. "Six fresh coconuts, please! We are thirsty," Steven said and handed over $10. "Yes, man!" the dark-skinned man replied in typically Caribbean style. A few seconds later he disappeared behind a dune and scaled up a large palm-tree like an ape. Within a few minutes ten fresh coconuts were set in front of us which our black friend deftly sliced with a machete, one after the other. The coconut juice was cool and delicious. At that moment I believed I had never drank anything so heavenly in my whole life.

When I raised the second coconut to my lips, the air was filled by deafening noise. A silvery spot which turned out to be a plane in the deep blue sky was approaching. "That type of aircraft noise is quite unusual, isn't it," I remarked, "particularly in the middle of paradise!" "That's because it isn't a usual plane," Steven's friend,

John, commented. "Have a closer look!" "This can't be true!" I exclaimed. "It's the *Concorde*!" "Exactly," John confirmed. "Once a week it flies out here with mostly rich English tourists who jet off from London on the weekend and arrive in Barbados less than four hours later to bathe in the sun." I shielded my face from the blazing sun with my hand at the impressive sight of the approaching Concorde, a phenomenon which I would have expected in Europe or in New York as opposed to this Caribbean paradise. What a pity that nowadays it is no longer possible to watch such an aeronautical phenomenon!

"Are you hungry?" Steven asked after we had spent hours frolicking in the waves and jumping into the crystal clear water from a high cliff. "It's lunchtime, and the flying fish are waiting to be devoured."

"Good idea," we replied. "We already look like roasted chicken ourselves after being in the sun so long. Let's go!"

Climbing up the cliffs was troublesome, but our hard work was rewarded: flying fish grilled in a pan and served with various sauces and a bottle of ice-cold white wine awaited us – combined with a view of the beach with its pink sand and the blue sea! What an extraordinary sight! One of my best friends whom I took to Crane Beach sometime later commented: "I could die here!"

However, it wasn't all fun and games on this particular day, Silly as I am, I forgot all the precautionary tales regarding the Barbadian yellow pepper sauce and put a heaping teaspoonful of the infernal stuff in my mouth. I had to drink nearly six liters of water before the sharp pain eased and I ended up with swollen lips as a side effect of my carelessness. My new friends almost died of laughter at my blazing red face and puffy lips. A word to the wise: you should always be very careful when you try foreign food.

"Damn sauce!" I cursed when I was eventually able to think clearly again. "Regardless I will take two bottles of it home, because one of my friends in Germany is a fanatic for spicy food. I am sure that he will spread the sauce on his sandwich instead of jam." Steven smiled at my plan. "I don't think so," he countered. "The stuff is extremely hot and can only be eaten in very small quantities. Only the Mexican *habaneros* and an Indian pod – I can't remember its name – are spicier than this sauce." "You don't know my friend

Kalle!" I sighed. "This guy is growing the *habaneros* you've just mentioned. He even takes a bag of them to the pizzeria! When the waiter takes his order, Kalle gives the bag to him, and requests, "Please ask the cook if he would be kind enough to use these pods as a pizza topping." One evening the waiter and the cook approached our table with reddened eyes and beads of sweat on their foreheads (wonder whether they tried the pods for themselves...?) and wished us "Bon appétit!" They hardly believed that this pizza could really be eaten since they had almost had to call the fire brigade to extinguish their fire. Smiling at their intolerance to the pods, Kalle bit into his pizza with gusto. To upset the cook and the waiter even more, he commented: "Not bad! But could you please bring me some Tabasco sauce?"

Steven laughed. "Was that a true story?" he wanted to know. "As true as I am sitting here," I answered. "Someday Kalle will pick up his burnt intestines off the street."

Our lunch was wonderful. The ice-cold wine was expensive since it had been imported, but it proved to be the perfect complement to the flying fish entree. After enjoying dessert, a cold cappuccino and a local after-dinner drink we relaxed and listened to Caribbean music for another hour. Next to the bar a local performed the most popular songs by Bob Marley on his steel drums.

At that point we realized it was time to leave. We had to take into consideration that we were about an hour away from the cruise liner and that a too late arrival would not be tolerated. Once again we admired the turquoise sea and its pink sanded beaches, took a few photos and waved to the locals who were again busy picking coconuts from the palm trees for new customers. It was only 3:00 p.m., but we were totally exhausted. We had to be back on board by 5:00 p.m. and car trouble during the return should always be factored into the travel time. The taxi driver who remembered our comments about Crane Beach on our way there welcomed us with a broad smile.

"Heaven," was the only word we could muster before we started back to our cruise ship.

If you, my dear readers, are now longing for the Caribbean Sea, I recommend paying a visit to the island of Barbados. But it is important to consider the following:

To get better acquainted with this fantastic island and its gorgeous beaches, it is best to start your cruise in Puerto Rico. Barbados is very far in the south, near Venezuela. You can reach the island only from Puerto Rico, unless you book a 14-day cruise to include Barbados. A flight to Puerto Rico has two advantages. On the one hand the island is located in the Caribbean Sea, which means that ships which have Puerto Rico as their home port are closer to more dream destinations than ships which leave the Miami harbor. On the other hand, Puerto Rico is beautiful and really worth the longer flight. You should ideally spend two to three days there to visit as many tourist attractions as possible before boarding the cruise liner. If you're wondering where to travel on the island of Puerto Rico, by all means a visit to Arecibo should not be missed, which is a synonym for high-tech in the heart of the jungle! What is worth seeing there, you ask? A suspended radio telescope and people who search for aliens! Ladies and Gentlemen, be assured that I am not joking. The radio telescope in Puerto Rico ranks among the most powerful telescopes in the world. From here, mathematical codes are sent out into space in the hope of receiving a reply someday.

If you don't believe me, you can find more information on the Internet. Or in the event you would like to see the telescope in an action film, watch the James Bond movie "Tomorrow never dies" featuring Pierce Brosnan. Except for the climax of the movie where water suddenly fills the telescope dish, all other scenes from the movie are real. In fact, the sight of the suspended telescope is overwhelming.

Moreover, I recommend participating in an entire tour of Puerto Rico with a local operator who will give you an understanding of the country, its inhabitants, the historical monuments and the numerous culinary highlights and maximize your anticipation of the cruise. The last evening before you leave the harbor should be spent in the bar, the casino or in one of the restaurants of the "El San Juan." It is known as one of the most wonderful hotels in the world and renowned for its hospitality. It is a great pleasure to enter the lobby with its unique bar which is made of polished mahogany wood. In its center, one of the most impressive crystal chandeliers in the world can be admired and you may enjoy a delicious cocktail or a glass of champagne. If you like Asian cuisine, you should try to reserve a table at the in-house Chinese restaurant. After the meal, I'm confident you will agree that the Chinese restaurant in the hotel "El San Juan" in Puerto Rico is undoubtedly the best in which you have ever enjoyed Asian food.

Chapter 30:   Man Overboard

Every week "Oscar – Oscar – Oscar!" echoes via the loudspeakers of cruise liners throughout the world. Most of the guests of course do not know the meaning of this announcement and only very few ask about it. Day by day unknown code words ring out aboard the ship. As evidently nothing peculiar happens as a result of the announcement, these words tend to be ignored after a while. The crew members who immediately have to react to certain emergency situations of course listen carefully to such announcements no matter whether it is an unexpected drill or a real emergency. Since the word "Oscar" sounds very harmless even in an emergency situation, the guests sometimes ask whether Oscar is a cook who has prepared unpalatable food and will now be given a good dressing down by the captain. In reply to this question I only nod. I won't explain to them that this code word can cause a lot of trouble aboard the cruise liner, since it means,"*Man overboard.*"

"Have you ever been on a cruise when somebody accidentally fell or deliberately jumped into the sea?" the passengers often want to know. My answer is brief: "Four times in more than twenty years!" Although this is not very often, each of these moments was one too many and, suffice it to say, really nerve-racking. They are difficult to forget and to my mind, not a particularly pleasant topic of conversation.

My candid reply is unfailingly met with wide-eyed and curious expressions by the guests. "What happened? How? And why?" they ask me. Taking a deep breath, I explain: "I don't know, because we are never informed as to why anyone would prefer to swim among sharks instead of lying in bed. All I can do is recount the occurrences I have actually seen and then it is up to you to consider the whys and the wherefores and try to make sense of it. One incident of someone jumping into the sea that I had witnessed firsthand was inevitable right at the beginning of the cruise. In most cases the safety precautions and the crew who are accused of being too inattentive are brutally skewered by the press. However, only someone who has dealt with such a world-weary individual during a cruise is, in fact, in a position to explain the true reasons for his/her behavior."

"Why do people jump overboard?" is the next question to which I always reply with the same response: "It is usually a chain reaction of circumstances involving frustration, alcohol, or other substances... Eventually, they no longer realize what they're doing" I am also often beset with the question whether I am allowed to talk about the times I actually saw someone fall overboard It's not a very nice topic, but passengers are curious and claim that if they hear about these incidences from a cruise member, it could help them understand why anyone would end his/her life in such a way. They claim that a firsthand account will determine whether to believe what's written in the press, which often tends to undermine tragedies and regard them as nothing more than a quick headline-grabber. I agree to alleviate their curiosity since they are so keenly interested.

These are the sad stories I tell the inquisitive guests:

The first instance involved a couple who was already very frustrated and ill-tempered when they boarded the ship. On the first day of the cruise when most guests are generally very happy, this particular couple hardly spoke to each other. Instead of enjoying their delicious dinner, they exchanged venomous looks. It was easy to see that the couple was on the verge of a divorce. The cruise was considered as a last-ditch opportunity to get together again, which unfortunately backfired. At the slightest provocation they would start arguing again and ignored their initial intention of salvaging their relationship. That evening the drunken husband was sitting forlornly at the bar; even the friendliest waiters from the bar who tried to cheer him up failed. This was not a good omen. The cabin steward who was asked about the couple the next morning replied: "All hell broke loose in their cabin last night. This morning I had to sweep up the pieces of the broken flower vase. None of the cans of cola whether empty or full were in their original places but were scattered all over the floor after they had obviously been used as projectiles."

When the couple showed up for dinner the next evening, they pretended that everything was fine. But the husband was again deeply saddened by the time dessert was served and tried to eat it as quickly as possible so that he could forego the remainder of the evening at the gloomy dinner table. A few hours later he was sitting in the bar, looking as despondent as ever. Although the bruises he sustained from the scuffle with his wife the previous night could hardly be recognized in the darkness, his facial expression spoke volumes.

All of a sudden, the Oscar-Oscar signal echoed throughout the cruise liner!

What happened? you ask... Well, in his morose state, the unhappy husband had just made the decision that a life without his "better half" would make no sense and jumped overboard soon after. But he was lucky to have been caught in the act. A lifebelt was thrown into the sea and the bridge was promptly informed of the incident.

After the captain had stopped the ship, the searchlights soon found the man who was disenchanted with life and got him back on board by speedboat. The husband's parents were informed and asked to not only keep their eyes glued on the couple during the cruise, but to also consult a psychiatrist with them once they had returned home. We have no idea how this family tragedy continued, but can comment on this event by expressing, "It could have been much worse!"

Conclusion regarding the first incident: the jump overboard was due to a severe underlying marital problem which a young couple was unable to settle. Love turned into frustration and finally caused the husband's rash action for which nobody can be held responsible. It is impossible to prohibit somebody with relationship problems from embarking on a cruise. Believe me when I say we witness quarreling honeymooners almost every week. Thank God most of these arguments do not tragically end with one of the partners going overboard...

In the second case a man disappointed by life didn't see any sense in living anymore. However, he had planned his death more precisely by ensuring he wouldn't be observed before making the jump. In this case nothing initially happened until someone made a missing person report. The "man overboard" signal rang out, and all guests – no matter whether they had already been sleeping or were still awake – were requested to stand in front of their respective cabin doors. All passengers were counted until it was confirmed there was one guest missing. Afterwards the crew was asked to search the entire ship. Once they had gone through every corner of the cruise liner, the captain was informed that not all registered passengers were on board. The cruise ship was stopped and the surface of the sea lit by search lights. At this time the wife of the missing person was questioned. I was told she was under the influence of alcohol and drugs (pills) and hardly fit for questioning. Her husband could not be found which was no surprise as the search operation had only started after he had been reported missing several hours after the fact.

What happened next?

The captain who is under obligation to do his utmost to save a human life notified all ships in vicinity to ours. Although the sea was searched for the missing man involving a joint operation of all ships, he was not found. The tragic victim was a slender Englishman who didn't have a snowball's chance in hell of surviving in the waters of Alaska. His wife who only realized the next day what had happened remained sitting in the drunk tank until the end of the passage. In Anchorage the police who had of course already been advised accordingly were waiting for her at the gangway and took her away in handcuffs. As previously mentioned, drugs had been involved, which also led to serious repercussions.

Conclusion regarding the second incident: this suicide was also committed due to marital problems and drug use, that is, for reasons which do not pertain to the safety on board. Consequently, the cruise liner was not held responsible for the fatality.

In yet another case, a guest who wanted to escape from this cruel world actually survived his attempted suicide. One night he climbed over the rail and jumped. Although many hours had passed before his disappearance was noticed, he was found. Thanks to the gigantic search lights, the heavyset man – weighing around 140 kg – was found floating in the water and subsequently fished out. Everybody felt sorry for the poor guy; nevertheless black humor was inevitable shortly after his rescue. The passengers discussed various scenarios as to how he would actually have been able to sink to his watery grave. Since such large masses tend to float to the top, however, all efforts to drown had failed.

Another example of a person going overboard included a 22-year-old assistant waiter who had shown signs of alcohol problems as early as during his first days of work. At the time of the pre-

251

employment examinations he had not attracted the doctor's attention and managed to control himself. This, however, changed very shortly thereafter on board our cruise liner. He was only able to properly perform his difficult job in the restaurant for one month before he ultimately lapsed and showed up continually late. One evening he did not show up at all. As he was my busboy, I called him in his cabin. Although he was drunk, he was able to sadly explain why he had not reported for duty, but instead chose to hit the bottle. He tried to talk his frustration away by telling me about his parents who had forced him to go work on a ship. Their logic was that this would be the best way for him to forget his girlfriend back home whom he loved from the bottom of his heart, but who was not tolerated by his parents. After attentively listening to his sad tale, my head waiter unfortunately appeared behind me; apparently he had overheard the conversation. He was angry that one of his waiters had deliberately decided not to come to work instead of doing what was expected of him. After he yanked the receiver out of my hands, he assailed the busboy with a stream of harsh words while simultaneously dismissing me by a wave of his hand. While straining my ears I managed to hear scraps of this conversation such as "blasted" and "dismissed" and thought: *Boy, oh boy, you could be more polite and diplomatic! Heaven knows why the poor guy is drinking so much!* It would have been possible to take him to task the next day after he had sobered up to find out more details, even though he had ignored one of the most essential rules which is: No alcohol while on duty and only moderate alcohol consumption after duty hours.

Unfortunately, there was no next day for the young guy. In the middle of the night he disappeared forever. Nobody noticed him leaving the cabin or climbing over the rail. The search was in vain. The next day nothing but a few blood-soaked scraps of cloth were fished out of the sea which pointed to a shark attack. The Irish head waiter who had made his final telephone call with the victim was aware he had inadvertently determined the fate of a human life the day before and possibly sent a young man to his death by his very harsh Irish-inflected barrage of criticism. Our officers questioned him again and again and clearly explained his misconduct to him. The head waiter's tone of voice and wording had most likely been too aggressive over the phone, which precipitated the young guy's emotional collapse. Consequently he had not seen any other way out of his dire predicament and jumped overboard. Strictly speaking, Michael, the head waiter, had done his job as he had the right to be angry if an employee did not fulfill his obligations and if the service that employee provided suffered as a result of alcohol abuse. Nevertheless he quit his job one week later and never again set foot on a cruise liner.

The phone calls between the shipping company and the busboy's family revealed that he had grown up as stepson in a very loveless and cold-hearted family who had never accepted him and tried to get rid of him by shunting him off to a job on a cruise ship..

Conclusion from the third incident: In this case a young person was no longer willing to continue living and to fight for a better future due to family problems.

The last example, which took place about twelve years ago, revolved around a very handsome waiter called Ali. He was Tunisian and had been working with the shipping company for some time. His black hair with a slightly blue shimmer, his delicately chiseled features and an athletic body earned him the nickname, "top model." Most of the ladies who cast their eyes on him would melt on the spot. Because of his mass appeal, Ali could - and did - select a different woman everyday who would gladly welcome him into her cabin with the intent of spending some pleasurable hours after he was off duty. The waiter's alluring appearance was the doom of a young man who had just gotten married and was spending his honeymoon aboard our cruise liner. Ali was responsible for the station next to mine and we got along well. Every morning he regaled me with his night-time escapades involving female guests, which certainly made the mundane task of setting the table more amusing. There was no doubt that his affairs would break his neck one day since our security guards are always on the lookout for cruise staff who violate the rules regarding illicit contact with guests. But at that time he – just like the rest of us – was a step ahead of the watchmen. One day a honeymooning couple was sitting in Ali's station and I realized immediately that the wife's eyes were fixed on Ali from the very first moment. The love-struck husband did not notice it at first. However, on the next day he was in a snit since his dear wife had sat down at the table before the restaurant was open in order to have sufficient time to flirt with her waiter. The husband who entered the restaurant with the other guests a short time later was very unhappy about his wife's behavior.

"Ali," I said while we were in the galley, "keep your hands off this woman, otherwise you will get into a lot of trouble!" "I'm not doing anything," he replied. "I'm only admiring her beautiful body and her ample bosom. What a hot babe!" At that point I was already aware that Ali was oblivious to the consequences of making time with a married woman and continued chatting her up.

He managed to avoid upsetting the husband for another two days. The honeymooner grew more anxious. When dinner was over he was observed talking beseechingly to his wife in front of the restaurant. He reminded her of the fact they had only been married a few days, but it didn't help. The next evening she suddenly disappeared from their cabin. Her husband of course guessed where he could find her, especially since he had previously learned Ali's cabin number whom he immediately suspected was the culprit in his wife's infidelity. On the way to my cabin after my shift I couldn't believe my eyes when I saw the young husband skulking through the corridors. He evidently figured he had nothing to lose by this point and tried to confirm his suspicion. I informed the security guards via intercom about a passenger straying in the staff corridors who might need some assistance. Of course I refrained from advising them of any further details, put the phone down and tiptoed towards Ali's cabin. The lovelorn husband was standing in front of it with his ear to the door. He needn't have guessed what was going on since it was impossible to misinterpret his wife's loud shrieks of pleasure. He refrained from angrily kicking the door down but instead turned around in my direction and asked where he could find the exit. After I had shown him the way out, I called the security guards a second time to tell them that the guest had already left the staff area.

Then it was quiet. I felt sorry for the man, but couldn't do anything for him. Since his behavior hadn't been volatile, I hoped that he had only intended to wait for his wife to return to the cabin before raking her over the coals.

The next morning Ali and I were again busy setting the tables for breakfast. When I asked him whether he had captured another woman's heart the night before, he denied any such behavior. At that moment the Oscar signal rang out. "This one's on your conscience, Ali! Now you're in for it," I berated. "That alarm is nothing but bullshit!" Ali countered. "It's either an exercise or somebody was tipsy and stumbled overboard." He had just finished his outburst when the first officer and the maître d' approached him to ask about a certain honeymooning couple in his station. Ali pretended to be ignorant, but the missing man's wife had already owned up and told everything.

"Let's hope for your sake that we'll be able to find him," the officer remarked in a severe voice before he ran off to assist in the search for the missing husband.

This was another instance where the passenger could not be found. Nobody had witnessed his jump into the sea shortly after he had spied on his wife. Several hours had passed before the Oscar alarm had sounded; all attempts to find the man failed.

Even Ali realized that he had really messed up. Although he was exonerated by the victim's wife who had taken the blame during the officers' and FBI's questioning, Ali felt guilty and quit shortly after the fatal incident. Five years later I met up with him again. He had lost weight, his hair had turned grey and he was working in a car cemetery. He admitted that he had never gotten over the incident and had actually succumbed to severe depression, which made any type of professional life impossible.

Conclusion from the fourth incident: Although it was partly the employee's fault, the provocative and weak-willed lady was ultimately responsible for her husband's rash action. Perhaps she had gotten married far too soon without fully realizing the consequences of matrimony.

I realize all of these stories sound very sad and should perhaps not be included in this entertaining and funny book. However, since I am so often asked about such situations, I had no choice but to comply with the passengers' many requests of this nature. At any rate you have now been informed of some of the situations that cause people to literally jump ship. Furthermore, this information has been provided by a person with an inside perspective. After all, you can't always believe what you read in the press!

Chapter 31:   Curse of the Casino

Crew members frequently face the rigors of a long term contract. Depending on the shipping company, it is typical for a waiter to work a four to eight month stint without a day off while under constant stress and above all without the sense of security and comfort a family provides.

However, many waiters, myself included, can easily adapt to the demanding and frantic pace because in many respects working on a cruise liner is much more favorable than working in a normal restaurant, when considering the waiter's job from a different perspective. For example, everybody knows which days of the year are the most important for a "normal" restaurant: Christmas, New Year, Easter, Catholic holidays, and even Carnival season in the Rhineland. On days with such high turnover there is a lot of work and time involved at most restaurants. In other words: all available waiters are obligated to show up on those days. During these public holidays in particular, an "onshore waiter" will only rarely be allowed to take time off and must sometimes even work from dawn till dusk, while other family members and friends are enjoying the festivities. I took a one-year leave of absence from the cruise liner and worked at a restaurant in Viersen during that time. Although I enjoyed working there, it wasn't long before I realized that I had very little time to spend with my friends. The few shifts I actually had off tended to be on the less interesting days such as Monday or Tuesday, whereas my friends were free on weekends. After a while I could no longer put up with the work conditions in my home country when it involved spending so little time with the people that meant the most to me. For example, I could only offer a dejected smile in response when my friends asked me what I had planned for the weekend of the Bon Jovi concert in Cologne. After all, it would have been a bit presumptuous for me to convince Jon Bon Jovi to postpone his concert until my day off on Monday.

Soon after my more conventional restaurant experience back home, I realized that working on a ship is actually preferable in those situations because waiters are off work for seven to ten weeks after their contract expires, and can actually spend time with family and friends as well as be a part of all festivities.

As you can imagine, the cramped living conditions on board create a major disadvantage for many employees, particularly for waiters, who are basically confined to the cruise liner with only very few days off, and there are far fewer options for spending free time than back home. Waiters therefore live every hour to the fullest which is not spent working or sleeping, whether this entails dining at expensive restaurants, hiring speedboats on the islands, upgrading from a Timex watch to a Rolex or splurging on the latest state-of-the-art mobile phone.

The waiters like to frequent one place in particular which offers both entertainment and an adrenaline rush. I am referring of course to casinos which await their victims in numerous harbors all over the world. In fact there are Caribbean cruises with at least one or even several casinos on every island where the cruise liner makes a port of call. The waiters zero in on the casinos immediately and make a beeline for them in their free time, regardless of the time of day or night. A few hours later they invariably return to the gangway either in a flush of victory or utterly dispirited.

After a few years I've realized that the thrills gambling offers aren't worth the risk. Like most waiters I had previously also headed for the casino on a regular basis to replenish my bank account. I once even managed to go on leave with exactly $2,200 after I had earned about $750 per week during the 6-month contract. Believe or not, I had in fact (involuntarily) left 90% of my hard-earned money at the casino. I explained to my parents that I didn't have the chance to earn money because the ship had remained in dry dock. I am ashamed of this lie even today, but back then I was young and had a lot of wild oats to get out of my system.

News about people who strike it rich after a single attempt at the one-armed bandit spread like wildfire. So much so that numerous people completely lose their mind and head for the casino three or even four times a week to give fate a helping hand. Thank God my gambling spree had come to an end during a transfer of ships which left from a harbor in California where casinos are strictly forbidden. Some of my colleagues weren't so fortunate: some of them succumbed to the lure of gambling and their addiction worsened over time; they were unable to concentrate on anything else. They only barely managed to perform their professional duties, due to the fact that their gambling was financed by the guests' tips. Apart from their work they were totally obsessed with the dream of hitting the jackpot someday and believed that frequent casino visits would inevitably increase their chances.

In this regard, I felt and still feel very sorry for one of the maître d's with whom I worked for some time. It was a real pleasure to work with Mendocino as he was a very friendly person who treated his waiters with respect and decency and who always tried to bring out the best in them. The Italian was not only a passionate gourmet but also an avid fan of the AS Rome soccer team. Considering himself a father figure, he listened to his protégés' problems and did his utmost to help them whenever they consulted him. He got along well with everybody and everybody liked him. However, due to his addiction to gambling, he was now in a real predicament.

Upon my return from holidays, I was transferred to a new liner from our shipping company. Its construction had been completed only two months prior and it was now waiting in the harbor for the guests and crew members to make its inaugural voyage. I was thoroughly delighted to see that we would be accommodated in twin bed cabins as opposed to the customary four- to six-bed cabins. "Oh, look!" the colleague with whom I had to share the cabin exclaimed happily. "Twin bed cabins for the waiters and a TV and shower in every room. No more communal showers or communal toilets! I could really get used to this place!" I was also very enthusiastic new vessel and looked forward to our head waiters and the maître d' who seemed to be very friendly and congenial. It was a massive improvement compared with my previous ship, and the change of scenery had a positive effect on me.

After two days on the high seas we finally arrived at the port of Puerto Rico. I have already told you about Puerto Rico and mentioned that several casinos are located on this island in addition to the radio telescope which added to the already extraordinary tourist attractions. This chapter concerns these casinos in particular.

We were in the middle of serving breakfast when I noticed our maître d' hurrying frantically across the ship. He kept looking out of the window to see whether the gangway had already been opened for the crew. Although I politely greeted him, he completely ignored me as though I were a total stranger and kept running. I had never seen him behave so erratically. While rushing past me he caught up with two of his head waiters who behaved in the same peculiar manner. They did not seem at all concerned with the hard work involved in serving breakfast, but were visibly preoccupied with something quite different.

"Look at them!" the Irish waiter Frank blurted out. "The boss and his gambling cronies are dying to spend their hard-earned salary!"

It seemed as though the entire restaurant was under a spell. I realized that not only were our bosses behaving oddly, the entire dining room suddenly transformed into a race track. Many of the usually calm and relaxed waiters served as quickly as they possibly could and sent their busboys scurrying around the guests at top speed. This accelerated service was, however, quite convenient for our guests as they were also interested in leaving the restaurant in record time so they could experience as many tourist attractions in Puerto Rico as possible. They didn't take offense and even laughed when the waiters recommended scrambled eggs with bacon instead of the more elaborate breakfast entrees that took much longer to prepare.

The gangway had only just been opened for the crew when our boss – who by that time had outrun the guests – was already waving down a taxi. The head waiters with whom he was speaking so animatedly beforehand were not part of this comical scenario; they were still at the restaurant preparing for lunch. Our maître d' was in a taxi speeding towards none other than the Condado Plaza, the nearest luxury hotel with a large casino.

The restaurant gradually emptied. The waiters who had worked the breakfast shift took a nap in order to be well-rested for lunch, while the others also hurtled down the gangway towards the waiting taxis shortly after their shift was over.

It's no secret that I would also have liked to join them and exercise my gambling tendencies at the casino, but I had to work that day, and I wanted to ensure a five-star rating by the end of the week. Although I could have easily paid a colleague $100 to work on my behalf, the price was a bit too steep for me.

After breakfast I hit the sack so I could recharge my batteries. About two hours later the following announcement echoed via the loudspeakers: "All head waiters are to immediately report to the maître d' in the restaurant!"

I of course also caught the announcement and the mischief maker in me commanded me to go upstairs to the dining room to find out why the boss was calling for his henchmen. To avoid getting caught on my impromptu spy mission, I took a secret route across the casino to finally reach the restaurant. I could not believe my eyes: Mr. Mendocino, the maître d', was kneeling on the floor while meticulously placing 100 dollar bills side by side; the chain of bills had already reached a length of about ten meters and was growing even longer.

The head stewards who had arrived in the meantime goggled at the sight on the carpet. Most of them believed they had been called to discuss an important work-related issue, but it turned out to be quite the opposite! The boss who was practically sweating bullets, his face flushed from exertion, stood up and pointed to the money, declaring: "Gentlemen, take a look! I was only in the casino for a couple of hours and grew richer by $24,000 dollars! That's the way it works, young men. If you like, join me tonight and we will get our hands on some more money." While hiding in the corner of the restaurant, I couldn't believe my eyes or ears. *I can't believe he's throwing his money around so flippantly!* I thought with dismay. *This is bound to end badly!*

Despite the fervor earlier in the day, dinner was served properly, albeit quicker than usual. It was evident that most of the waiter brigade was preoccupied with something else entirely, namely, the casinos which were awaiting customers from the cruise liners.

Our maître d' didn't show up in the restaurant that evening.

The waiters assumed he was undoubtedly sitting in the hotel and gambling away the money he won earlier that day since this was his pattern.

Since I was extremely curious, I also took a taxi which was waiting for customers in front of the ship late in the evening after dinner was over.

The impressive casino was only a short cab ride away and as soon as I arrived, I watched the throngs hurry upstairs in order to get a prime spot at one of the innumerous gambling tables.

"Where is our boss?" I asked. "I don't know," one of my colleagues replied. "Maybe he is still at the gourmet restaurant enjoying the finest cuisine on the house."

At first I did not understand what he meant, but was very curious to see what type of entrees were served in this first-class establishment all the same. I approached the entrance of this gourmet temple and studied the menu.

"Hey!" my boss' voice boomed. "I know you – you're the friendly German waiter. Come here and join us! Do you like Beluga caviar and Dom Perignon champagne?" "Do fish swim in the ocean?" I countered indignantly. "Is there anyone who *doesn't* like champagne and first-class caviar?!"

My boss was holding court at his table while surrounded by lobster, caviar and the most expensive champagne – on the house. I was sure that he was one of the favorite regular customers, perhaps more accurately, one of the favorite regular losers who frequented this casino as often as possible and was now enjoying the sensation of being the biggest winner for once in his life.

I was only too happy to join them and enjoyed some toast with caviar, two large pieces of lobster with mayonnaise and a glass of Dom Perignon that was served by the patronizing maître d'.

"Are you a gambler?" my boss wanted to know. Slightly ashamed, I answered in the affirmative, but he was delighted. "You need know some important rules of gambling," he advised with slurred speech, slightly addled by the champagne. "Never gamble with small amounts of money," the boss continued explaining. "Showing a great game and aiming for a favorable run will make you rich. If you ante only a small amount and win, you will always wonder about the high profit you would have made with a large amount. Take my advice: it always pays to do things on a grand scale!"

While I didn't exactly agree with his modus operandi, I followed him to see if his grand scale approach would actually pay off.

Without hesitation, he headed for the VIP tables at the back of the casino where the dealer warmly welcomed him by name. My boss took some of the money he had won in the morning out of his pockets which was exchanged for 500-dollar and 1,000-dollar chips (I felt dizzy just watching the transaction!) in less to no time. Small piles of chips were then placed in front of him.

"Another bottle of champagne!" he commanded the dealer who immediately beckoned to a waiter.

The game started. I thought to myself: *Oh boy, so much money! That can't be happening. He's acting like Bill Gates, he's only a restaurant manager. Five hundred dollars in one shot! If it were me I would probably pass out from a panic attack.* If it had only been 500 dollars......! This, however, was definitely not the case! Now my boss proceeded to pretend he was sitting at a table with numerous gamblers, although he was the only player. He put one of the chips on every game box and thus anted up a total of 4,000 dollars. *This is the equivalent of the monthly wage of a father with a wife and four children – and only fate will decide their futures within the next two minutes!* I thought grimly.

His impetuous actions actually paid off – he got lucky! The dealer dealt a 9, a 7 and a 10 and thus had by far exceeded the permitted blackjack maximum of 21. A chip was added to each of the eight chips. With only two chips the boss won an additional 750 dollars as he showed a 10 and a face card, the so-called blackjack, which yielded one and a half times of the stake. He had won 4,500 dollars in less than two minutes! Unbelievable! When I looked around, I realized that three of his head waiters had meanwhile gathered at the table. They were calmly talking to their boss while keeping a straight face. The next game took a disagreeable turn. The dealer had a score of 21 and won the money in all five boxes. The sensational winnings from the first game had already been lost, and our boss had to start all over again.

"Johannes, come here and play with us!" one of my waiter-colleagues yelled and waved to me from a table in the main room. Accepting this invitation, I sat down at a table which allowed me to keep an eye on my boss' gambling activities. Betting only a small amount of money, I focused more on Mr. Mendocino's body language which foreshadowed a disastrous outcome after only half an hour. He was loudly and frantically consulting with his head waiters and nodded his head after every round. Two of the head waiters suddenly left the table and went to the cashier where they took out their credit cards. About ten minutes later they returned to their boss and gave him several bank notes. I surmised it must have been quite a lot of money because I could not imagine that our boss would have continued gambling with low value chips after having lost all his winnings from that morning.

I will refrain from describing what ensued at the gambling table that evening. Besides, my cherished readers will no doubt be able to imagine how the game ended for the three gamblers. As I was told later, our boss had not only gambled away the king's ransom he had won that morning, but he had additionally asked his head waiters to withdraw 16,000 dollars from their accounts. Nobody knows how he managed to pay back such tremendous debt within such a short time, but he did. In this regard he was a man of honor.

I found it somewhat bizarre that gambling activity was not confined to the casinos in the harbors. I remember one day quite well while in conversation with one of the head waiters which ended with the following remark: "We've noticed that you also occasionally go to the casino. How would you like to meet us at our maître d's cabin to play poker after work? You could win a lot of money." "And lose money!" I added. "Yes, of course ... but most of the time we win." At that moment I didn't realize the significance of my colleague's statement, but for the first time in my life I was given the chance to peer into the very deep abyss of a human soul. Worst of all, I was part of this abyss for some time.

At around midnight one of the head waiters advised me that a few gamblers – the maître d' Mendocino, four head waiters and some gambling-addicted waiters (I was obviously one of them) – would meet in a colleague's cabin that evening. I accepted the invitation as I was very curious to learn the meaning of the head waiter's words: "Most of the time we win."

The answer was revealed that very evening. After work that night I went to the cabin where illegal games had become commonplace. One of the waiters standing at the door stopped me. "Do you want to win or lose?" he asked while taking a last drag on his cigarette before he ground the cigarette butt under his heel. "What a silly question!" I replied. "My last visits at the casino were a nightmare because I always lost." "Okay," my counterpart explained, "go on in, watch our boss' mannerisms and keep an eye on him! He is always upping the ante because he doesn't have use for small amounts. Take a close look at him! If you see him reach for his coffee after dealing the cards, and then notice him take a drag of his cigarette, this usually signals a favorable hand on his part and you need to be careful!! If he only takes a drag of his cigarette when he's frowning, it means the cards are stacked against him. In that case you can take him to the cleaners since he always tries to bluff without being aware his body language is so easy to read. Of course we let him win from time to time so that he won't get suspicious. But the big winnings are always pocketed by one of us."

And that's the way it carried on. Our perpetually perspiring boss did not have a clue what was happening to him. If it was possible to win a small amount, he was successful. If several hundred dollars were lying on the table, all gamblers except those with a good hand suddenly stopped playing. It was quite amusing in the beginning. Sometimes you won, sometimes you lost – as is quite common in card games. The colleague who had the best hand while the boss was bluffing often won several hundred dollars. Everybody would wait with bated breath for our maitre d' to raise the stakes while he sternly took a drag on his cigarette then ignored the coffee next to him and thus inadvertently signaled a bad hand. Shortly thereafter he would once again lose to one of the other gamblers. Occasionally I also enjoyed moments in which I won a lot of money with a straight flush, while the others were stuck with a less advantageous hand. With rare exception, these rounds always had the same outcome for our boss: he would take a big loss and have no idea how it happened. I must admit that I did not have any twinge of conscience regarding this set-up at the beginning since winning a jackpot was the only objective. After a few weeks, however, I felt very badly about it and withdrew from the games. Today I am very ashamed of my unscrupulousness and don't relish these memories. The next day, Mendocino was predictably sitting in the posh hotel, stuffing himself with vast amounts of caviar on the house and throwing a lot of money down the drain. Even today I have no idea where he acquired the money for these escapades, but he in fact always had the cash at his disposal. When he visited the casinos in the harbors, he seemed to have already forgotten the evenings spent in cabins where he always ended up on the short end. We often watched him going to the casino by taxi either in broad daylight or at night after work. The next day he was either sitting in his office in high spirits or totally dejected. It was a

266

tragedy to witness such an amiable and charismatic man sabotaging himself. I offered him my advice on one occasion when had won as much as $55,000 in less than an hour, represented in the form of chips which were piled up in front of him. Patting him on his back, I suggested that I could take most of the winnings with me and return them to him later on board our ship. He was wide-eyed with surprise when he saw me. He might have expected this piece of advice from one of his head waiters but none of them had accompanied him that evening. Although he greatly respected me as one of his best waiters, I did not manage to bring him to reason. "Look!" he said. "These chips add up to almost $60,000. Today is my lucky day. I want to win *$300,000* so that I will be in a position to quit my job on the ship and buy a restaurant of my own." *Dream on!* I thought cynically and stepped back to continue watching his game. Perhaps I would witness a gambler whose clever tactics enabled him to extract a large sum of money from the casino, despite my sense of foreboding.

However, in less than two hours the large pile of chips in front of him turned into a small heap, the small heap then dwindled into a meager handful, until by the end of the night there was not even a single chip left.

"May we offer you a limousine back to the cruise liner?" I heard the casino manager ask our boss. The whole time he had been in the back watching the games at the gambling table. Sweaty and downcast, a broken Mendocino got up, shook his head and left the casino without saying a word.

We don't know how he managed to get back to the ship. He had either paid a taxi to the liner with whatever was left in his wallet or had walked.

It was the same procedure day after day, week after week and month after month. I could regale you with plenty of positive and negative moments in his gambling career, but I will refrain since you are most likely only interested in knowing what became of Mr. Mendocino.

One day I saw him strolling through the dining room hand in hand with a cute little girl and an elegant, well-dressed woman behind him. "Would you like to meet them?" I heard him ask. "This is my wife and my daughter." All of us were lost for words because with the exception of his head waiters, nobody had even suspected that he had a family. We cordially welcomed them upon introduction. Both of them smiled back at us, but unspeakable sadness was reflected in their eyes.

Poor family! I thought. *Who knows how long they'll stay with him if he doesn't do something about his gambling obsession.*

In fact it turned out that his wife left him a year later, and he was only seldom allowed to visit his daughter, as fate did not smile upon him.

He continued working as a maître d' with great success since he had the competent assistance of his waiter and head waiter brigade and was considered a role model for all employees in his field. Everybody who ever worked with him had given up trying to rescue him from his dark side, while others simply turned a blind eye.

One day we were informed that our restaurant manager Mendocino had fallen in the dining room and sustained very severe injuries which confined him to a wheelchair for the rest of his life.

Since the accident had happened on account of a wet floor on board, he sued the shipping company and was compensated with a very large amount of money which allowed him to live without financial problems. But what did Mendocino do with this amount of several millions? Well, he first went into therapy to fight his gambling addition, but nothing changed since the gambling virus had already totally consumed his brain. In less than a year he had spent the entire remuneration at casinos in Las Vegas and Atlantic City. After he had lost the money, his so-called friends abandoned him. As his family was already living far away, nothing else was left for him but to die lonely and impoverished.

Those who knew him remember him as a wonderful and competent boss. However, Mendocino's name is still used as a cautionary tale nowadays while explaining the curse of the casino to the new generation of waiters.

269

Chapter 32:   Thrifty Daridor

Now that I have told you in detail about our lavish Mendocino, I will refer to the waiter Daridor from India who was exactly his opposite. Daridor can undoubtedly be described as abnormally avaricious, but I am not sure whether even such a vivid description truly captures his persona ...

As already mentioned, Daridor was from India, but not from a poor background – as you might have assumed – but from quite a wealthy family. His father was a goldsmith, his mother worked as a seamstress, while he and his four siblings were employed in the tourist trade.

Daridor only cared about two things: doing his job well and not wasting money. He never allowed himself to visit the casino or a restaurant, nor did he go to the beach unless it was in close proximity to our cruise liner. He never attended a shore excursion or even bought a can of coke which was only 50 cents, the price offered to employees of the shipping company at that time. He had one pair of sneakers with the original 'R e e b o k' label. After numerous months, however, only the letters '_ _ _ b o _' were still visible. When these shoes eventually crumbled to dust one day, Daridor asked whether he would be allowed to work barefoot on board the ship; his request was denied. His waiter colleagues had fun collecting some coins to buy a very old pair of sneakers for Daridor at the local flea market. Since these tennis shoes were barely held together by dried glue, the waiters expected Daridor to be very angry. Far from it! He was thrilled to bits, gratefully accepted the shoes and whenever they were on the verge of falling apart, he found more glue on the ship and repaired them. He even repaired the disheveled footwear which other waiters had thrown away and wore them for another several million steps on board. Did he ever phone his wife and children at home? No way!! Far too expensive!

After the captain had finally also been informed of this particularly parsimonious waiter on his team, he felt sorry for Daridor's family. One day the captain showed up at lunch time and approached Daridor, took out his wallet and handed him a 10-dollar bill. "Take this money and buy a telephone card, my son," he said sternly. "Go and call your family now, otherwise I'll be very angry!" When the sound of laughing and chortling echoed throughout the restaurant at Daridor's expense, we assumed he would be ashamed over the captain's gesture. Not a chance! He politely thanked the captain, triumphantly held up the money to show everybody, hurried to the crew bar and in fact bought a phone card. But this was not the end of his thrifty ways.

When the first waiters entered the dining room at dawn to set the breakfast tables, we heard Daridor offer the following, "Who would like to be off at lunch today? If you pay me 100 dollars, you will have a chance to go to the beach and visit the casino instead of having to deal with a large station in the restaurant at lunch time!"

In those days it was permissible to let a colleague work on another colleague's behalf against monetary payment. Tired waiters who urgently needed to sleep after an all-night party, not to mention the gamblers who hoped to recoup their losses from the casino were queuing in Daridor's station early in the morning to take him up on his proposal. We quite often witnessed the outbreak of a price war as a result. The colleague with the best bid was substituted by Daridor at lunch time. He, however, was not only willing to take over a colleague's work at lunch, but also at the midnight buffet. Not surprisingly, this waiter earned a small fortune every week.

Very early one morning there was a knock at all our doors. We couldn't believe our eyes: Daridor was standing in front of the door and offering freshly squeezed orange juice. After he had stolen a large crate of oranges in the warehouse in the middle of the night, he had prepared fresh juice which he now offered for purchase. In no time at all he had sold all of his juice since most colleagues were only too happy to be served such a delicious beverage in their cabins. When he prepared orange juice for the next round, Daridor was of course caught red-handed by the executive chef who had already been frantic over the whereabouts of his missing oranges and Daridor was consequently given a written warning. When I learned of the disciplinary action, I went to the executive chef's cabin, a German with whom I was in close contact, and suggested he summon Daridor into his office just for fun. Manfred, the chef, would then inform Daridor that he was obligated to pay for all the oranges he had stolen over the past month. Manfred liked this idea

271

very much and promised to me give me call when the thieving waiter was expected in his office. I will never forget Daridor's facial expression when Manfred presented him an invoice amounting to more than 4,000 dollars for the oranges. He recoiled in horror as if Freddy Krüger, Dracula, the Predator and Saw were about to gang up on him to unleash their torture. Once the shock had worn off, he convulsed with pain and started whining like a little child whose favorite toy had been taken away. He was wailing and begging, but we kept up the suspenseful charade. He was utterly relieved when he was finally told that the executive chef had only wanted to teach him a lesson. He was admonished to never again steal from the galley and cellar for the purpose of lining his own pockets. Trembling from head to toe, he fell to his knees, thanked Manfred profusely, then fled the office. It didn't take long before everybody learned that Daridor had been held accountable in the executive chef's office for stealing, which was just what the other waiters had been waiting for. They continued to make fun of him for several days after the fact. One time they set a large bowl of mixed fruits on a table in his station with the note, "Make some fresh juice for everybody, please!" On another occasion a large bag of pears was left in front of his cabin with the instruction that since there was no more fruit brandy available in the bar, would he be kind enough to distill some pear brandy overnight. Daridor stayed calm because he was so happy and relieved not to have to pay a single cent back to the shipping company.

Daridor had been working for eighteen months consecutively, although six months is the usual stint. Slogging away day and night, he took every extra job in addition to his hard work as a waiter; it was no surprise that he looked like death warmed over on the day of his disembarkation.

I will reveal the amount of money he had saved, but not just yet. Although he was bone-weary and exhausted, Daridor happily shook hands with everybody he had met and said his goodbyes. I was enjoying an espresso in our cafeteria during my short break when I saw Daridor walking along the street with two age-old suitcases and a carrier bag around his neck. I was totally surprised since the crew usually orders a taxi to either the hotel or directly to the airport and they usually have sufficient money for the fare that day. Moreover, most employees try to skedaddle as quickly as possible, before the boss has a chance to cancel the long-anticipated home leave and postpone an employee's departure for a week in the event a colleague has fallen ill. Consequently it wasn't unusual to watch as the taxis passed the liners in the harbor and disappeared into the distance. Our Daridor, however, was too chintzy to spend three dollars for the taxi ride to the "HO EL" which I have described in one of the first chapters of this book. He would have had to pay only a few dollars for a taxi and another 75 dollars to stay in a first-class hotel affiliated with our shipping company. But some people are unfortunately obsessed by miserliness and do not realize their strange behavior can actually have dire consequences.

After an exhausting hour-long walk Daridor eventually reached the cockroach hotel, checked in and went to the third floor with his heavy baggage. He shot a contemptuous glance at the porter who had offered his help since Daridor knew he would be expected to give a tip, which was totally against his nature.

Upon his arrival in one of the squalid rooms Daridor realized that he had forgotten his meal vouchers at the front desk which allowed him to have dinner at the expense of the in-house restaurant. He couldn't believe he'd been so careless! He quickly shut the door behind him and hurried downstairs to retrieve the shipping company's coupon.

Since he was so obsessed with the savings he stashed away in his suitcase, he bolted upstairs to his room less than five minutes later and froze at the sight that confronted him: the door was open and his suitcase in which 38,000 dollars had been hidden among the dirty clothes was now empty and all that remained was the pair of broken shoes.

At about 3:00 p.m. Daridor – who by then was totally distraught and trembling – showed up at our cruise liner accompanied by a policeman. I was buying some refreshments at the kiosk in front of our office when I saw the two men. I watched the policeman disappear into the office to speak to a crew supervisor. Daridor was sitting on a bench, understandably extremely upset when I approached him a moment later.

"Let me guess!" I said to him. "You were too thrifty to buy traveler's cheques for 50 cents per cheque which would have allowed you to safely exchange all the money you earned over the past 18 months. You were also too cheap to pay for a taxi which would have taken you and your hard-earned money quickly and safely to a reputable hotel. You were too thrifty to buy a solid suitcase which couldn't have been broken into so easily. And you stayed at the …. 'HO EL cockroach hotel,' didn't you?" Daridor looked at me despondently and nodded in silence. "I was at the front desk for only five minutes. *Five minutes*! How could it have happened?" Then he started crying. "Very easily, actually," I replied. "Your strange behavior and abnormal sense of thriftiness that you were so damn proud of made you enemies who only had to wait for you to disembarked the ship. They knew that you had stashed your money in your cabin for 18 months because you didn't want to spend any money on traveler's cheques or a bank transfer. They followed your departure from the liner to the hotel, watched as you checked in at the hotel; they only needed the five minutes you spent at the front desk to break down the rickety door in this trashy hotel and empty your shabby old suitcase!" "I hope that the police can help me," he murmured in a barely audible voice. "Get real!" I scolded. "You're in Miami – the criminals here are unscrupulous!"

Once the police had arrived on board, everybody was questioned and it soon became evident that the culprit was likely one of the crew members. As the victim had neither friends nor enemies who could provide any information, the interrogation only lasted a few minutes. The thieves were not on board during questioning and had undoubtedly long disappeared with the stolen goods as quietly and furtively as they had entered Daridor's hotel room. The police also investigated the hotel employees, but their inquiry regarding the use of security cameras on the premises which might have caught the burglary on tape was only met with an apathetic smile.

The shipping company learned a lesson from this event and immediately changed the hotel it offered at its employees disposal, which heralded the end for our 'HO EL.' The ill-fated establishment didn't do much business without the ship crews. By all accounts the owners of the so-called 'cockroach hut' disappeared soon after the incident, leaving behind a lot of liabilities in their wake. The hoteliers seemed to have invested their earnings over the years in private pursuits rather than in bolstering their reputation in Miami. Three months later a construction team was brought in to bulldoze the hotel.

An impressive monument has meanwhile been set up at this site, yet even today shipping company employees often stop to point and comment: "Can you believe that was once the horror hotel?!"

Chapter 33:   How Hadji Mehmet Crossed the Panama Canal

"Head waiter Fabian, please give me the list with the names of the new waiters who are expected on our ship today!" the maître d's voice sounded from the office. It was the last breakfast on the day of disembarkation and the maître d' wanted to know which of the new and which 'old-timer' waiters would be working on our liner for the next cruise. Fabian retrieved this list once it had been faxed from the office in Miami to the head waiter's attention. Upon quickly glancing at the message, he grimaced then frantically hurried to the maître d's office.

"Hadji Mehmet is coming back to us!" he gasped. "You've got to be kidding!, the maître d' anxiously replied. "He is the last person I would ever want to see on this ship again," he added, visibly distressed. I will try to prevent this disaster, otherwise he will put an end to the peace and quiet in my restaurant I worked so hard to salvage after his first stint here!"

Since I was responsible for the station next to the maître d's office that week, I overheard his tirade which immediately piqued my curiosity. I went to see my teacher Jesus who was busy placing a pile of doilies on his gueridon. As usual, he refused to change the tablecloths after the first sitting.

"Who is Hadji Mehmet?" I asked. "Hadji!" Jesus cried out. "Are you telling me he's going to work with us again?" "Well, it looks that way, doesn't it?" I countered. "What's the matter with this guy?" "The only thing that's wrong with him is that he's a veritable catastrophe!" Jesus lamented. "He drives everybody crazy – the guests as well as the crew. He is half Turkish, half Greek, looks like a bowlegged pot-bellied bulldog and doesn't waste any opportunity to make his colleagues look like fools and ridicule them in front of their guests. Lord help us!" "He actually sounds quite interesting," I smirked. "Tell me more about him, please! I am curious." Jesus hesitated for a moment, then laughed and agreed to recount the story of Hadji:

"Two years ago Hadji started his career with us," Jesus informed me. "By the second week as a busboy on one of our ships in Europe he had already made a lasting impression on us. On the day he first boarded our ship to report for duty, he was informed while still in

277

the harbor of Venice that he would be responsible for selling wine in the terminal. As we had learned from his application documents he was familiar with wines, but he seemed to have problems with the term 'terminal...'"

"Yes, I know what you mean by the wine sold at the terminal," I answered. "As soon as our guests have arrived at the harbor, they are immediately sent to a wine stall where they can pre-order one or two bottles for dinner." "You're right," Jesus said, "On that day it was our Hadji's task to receive the wines with the coolers, a folding table and decorations from the cellar at lunch time. Then he had to go to the terminal where everything was to be attractively arranged so that the wine could be easily sold.

At about 11:30 a.m. on a bright summer day in Venice, Hadji bounded down the gangway. Equipped with the valuable goods, he welcomed everybody with a big grin on his face.

At lunch time the first guests checked in, admiring our beautiful ship as they roamed around.

"Where can I order the wine for dinner?" a guest asked who apparently had already attended another cruise on one of our liners.

in charge is expected here at any moment with our wines," a head waiter explained to him who had just arrived at the terminal to check if everything was in order. By 12:30 p.m. there was still no Hadji in sight! The head waiter nervously checked the time and shook his head. "Where is that dumbass?" he cursed almost inaudibly to a bar waiter who was busy setting up his own station for the advance sale of tasty cocktails. He wasn't much help and only shrugged his shoulders; he didn't seem to be terribly interested in the activities of a busboy.

Startled by the bar waiter's indifference, the head waiter alerted the other colleagues. Shortly thereafter, the maître d' and four additional head waiters arrived in the cruise terminal hall and stared in disbelief at the empty location where a busboy should have attracted attention while peddling his goods. The gentlemen were completely stymied and once again took a walk around, consulted the officers who were on duty outside the ship and eventually called the F&B manager as well as the hotel director to notify them of a busboy who had been missing since 11:30 that morning and had wine bottles worth 2,000 dollars in tow. At about 2:00 p.m. all the

278

previously mentioned managers assembled once again for an emergency meeting in the terminal. The F&B manager's assistant suddenly and frenetically approached the group, holding a mobile phone in her hand, yelling: "Urgent call from a busboy for the head waiter!" Frowning, the restaurant manager took the call and asked for the caller's name. His face turned red with anger and disbelief. This is the way I imagine the phone call during the next three minutes must have unfolded:

Restaurant manager Thomson: "Thomson speaking. Who is on the phone, please?"

"Hadji speaking, I'm a busboy."

Restaurant manager: "Where the hell are you? Tell me *now*!"

Hadji: "The terminal, and I have a lot of wine with me."

Restaurant manager: "You must be out of your mind! Where *are* you? We've searched the entire terminal, and you definitely aren't here!"

Hadji: "As I said, the terminal, with a lot of very expensive wine, but I only sold a few bottles."

Restaurant manager: "Well, I'll be damned! But *which* terminal are you talking about for Christ's sake; we're at the terminal right now but there's no sign of you!"

Hadji: "The only terminal I know about is the terminal at the airport. Is there another one? I really have no clue."

Looking at his colleagues in utter incredulity, Thomson was unable to speak for a few seconds.

Restaurant manager: "Airport? Why are you talking about the airport? Why would you be there, of all places?!"

Hadji: "The head waiter sent me to the *terminal* to sell wine there, but business is bad. The airport police told me that I am not allowed to sell wine. What am I supposed to do now?"

Staring at the other officers in disgust, the restaurant manager tried to regain his composure. "He's at the *airport* terminal!" he gasped. "The idiot has gone to the airport terminal! Can somebody please pinch me and tell me this isn't happening?!" "Hadji!" he shouted into the mobile phone, "Can you tell me how you managed to take the damn wine, the tables *and* the ice buckets to the airport? This stuff must weigh a ton."

Hadji: "I asked the bus driver whether he could carry the goods into the bus. He was friendly enough to do so then informed me that he would send the invoice to the ship. But what shall I do now? I am thirsty. May I drink a bottle of wine?"

Restaurant manager: "NO, you may *not*! Don't even think of opening a bottle! You'll wait for us. We'll come to pick you up at the airport, so stay where you are. By the way, how many bottles did you sell and to whom?"

Hadji: "I asked passengers whether they were taking a cruise on our ship. Then I sold the wine, but only a few small ones. I have some money in my pocket to pay for a taxi to the ship!"

Restaurant manager: "Stay put, you imbecile! Don't move. Like I said, we'll pick you up." "Yes!" Hadji shouted into the phone. "Come here and afterwards we'll go cross the Panama Canal." "Exactly!" the restaurant manager replied. "Which will give me the perfect chance to throw you overboard."

"That's not such a good idea," Hadji countered. "The sea is already rather polluted. Ha, ha!"

Shortly afterward the restaurant manager and his assistant took a mini truck which offered sufficient space for three people and the wine bottles. They disappeared towards the airport to pick up the busboy Hadji and the wine assortment.

That evening we could not stop laughing about this story which of course spread like wildfire. But this was only the first of several amusing antics by this thick-headed busboy. He was working as a waiter's assistant at the beginning because of his rather bad command of English. Moreover he had made a huge misstep with his ineptitude and cluelessness at the terminal and the managers had consequently lost quite a lot of confidence in him. Yet it didn't take long until he was promoted to waiter since he proved to be very skillful and clever. He benefitted from the experience acquired during his employment at a few reputable hotels in Turkey and additionally improved his English knowledge within a very short time. During his employment as a busboy he was rather reserved because he did not want to jeopardize his promotion to that of a waiter - or the doubled salary that came with the added responsibility. However, the more he brushed up on his English, the more he took advantage of using it at others' expense. Shortly after his promotion to waiter he considered it appropriate to strut across

280

the ship and to insult any busboy who had not yet had the wherewithal to be promoted. Snide and taunting remarks such as, "Hey bonehead, are you *still* working as busboy?" "You will soon have to work with me and you can be sure I'll have your butt in a sling in no time!" or "Hey, idiot boy, how're you doing? I've noticed your parents' intelligence hasn't rubbed off on you, has it? What a shame!" echoed throughout the entire cruise liner. Today it would be impossible to talk in such a disrespectful manner since this would automatically mean a written warning would be given. But in those days the law of the jungle prevailed.

Not a single meal could be served in the restaurant without Hadji picking a fight with somebody. For example, if he didn't like the appearance of the waiter who was working next to him, he would wait until this particular colleague disappeared into the galley and then take great pleasure in disparaging him in front of his dinner guests. He followed him into the galley but first paid a short visit to the guests in the neighboring station. "Hi, folks!" he smiled at them. "Who's your waiter?" "Antonio," they replied in bewilderment because they had no idea why this bulldog-like waiter would approach them in the first place. "Antonio?" he spat maliciously. "He's a moron and really clumsy. Let's hope he will manage to serve your dinner before breakfast tomorrow... You are really unlucky to be traveling across the Panama Canal with Antonio as your waiter." The guests all had blank expressions since they had not at all expected such venomous comments about a fellow waiter. When their own waiter arrived at his station with their meals, they of course told him about Hadji's impertinent display at their table. But Antonio only laughed and tapped his forehead, saying: "Don't take him seriously, he's not exactly the sharpest tack in this restaurant." Antonio had just returned to the galley to get the soups and salads, when Hadji arrived again at Antonio's station and smiled provokingly at the guests. He had piled 18 main courses on a tray atop his shoulder which were not expected to be served so early in the evening. If you're wondering how Hadji had managed such a feat... Very easy to answer! Aside from a simple appetizer such as a shrimp cocktail and one or two main dishes, he had declared to his guests that all the other meals were inedible. Strangely enough, his guests believed him.

281

Guest: "Hadji, what about the onion soup?"

Hadji: "Far too salty, Sir."

Guest: "Can you recommend the fish tapenade?"

Hadji: "Sure, why not, if you enjoy picking out all of the fish bones before you can actually taste it."

Guest: "Would you recommend the steak?"

Hadji: "Most definitely, Ma'am, it's very juicy and tender – just like a baby's bottom."

Shielding his face with his hand, he turned to his busboy and whispered: "Always recommend the steak; the meat is really good and very easy to serve." Hadji's busboy nodded sympathetically. In the end Hadji recommended only two courses: an appetizer and a main dish. The guests had been put off the other meals to such an extent that they did not dare order any of them. Considering their meager orders it was not surprising that Hadji was always the first to arrive in the galley. The executive chef was astonished that Hadji of all restaurant staff was collecting the main courses in next to no time. But even they had to withstand Hadji's insults while they were still busy preparing the meals; waiters weren't the only ones who bore the brunt of his ill behavior. For example, he would ask the chefs why they were so slow and whether they knew how to properly use a knife or a soup spoon. Once one of the chefs was so furious with Hadji that he banished him from his work area, and seconds later the heavy soup ladle which came suddenly flying out of the galley missed our dear Hadji by a hair's breadth. Unfazed, he simply turned away and headed for his own station. Antonio's guests were visibly unhappy, and undoubtedly thought they had received poor service. After all, they were none the wiser that not a single soup and only very few salads had been served in Hadji's station. When Antonio returned from the galley with the salads, he immediately realized that something was wrong. A glance at Hadji's station then at his own tables, which were full of stone-faced guests, spoke volumes. "Oh, I see! My neighbor has paid you another visit," he said with a thoughtful smile. The guests answered by nodding silently. They really did not know what to think about the strange demeanor by the pot-bellied waiter from the neighboring station. "Don't worry!" Antonio assured them. "His guests get only half of the food that I am serving to you. Therefore

282

it's quite understandable that I need more time." Assuming that the same amount of food would be offered and served at all times, the guests were slowly catching on to what Antonio was trying to explain to them and contented themselves with his reply. During dinner they would occasionally steal a glance to Hadji's station to see how his guests were faring. Antonio's guests were still enjoying the main course while Hadji busied himself by placing the desserts on his gueridon then clearly and succinctly describing each dessert in a loud voice. Guest no. 1: "A piece of cheesecake, Ma'am." Guest no. 2: "A piece of cheesecake for you, Sir." Guest no. 3: "This cheesecake is for you; enjoy it." Guest no. 4: "A piece of cheesecake with vanilla ice cream for you, Sir." He continued in that matter-of-fact tone until a piece of cheesecake had also been served to guest no. 16.

"Incredible!" the guests at Antonio's tables were whispering. "None of the guests order soufflés, cherries jubilee or mango parfaits. Wow, we are very lucky not to be served by such a bizarre and rude waiter."

That's just the way Hadji was. Due to his harsh behavior and his frightening appearance Hadji had his guests under his thumb and they didn't have the heart to contradict him in any way.

As already mentioned, he made both his guests and his colleagues dance to his tune. He was particularly fond of annoying the newcomers. I will never forget the moment when a new Jamaican busboy was assigned to Hadji to help him at his station during the week. "You look like a rookie," Hadji commented upon Winston's arrival at his station. "But don't worry; I'll make an excellent busboy out of you. If you do what I tell you, you will always finish your shifts in the evening as well as the other meals in next to no time." "I know," the Jamaican replied, "I've already been told that your guests don't get much to eat." Smiling at his assistant, Hadji seemed to be satisfied with Winston's answer. Although Winston had already been informed about this strange waiter, he did not at all expect the incredible bold faced lies Hadji was telling about him during dinner that evening.

Once the restaurant doors had been opened for the first dinner sitting, the guests sat down at their tables. They were all waiting for their appetizers and meals to arrive, when Hadji pulled his new

283

busboy by the sleeve and took him to the tables. "I will introduce us now," he quietly assured him. "Okay," Winston agreed. "It's a good idea to let your guests know right from the beginning which dream team is going to take care of them," Hadji said benevolently, though his subsequent actions were anything but.

Smiling at the dinner guests, Hadji began his spiel "Good evening, Ladies and Gentlemen! May I introduce myself? My name is Hadji Mehmet and I'm your waiter." He then pointed to his dark-skinned assistant and explained: "This little black boy, I found him in Africa, swinging from banana tree to banana tree. One day, this little black boy fell down from the banana tree and hurt his head very badly. Since then, he is a handicap. So Ladies and Gentlemen, if he forgets to bring your coke, your ice tea or your salad dressing, don t worry, he is a handicap!" Hadji's monologue was met by dead silence at the table. The perplexed guests were looking at each other in utter disbelief. Some of them had already been on several cruises, but so far none of them had ever heard such a thing. To their credit, they did try to see the humor in Hadji's introduction, but all they could manage was a strained smile. Winston was also not at all amused as at that moment he caught the eye of a head waiter who had witnessed Hadji's failed attempt to set a relaxed tone. Winston pointed at the waiter and asked, "Has this ugly, white guy been saying nasty things about me when he introduced us to the guests just now? If so and if the management doesn't take appropriate actions, he will have four hours to live before I throw him overboard to the sharks." Nodding understandingly, the head waiter promised to take Hadji to task. He did indeed fulfill his promise after he had asked Hadji to come to his office when his shift was over. "Mr. Hadji," he said in a stern voice, "we have been keeping a close eye on you for some time and are quite aware that you are off the wall, but don't you think that you went slightly overboard today by the way you introduced your busboy?" Smirking maliciously, Hadji remarked: "Why shouldn't I tell the truth? It's obvious that my assistant is a loser." "You cannot judge him before you've even worked with him," the head waiter argued. "Who cares!" Hadji replied. "He's still a loser." The head waiter's blood started boiling. "I give you my word that you will have to swim back to port after we've crossed the Panama Canal, should I receive even *one* negative comment about you by the end of the week or get a bad rating about you or a letter of complaint about your despicable behavior!" "Don't worry, Boss," Hadji said. "I am the best and nobody will complain about me. I know how to juggle with words." "Fine," the head waiter commented. "I hope that you also know how to handle a flight ticket back home in case you get any complaints. Get out of my office *now*, before I lose my temper!"

Hadji whistled on his way out of the office as though nothing had happened, then returned to the dining room. He was still looking for an opportunity to harass his colleagues. Shortly after he had been told he had been assigned to the midnight buffet he saw his chance – he just couldn't help himself.

It's not difficult to imagine that no waiter is especially eager to work at the midnight buffet after an already long working day only to serve his customers who had enjoyed the last meal only a few hours previously. By this time of the evening, the waiters don't particularly like to reenact their canned speech about wines and cocktails or listen to the guests' problems and complaints. They would far prefer if the customers were satisfied with iced tea, coffee or water so that the tables could be cleared very quickly and be able to leave the restaurant as early as possible. Unfortunately only the waiters who were not working next to Hadji's station succeeded in doing so. God help anyone who was in Hadji's line of sight!

For example, one evening our waiter Fred from Wales was working next to Hadji, and found out about his evil nature the hard way. Watching the guests like a hawk who were sitting in Fred's station with fully loaded plates, the pot-bellied Hadji waited until Fred headed for the galley to get some water and iced tea and then descended on the neighboring station.

"Hi, folks!" he welcomed the customers. "I am happy to see you. I am the head waiter and would like to recommend the beverage specials offered tonight. In addition to the usual and boring beverages such as iced tea or coffee, today we offer freshly made orange tea, sugared iced coffee with whipped cream, and homemade cappuccino. If you like, we can also prepare some nice hot apple juice with crushed mint for you, which is a specialty from Panama. Your waiter is looking forward to your order. We hope that you'll enjoy your meal!" With these words he left the station.

285

After listening to Hadji's recommendations, the guests were wide-eyed with anticipation. "This shipping company is really great," one of the highly satisfied guests commented. "We can even expect to be served the most delicious and exotic beverages in the middle of the night."

A moment later waiter Fred returned from the galley. Tired and stressed out after a hard day of work, he put his jugs with iced water and iced tea on his gueridon. Greeting his guests with half-closed eyes, he politely asked them: "What would you like? Iced tea, water or perhaps a cup of coffee?" "Nothing of the sort!" they exclaimed indignantly. "We want the midnight specials which were offered by the head waiter!" Fred looked distraught. "Come on, come on!" the guests cried out as they egged him on. "We would like to have two glasses of apple juice with mint, four orders of orange tea and two sugared ice coffees with some extra condensed milk, please!" When Fred took the order, he looked as though he was about to cry. But he had no choice! If a head waiter recommends these beverages, the waiter is obliged to serve them – whether he wants to or not. Fred, however, did not have a clue why his superior had recommended such elaborate cocktails at that time. "What are you doing?" Hadji taunted when he watched his colleague Fred busily arranging glasses and jugs in the galley. "Well," Fred sighed, "some stupid idiot of head waiter who evidently doesn't like me has recommended some freaky beverages to the guests which I have to prepare now. Tomorrow I will go to ask the maître d' whether this harassment is legitimate." "Of course it is," Hadji replied immediately. "The guest is your master and thus entitled to be treated like royalty – even at midnight." "I will wring the head waiter's neck," Fred announced contemptuously. "But first I have to find out who it was."

Beads of sweat appeared on Hadji's forehead when he watched Fred entering the office after the midnight buffet to ask whether orange tea with mint was usually recommended in the middle of the night. It didn't take long until a head waiter approached Hadji's station and politely invited him to come to the maître d's office. Alarmed at the sound of Fred's yelling, everybody who was going past the office at that moment stopped in their tracks. When the door opened a minute later, four head waiters, Fred – still trembling with rage – and the 'impostor head waiter' Hadji, brandishing a written warning, all left the office.

If you believe that Hadji decided to mend his ways and suddenly stopped treating his colleagues disrespectfully, you are wrong! During lunch he again had the opportunity to give evidence of his skewed sense of humor. Hadji was busy serving beverages when a purser and his family sat down in his station after he had obtained the staff captain's and maître d's permission to have lunch in the dining room. Sizing them up, Hadji asked: "Was there no room left for you in the canteen? Do you have to blight my existence up here?" Seething with anger at Hadji's flippant remark, the purser stated: "We are part of the first class crew and are allowed to have lunch here today." Hadji countered right away: "First class crew! Who cares?! I earn 5,000 dollars per month! How much do *you* make?" The purser knew that he could not compete with the salary and enormous tips waiters receive for working twice as much as he did. He blushed and didn't say anything. Fortunately the maître d' came along at that moment and gave Hadji a withering look. He knew instinctively that the purser had been treated highly unprofessionally by his star-waiter. Thanks to the maître d's sudden intervention the purser and his family were able to enjoy lunch, Hadji's despicable behavior notwithstanding.

Hadji capitalized on every opportunity to annoy his colleagues and was in the restaurant for every meal. Thus he was also very attentive during the breakfast sitting. After he had served his guests the most prosaic breakfast of scrambled eggs and porridge in less than no time, he was now busy polishing the cutlery, while his right eye watched the entrance and his left eye focused on his watch. He was eagerly waiting for the guests who showed up for breakfast at the last minute, shortly before the restaurant was closing. Then he hurried to the door, gave the 'late arrivals' a smile, yelled, "Good morning!", offered his arm to the ladies among the guests and accompanied them to their seats. If he did not know the waiter who was responsible for the lady, he would shout loudly and clearly: "Hey, is anybody there? Who is the lucky waiter?" However, if he knew the waiter was the rather hot-tempered Antonio from the Canary Islands who was not at all in the mood to serve guests who showed up for breakfast at the very last minute thus shattering his

287

dream of a break between meals, Hadji would shout from the restaurant door in a deafening voice: "Antonio, have a look who's here! Aren't you thrilled? Your cherished guests have just told me that they've missed you terribly since they saw you a few hours ago!" Antonio would have preferred to grab Hadji by his throat, but he had no option but to politely welcome and serve his guests. He would have loved nothing better than to offer scrambled eggs with bacon. But our dear Hadji, who had just helped a lady in Antonio's station with a package of cornflakes by tearing it open with his teeth, immediately rose to speak.

"I recommend today's special " he announced after all guests had sat down. "The eggs Benedict is excellent, particularly if you order it with salmon to put between the bacon and the poached eggs, or even spinach if you wish to add it to the meal. All you have to do is place your order with the waiter and he will gladly bring it to you Anything to make our customers happy!" "No kidding?" the guests asked in response to Hadji's burst of hospitality. "Well! Antonio, you never told us about this breakfast special. We'll have to try it right away!" Antonio was incandescent with rage because he knew exactly that such an elaborate order taken at the very last minute before the galley closed in the morning would incense the chiefs. Moreover no time would be left for him to have a break – even a very short one – before lunch. I shall refrain from describing the argument between Antonio and the chef. But suffice it to say that the restaurant staff enjoyed listening to them while they were polishing the cutlery.

The days went by, and the cruise liner approached its main destination, the Panama Canal. It was getting hotter and muggier. The passengers were all sweaty when they returned from the weather decks to rest in their cabins; nervousness was creeping in.

"It's so hot and muggy," a male guest remarked who was standing on the upper deck with some friends trying to see even a small branch of the canal.

"You're right", his wife replied while pointing upward. "Looks like they've even switched the fan on."

As I passed by, I stopped short when I overheard her comment. Which fan? Looking up, I realized what she had been talking about. She pointed to our radar which was quickly spinning around.

"What's the matter with our passengers?" I asked our head waiter Darius. "They all seem to be beside themselves. The ladies on deck are mistaking our radar for a fan and the gentlemen ask when we will eventually arrive. Is this usual behavior on a cruise to the Panama Canal?" "It is," Darius told me. "But this is only the beginning. Wait and see how our guests behave when we approach the Panama Canal tomorrow at dawn. The canal is one of the Earth's miracles of construction; crossing it is an unforgettable event. Everybody wants to watch the cruise liner pass through the canal without being hit or scratched on the left or right side. It's strange that most of the guests like to have breakfast while they are crossing the canal. You will be surprised over the hustle and bustle in the restaurant and the Windjammer Café on the upper deck tomorrow in the very early morning, when they will all be fighting for the best window seats." "I am very curious," I replied and frowned while imagining how to provide proper service to the madding crowd during the breakfast session.

"Tomorrow morning we'll reach the Panama Canal," Hadji informed his guests. "We know," they said. "Is there anything special we have to pay attention to so we don't miss anything?" they asked. "You have to get up very early, if you want to catch every detail," he replied. He had hoped to be asked this question so that he wouldn't have to serve so many guests during breakfast. "I recommend having breakfast in the Windjammer Café since it offers the best view."

Hadji was right about this statement, but he was also fully aware of the consequences. This information spread like wildfire among the passengers who had never before crossed the canal. Everybody had the same intention of being one of the first guests in the Windjammer Café the next morning and to be close to the action.

Now the fat was in the fire! Not only the passengers who had already previously crossed the canal now knew where and when they should sit in order to witness the arrival without missing a delicious breakfast, but also the guests who had been let in on this secret thanks to Hadji's advice.

Numerous guests skipped the dinner on the evening before our arrival. They opted instead to go to bed early so they could grab one of the prime seats in the Windjammer Café at dawn.

Hadji was secretly delighted because he had ensured his station would be almost empty during breakfast since his guests would surely be fighting for the seats in the café instead. The mere thought of so little work the next morning had to be celebrated. Following the pattern of our 'hero,' only one kind of celebration would fit the bill: He was in need of some victims among his colleagues to either offend or humiliate. Heading for his cabin after he had finished his work, he passed the dry cleaner's where a few hard-working Chinese employees were still busy. "Dry cleaner's, dry cleaner's," Hadji mumbled. "Very good idea, I haven't been here for a long time. I think one of those Chinese dudes will be pleased to see me."

On the evening prior to our arrival at the Panama Canal the managers of the restaurant and the Windjammer Café discussed all details for the next morning in a meeting. Expecting some guests in the café very early the next morning who wanted to combine the arrival at the canal with an excellent breakfast, they wanted to be well prepared. None of them, however, had anticipated what in fact did happen the next morning.

The arrival at the first canal lock was scheduled for 6:30 a.m. All waiters, busboys and managers had gone to bed fairly early so as to be refreshed and energetic enough to prepare for breakfast at 5:00 a.m. Only a lonely guard on night duty and the cleaner were working throughout the night according to the service schedule.

At about 3:00 a.m. when it was still dark, our diligent cleaner was busy mopping the floor in the Windjammer Café when there was a loud knock at the door. Five seconds later there was another knock – louder and more forceful this time. When Pedro, the cleaner opened the door, he couldn't believe his eyes. About 200 guests had gathered in front of the café and noisily demanded to be let in.

"Is breakfast being served already?" a guest asked. "I sure don't smell any fresh coffee," another one remarked. "Breakfast, breakfast!" they all chorused while pushing and shoving towards the tables at the window. Pedro just stood there at a complete loss as to what to say or do. "Coffee, coffee!" the customers yelled, waving the cups they had found in the café. "Are you the manager?" the terrified cleaner was asked, although the mop in his hand belied that possibility. "No, Señor," he replied. "I do the cleaning when the café is closed." "*Closed*?! Why is the café closed?" an indignant British guest wanted to know. "Doesn't the management know that we will arrive at the Panama Canal any minute now?" When he realized that grilling poor Pedro – who was obviously not in a position to provide any information – wasn't helping the situation, he turned around and saw his wife trying to wrangle some prime seats. An increasing number of Panama fans who had also woken up very early in order to grab a window seat were furiously looking around at the sight of the occupied tables. They left the café hoping to grab a table at the pool outside which would also grant a view on the Panama Canal. Unfortunately, all of these seats were already occupied as well. In most cases the husbands kept a close watch at the tables, while the wives were busily ferreting around in the hopes of finding some coffee left over from the midnight buffet. Pedro was growing increasingly frightened since he was the only one in the café who had to deal with the angry mob that kept demanding breakfast and coffee. Panic-stricken he hurried down to the reception desk to report the pandemonium that was taking place.

At about 3:30 a.m. the alarm bells were ringing in the cabins of all head waiters, the maître d', the F&B manager and even the hotel director. About 20 minutes later all staff who had been summoned arrived at the Windjammer Café and couldn't believe their eyes. Approximately 400 guests were already inside or standing around the café, requesting admission. The manager circulated the area and tried to calm down the upset crowd, but nobody was paying him any heed. When the hotel director advised them the café would only open at 6:00 a.m., they became even more disruptive. They expressed their desire for coffee by pounding their cups on the tables.

"What the hell!" the hotel director said, as he surveyed the unruly horde. "Let's prepare the coffee and call the bakery for some rolls and croissants for the café. Maître d', please call as many waiters as possible and ask them to immediately come to the Windjammer Café to give us a hand." The maître d' followed his instructions and phones started ringing off the hook.

It was funny to watch the hotel director, the F&B manager and the maître d' switching on the coffee machines and arranging the rolls

291

and pastries on the trays so that the boisterous throng sitting outside could be served.

Half an hour later all the busboys had arrived at the café and started to work, although their usual shift would have started only two hours later according to the work schedule. They were understandably dead tired and still half asleep when they showed up and struggled to carry the coffeepots, hot water and tea bags on their trays without spilling anything.

The news of the breakfast service having already begun in the Windjammer Café circulated instantly. More and more guests forced their way in, still hoping to find an empty table with a breathtaking view of the canal. On that particular eventful morning, however, this hope was dashed. Anybody who had grabbed a favorable window seat refused to move an inch. Day was dawning, but the canal could not be seen, which was no surprise as it was 5:30 a.m. and the arrival was only scheduled for 6:00 a.m. The guests had briefly calmed down in the meantime, but became grumpy and unruly again. Silly comments echoed throughout the vessel. "Go tell the captain to speed it up!" one of the passengers shouted. "Shall we get out and push the ship?" another one asked. "If it takes any longer, I'll have to set up my bed here," a third passenger groused. As you can imagine, it was a very friendly and pleasant atmosphere conducive to working at this early hour!

"Ask Hadji to come here!" one of the busboys proposed. "Why should he be spared from burning the midnight oil among these nagging and grumpy customers?" The maître d' who had overheard this suggestion was in favor of the idea and approached one of his head waiters: "Go and call the big mouth. He should be here right away to assist us. I am sure that the hard work here will take up all his energy which is usually wasted by his vile behavior."

Half an hour passed and Hadji still hadn't shown up. One of the head waiters announced that Hadji was nowhere to be found. "We have called him, looked for him in his cabin, in all the bars and canteens, but we still can't find him. He doesn't have any friends on board, and even his enemies we encountered during our search didn't have a clue where he could be." "Okay," the boss decided. "Then we will continue working here without him and I will take care of him later."

By that time we had reached the Panama Canal. Not a single passenger remained inside the ship since they all wanted to witness this gigantic tub passing the canal firsthand. In next to no time all rails and windows were crowded with passengers watching and waiting with bated breath.

Everybody froze in place when the liner entered the first lock and stopped. The water did not stop flowing in from all sides until the swimming ship had reached the next level. The passengers all held their breath. Our ship was lifted and pushed into the next lock three times. After it had reached the top level, it had arrived at the true canal and was then tied down. "Ah, I see," one guest remarked. "The ship doesn't cross the canal on its own. Instead, it is pulled through the canal by small trains on the rails from both sides of the ship which are firmly tied to the ship with steel hawsers. This prevents the cruise liner from slipping out of place either on the left or right side." The guest was totally correct. Gradually our ship proceeded until it had reached the open canal and continued its way on its own. All passengers were startled by a loud tooting and curiously looked down and saw several other ships – among them a cruise liner, a container vessel and a destroyer from the American navy. Some of these ships were far larger than our cruise ship. It was immensely interesting to see that this was nothing but daily routine for these giants to pass the critical first section of the canal with the help of the small trains. With reference to the destroyer, a space of exactly two centimeters is left to the concrete walls on the right and left sides, but the steel hawsers had a lock on each of these swimming giants and helped them to safely pass the canal. "How much does it cost for our ship to pass through the Panama Canal?" a curious guest asked the hotel director who was busy filling some glasses with orange juice. "Roughly 80.000 dollars," he replied. "This very low price is based on the fact that we do not cross the entire canal, but leave it after a few kilometers." "Very low price indeed!" the totally astonished guest replied.

By that time the atmosphere on board our cruise liner had considerably improved. There was no more clamoring for window seats or malicious comments. The rather sleepy waiters did quite a proper job, but were still annoyed that Hadji had avoided duty.

Another search for the surly waiter started but again failed. The crew gradually became nervous since a missing person – no matter whether it is a passenger or an employee – is always a serious matter. "Stop!" one of the head waiters yelled. "I think I now know where to find this crazy guy. Each of our waiters and busboys has to perform an extra side duty every day. As far as I know, Hadji is responsible for tablecloths and napkins. After they have been washed, they have to be collected from the dry cleaners and stored in the restaurant. I am quite sure that he must have started arguing with one of the Chinese staff there and was shut up! Let's go downstairs and have a look whether I am right!" Everybody frowned at this hare-brained notion, but nevertheless followed his suggestion and went down to the 'holy catacombs' of the Chinese 'linen gang.' Although we were still two decks away from the dry cleaners' room, we heard a loud rumbling and a voice which resembled a wild gorilla stuck in a cage, yelling, "You rotten bastards! You creeps! Open the door!" Shortly thereafter we were standing across from him. Clinging to the locked grille of the drying room where the laundry was hung out, Hadji stared at us. "Those shitheads! Those assholes!" he shouted. "They locked me in here all night!" Giving Hadji the once-over, the boss commented: "They would have had every right to do so, dear Hadji! Who knows what kind of nonsense you stirred up here last night. Before you can go anywhere I will talk to the dry cleaner's manager. You'll stay put until I return. To be honest, I am very amused to see you in the cage! It really suits you!" Hadji kept quiet. After all, it was his boss talking to him and Hadji did not want to spoil his rapport with him.

The manager went to see the boss of the dry cleaning staff to find out why Hadji had been put behind bars for the entire night and during the passage through the Panama Canal.

"It's very easy to explain," the old wise Chinese man replied while he was busy working. "This ugly and stupid roly-poly walked into our room while we were having supper. He indignantly looked into our cooking pot and said: "Hi, you Chinks! What's in the pot? Dog? Cat? Hamster?" The guy was acting so silly. He was on his own, yet he managed to insult all 25 of us men. Two seconds later he was being carried by our strongest employees who took him into the drying room and locked the door behind him. Do you understand? He was shut away in a cage like a dog, a cat or a hamster. Now you may take this imbecile away, but tell him that if he is ever rude to us again he will be thrown into the sea as shark bait."

Following this instruction Hadji returned to the dining room, accompanied by the manager; he first had to see the hotel director in his office. Once again our 'star' had to sign a written warning. He was again warned that he would be sent home immediately in the instance of any other infractions. Hadji had no sooner left the hotel director's office when all the managers burst out laughing until tears were running down their faces. It had been too funny seeing this pot-bellied waiter clinging to the bars of the 'cage' like an orangutan and cursing the Chinese..

At this point you may wonder whether our top insulter was eventually dismissed because of another set-to with one of the colleagues. Rest assured that he *was* fired, but for a different reason: he had doubted his guests' memory.

On the next cruise Hadji had to serve a group of young guests who were soon wise to the fact that their waiter was a bit of an oddball, but didn't let on. As I was working in close vicinity to Hadji's station, I was able to carefully observe these guests' body language. As soon as Hadji had disappeared into the galley, they either flipped the bird at him or sneered. They didn't say much to their waiter, but always listened attentively to his gibberish. They kept particularly silent on the last evening of the cruise. After a short 'Thank you' they simply disappeared. Tip? No way!! "Bastards, assholes, swines!" everybody heard Hadji swearing when the guests were out of earshot. "I'll get even with them tomorrow!"

The next morning the young gang indeed showed up for breakfast and were welcomed by Hadji with the words, "Yesterday evening you forgot to give me a tip." Not reacting at all to his sarcastic comment, the guests instead ordered a huge breakfast which they thoroughly enjoyed.

The news that Hadji had to serve guests in his station who made a fool of him instead of the other way round had quickly spread throughout the ship. Many waiters came to see Hadji that morning. While Hadji was piling the main courses on his tray in the galley, they mocked him and asked him about his tip from the previous evening (although they already knew the answer). "Hadji," they taunted, "were your guests generous last night? Have you already ordered a Ferrari?" Without dignifying their catcalls with a response, Hadji went to the dining room to serve the meals. He put the food grumpily in front of his guests and then committed the crucial mistake which brought about his downfall. He pulled his busboy in a corner and hissed: "No more coffee, water, or pastries! These knuckleheads didn't give me a tip last night. In return they have to be satisfied with the food and beverages served this morning." The busboy to whom the guests had granted a tip last night after he had done his job without any silly comments, obeyed his discontented boss; he was too inexperienced to contradict a superior. Both of them waited until the esteemed customers had left the table and then started cleaning the table and griping over the missing tip. To be more precise, Hadji was the only one who was upset; there was no reason for the busboy to complain. He had already padded his wallet with the tip he received and would shortly deposit it into his bank account.

What do most of the guests usually do after the last breakfast sitting? They return to their cabin to check whether everything is in order before they leave the cruise liner. Hadji's guests, however, made a detour to the complaints department and insisted on talking to the hotel director.

The breakfast sitting was already long over, when the maître d' suddenly showed up next to Hadji who was still cursing about being stiffed for a tip the previous evening. Hadji was summoned to the captain right away. "Whatever does he want?" our super waiter asked. "You will find out in a minute," the maître d' calmly assured him.

All of the high-ranking officers had gathered at a table on the bridge. They held a few documents in their hands and offered Hadji a seat.

The meeting was very brief. Wielding the long written complaint like a weapon, the captain read the indictment to the attendees.

"Mr. Hadji," the captain began, "you were responsible for table 49 last week?"

Hadji: "Yes, Captain, the guests at this table were, in fact, real penny pinchers." Captain: "Since they obviously didn't give you any tip, you thought it appropriate to remind the guests about their

296

memory lapse. You realize this violates our company's rule, don't you?"

Hadji: "Well, Captain, look at it this way! If our company informed you at the end of the month that you wouldn't get any salary for the last four weeks that you worked, would you agree to it in a friendly way or would you complain about it? Just like you, I have to take care of my wife and my children and I don't have a part-time job in addition to this one. You must understand where I'm coming from!"

The captain swallowed hard because he had not expected such a defiant and disrespectful reply, although it was reasonable to some extent. After he had again looked at the officers and at the guests' complaint who had indeed written a very indignant letter to the shipping company, he turned to Hadji for the last time. "I am sorry, my son, but I have no choice but to dismiss you."

Although I would like to inform you that Hadji left the ship in a huff as soon as we arrived in Miami, this story isn't quite finished. His send-off was in the form of a party arranged by all of the waiters, chiefs and cleaning staff who had shown up in front of the ship and on the weather decks after Hadji's dismissal had been announced. Some of them had brought drums, cooking pots and even compressed air horns with them which are often used in stadiums. 'GO HOME, IDIOT' had been written on an old bed sheet which was raised when Hadji – escorted by the first officer and the hotel director – walked down the gangway. Due to the loud applause, singing and music, numerous others who were in close proximity to the cruise liner came running to find out which important person was being celebrated. All this fuss left Hadji rather cold. In the middle of the gangway he suddenly put down his suitcases, turned around in front of his admirers – and gave everybody the finger. After a last asinine smile he disappeared into a waiting taxi.

Are you curious as to how his life continued? Someone told us that he had established an avocado plantation in South America. However, after a while his staff poured petrol over the plantation and set it ablaze; in other words the plantation was razed to the ground. Nobody knows how Hadji managed to again raise the shackles of his poor workers who were only interested in earning

297

some extra cash for their families by working on the plantation, and none of us were particularly interested in finding out."

After Jesus had stopped regaling me about his experiences with Hadji, I was indeed a bit jealous that I didn't have the chance to witness Hadji's capers first hand.

299

Chapter 34:   MANTA MANTA

Jesus also let me know that all of the guests – no matter whether they were standing on the decks or at the windows – were still thinking of the Panama Canal which was already far in the distance. A lot of the passengers were rather ashamed of losing their self-control and their misconduct while they madly scrambled for seats at the best vantage points while simultaneously enjoying breakfast.

It was getting dark and the diesel engines were running at full speed (23 knots or roughly 40 km/h), which caused a rather unpleasant sensation to those guests whose cabins were located directly above the aggregates. Many passengers with such a cabin feared they wouldn't get a good night's sleep. A waiter advised topping off dinner with two or three glasses of exquisite red wine. This recommendation was in fact gratefully accepted, since the alcohol in the blood helped to ignore the ship's noises and vibrations as well as to quickly fall asleep.

Note: Nowadays there are no cabins in which it is impossible to relax or sleep due to engine noise. Not a sound is heard even in the cabins on the lowest deck which are available at the most favorable prices. However, if the liner is vibrating due to high speed or rough seas, this sensation will be noticed regardless of your location on the ship.

This much was certain: everybody – whether well rested or not – was looking forward to the last destination of our cruise: the Cayman Islands.

It took two days until the famous Caribbean island paradise emerged in front of our liner. We were all thrilled by the shiny water and the large palm trees waving towards us. Everyone had made detailed plans for the day: diving in the fascinating underwater world, visiting the turtle farm or going to the bank to check the interest which had accumulated during the last few months by virtue of the Caymans' status as a tax haven. Most of the passengers, however, booked an excursion which offered something very special: a visit to Stingray City, the manta ray bay which is famous throughout the world, not to mention the Cayman Islands' most popular tourist attraction.

After I had received a rating of five stars by my dear guests the week before, I was granted a day off and could mingle with the tourists.

Smiling from ear to ear, I said my goodbyes to the colleagues who were preparing the lunch buffet. Green with envy, they watched me while I headed for the gangway.

"Where are we going?" an older lady asked who seemed to be on edge. Aided by her grandsons, she was limping towards the ship exit in order to sit down in the tender (lifeboat). "We are going to show you something marvelous!" the teenagers replied. Smirking impudently, they carefully put their reluctant grandma in the boat. "I have a bridge tournament this afternoon," she grumbled. "I even dressed up especially for the occasion and hope to be back on board on time." Curiously, we looked at the lady who indeed was elegantly dressed in fine light silk. She also wore a fashionable sun hat and shoes made of what looked like crocodile leather (I don't know whether it was genuine!). She was now being escorted into the tender by her young grandsons and the square-shouldered security staff. We soon learned that her grandsons were responsible for her unhappy facial expression because they had booked the excursion without grandma's permission. But it was mandatory for them to be in the company of an adult acting as their guardian during this 'manta tour.' The bridge-loving grandmother would have never agreed to participate in this excursion because of her age (she was nearly 90 years old) and primarily because she did not like fish. Since the grandsons were fully aware of grandma's objections, they had to resort to trickery to make her leave the ship. Thus they had lured her with the promise of a spectacular excursion.

Now she was sitting across from us, staring at her expensive shoes. She was most worried about these shoes getting dirty or wet, while the nature's breathtaking beauty was only of minor importance.

All passengers were enthusiastic about the perfect weather, the crystal-clear water and the welcoming palm trees on the white beaches. During the short trip to the dock most of the passengers had already gotten up and were eager to explore the island. Only our special lady was not at all in a hurry and the prospect of

301

boarding another ferry to get to the 'spectacular sight' did nothing to mollify her.

Waiting for us at the dock, the organizers raised plates with a large manta on it. After they had warmly welcomed us, we were asked to follow them. It didn't take long until we were all sitting in the tour boat, waiting in pleasant anticipation.

"The trip was just fine," we heard the lady say rather reluctantly. "But can't we go back to our cruise liner now?"

"We will be back in no time," the grandsons assured her immediately. "First we would like to show you some of the beautiful Caribbean nature." "Okay, I guess so," she mumbled and once again checked her clothes and shoes which were totally ill-suited for an adventure tour.

As we traversed the shallow waters, we passed the Caymans' endless beaches until we finally moored in a magnificent bay.

Everybody was eager to be among the first passengers to buy food for the mantas. The so-called 'squid' from the family of cuttlefish was their favorite food and the only food allowed to be fed to the mantas. Loud protest was heard from the boat again: our lady refused to walk on the beach with her fancy designer shoes. Since her grandsons didn't leave her any choice, she was soon standing barefoot in the shallow water, holding a bag of squids which the boys had given her.

"What's that slippery stuff down in the water?" she asked, then pointed to some black shadows in the water and warned her grandsons: "Be careful, there are some large rocks in the water. Make sure you don't stub your toes on them. Once I have….. What the hell! It looks as if the rocks are moving! How can this be?" Laughing at her expense, the youths explained: "Grandma, these aren't rocks. These are mantas that want you to feed them! Isn't it great?" The silence was interrupted by a loud cry. "Don't tell me that I am standing in the water and am about to be eaten alive by the mantas!" our little grandma wailed. "No, Granny!" the grandsons assured her. "They don't want to eat you, just put the food in there." They took out a fist full of squids from the bag and put their hands in the water. One of the mantas immediately swam to them and greedily snapped at the food. Being touched by humans didn't seem to bother the manta; it even seemed to enjoy it. "Have a look,

302

Granny!" one of the grandsons yelled. "They feel like warm soft leather. Would you like to......?" "No, no, I certainly would *not*!" the grandmother shouted. "I am afraid those slimy creatures will also eat my hand!" "No problem," the grandson giggled. "You can still play bridge with only one hand." "You little monkeys are such monsters!" the grandmother chided. "That's enough for me. Let me get out of the water – I'd rather relax in the shade, anyway. Better you getting devoured by these critters than me! In fact, I hope there won't be anything left of you, since you already ruined my bridge game."

"Okay," the two teens snickered in reply and helped her slowly get out of the water. While they calmed her down and promised to return to the cruise liner straightaway, frantic cries were suddenly heard from the water in the distance. While everyone there was looking around, trying to pinpoint the location of these cries for help, they noticed a young panic-stricken man clad in snorkel gear who was thrashing about in the water. "Look over there!" the grandma exclaimed, her face contorted into a mischievous expression. "It was bound to happen – the first human is being devoured by these beasts in front of our very eyes. I saw it coming!" "No way!" one of the islanders scoffed who was standing in the water demonstrating to a group of tourists how to handle the mantas. "There aren't any sharks in these waters, but I think I have an idea of what's going on." Meanwhile the snorkeler, who by then had managed to swim to safety on the beach after racing at a speed which would have rivaled Olympian champion Michael Phelps, was shaking from head to toe.

What happened? We learned that this amateur diver wanted to try something clever while feeding and watching the mantas in the open sea. He had brought a tube of easy cheese with him, that is, cheese from a spray bottle, similar to perfume or hair spray. He had tried to use this kind of cheese under water for feeding the manta rays. It had worked pretty well, at least at first, but unfortunately our hero had not counted on being assailed by the small yet very aggressive fish known as sergeant majors. This species of fish, which is usually docile until it encounters something edible, also inhabits the waters of the Cayman Islands. When they detected the easy cheese, they immediately started behaving like piranhas.

About 20 seconds later a school of wild little creatures was chasing the swimming cheese. Unfortunately some of the cheese had become stuck to the diver's body, which didn't deter the fish at all. Understandably the diver panicked as they latched onto him, puckering at the food all over his body. The diver did his utmost to propel himself back to the beach, yelping and whining all the while, but the fish were persistent and kept on his tail since they were not yet sated from the cheese. The snorkeler had barely managed to get to the beach a minute later and did not look happy at all. Everyone on the beach had of course witnessed this spectacle and was informed about it in detail by the islander shortly thereafter. Naturally they were very curious as to why the young man had been swimming at top speed as though he were being pursued by a shark. By this time a group of teenage boys had assembled at the scene and were taunting the snorkeler as he was trying to recover from the near disaster on the beach. The grandmother who also was very amused after she had been told by her grandsons what had just happened. The poor snorkeler surveyed the sniggering youths, the ringleader of which was a rather chubby boy, and decided to seek revenge. It didn't take long before he was able to devise a suitably diabolical plan. He went to the food stall then returned to the seashore with some squids which he kept in the pocket of his swimming trunks. He waited for the spectators' laughter and gawking to subside before he took action. Soon afterward, he again plunged into the water. Squids in hand, he stealthily approached the pudgy leader who had mocked him. In the meantime the nasty youth had separated from his friends and was now standing in the deeper water, feeding a manta. As he held his head under the water, he didn't realize that somebody was creeping up on him. The snorkeler did indeed manage to reach the victim's long swimming shorts and then slowly deposit the squids in his back pockets without attracting his attention. The hobby diver disappeared as silently as he had crept up on him. He was totally content with himself since his efforts proved to be successful. Moments later, everyone in the vicinity was agog with surprise that yet another tourist seemed to be having the same problem as the diver so soon after the first occurrence. The second victim was evidently likewise panic-stricken and tried to get out of the water as quickly as possible. Everyone who was in the young man's line of sight noticed that the ill-fated swimmer was surrounded by at least six or seven mantas which were greedily snapping at food. Nobody could figure out why the mantas were repeatedly puckering on his swimming trunks and preventing him from escaping. Only the snorkeler knew exactly how awful it felt to be surrounded by greedy, hungry mantas which cared only about being fed, regardless of the source. Laughter was heard across the beach. Who do you imagine was the most amused tourist? Right, it was our 'posh granny,' who had witnessed the entire bizarre exhibition. She hugged her grandsons and apologized for her initial foul mood, then thanked them for such an entertaining excursion which she wouldn't soon forget.

The day was coming to an end, and the guides advised it was time to leave. The swimmers, snorkelers and all other tourists were exhausted and ready for a shower on the cruise liner.

The tourists took a last look at the manta bay before it gradually disappeared into the distance. Except for two fellow passengers who were still taking care of their minor injuries, all tourists were keen on recommending this excursion to the bay of the gentle yet greedy mantas as well as taking part in this tour with other family members or friends during another cruise into this part of the Caribbean Sea. As far as I know, Stingray City is the only place in the world where you have the opportunity to be so close to these majestic creatures which you can normally only see on TV.

Boats and buses coming from all parts of the islands arrived at Georgetown, the capital of the Cayman Islands. All travelers exchanged their experiences they had gathered during the day. While some of them were thrilled about the wonderful, white beaches of the island and the underwater world they had become familiar with during diving or snorkeling, others were raving about the large turtle farm. I won't refer to this particular tourist attraction in great detail since there are numerous farms of this type which can be visited all over the world. The very few passengers who were affluent enough to stay in the large suites had paid a visit to the banks and were very content after they had checked their deposits. In addition, two of my Romanian colleagues had gone to the Royal Bank of Scotland, but for an entirely different purpose:

they wanted to cool down for a short while from the sweltering heat outside. They were laughing as they told us what had happened to them in the bank. According to them, they had scarcely arrived at the bank and were already given preferential treatment. They had been offered a seat and a glass of ice water or iced tea. One of the waiters continued to recount their tale. "Okay, both of us were dressed up, too dressed up for this terrible heat that we hadn't expected. The bank manager seemed to be very impressed by our appearance and the fact that we were Europeans who did not look at all as if we were visiting the island for its turtles, mantas or beaches. Therefore the employees most likely hoped to convince us to transfer our entire or at least a part of our savings to an account at their bank. We could barely get a word in edgewise, but were immediately provided with an information brochure with several investment options. At the same time they started to explain the advantages of a bank account on the Cayman Islands. We listened attentively because it was quite interesting to be informed about their offers. At a favorable moment we asked the manager about the minimum investment required which is different for all banks. "This year we have lowered the minimum investment amount," the manager explained to us. "Consequently more customers are now granted the opportunity to invest money with us. One hundred thousand dollars is all it takes to start doing business with us. May I ask you, my dear gentlemen, in which industrial sector you are working? Or your company name?" "We are waiters," was our disappointing reply. The manager gaped at us and tried his utmost to maintain his composure. "The iced tea was very delicious," we continued. "The best beverage for this baking heat. Many thanks. Be sure that we will definitely recommend your bank! We regret we have to leave now, but must return to our restaurant and earn as many tips as possible. Maybe we will return someday to open an account with your friendly bank that serves perfect iced tea." After shaking hands with the flabbergasted manager, we left the bank and split our sides laughing outside. It was most hilarious to watch the manager's facial expression when we told him that we earned money by serving iced tea and food to our guests!"

This little story shared by the two waiters on our way back to the cruise liner caused general amusement and intensified the sense of well-being after spending a gorgeous final day in the Caribbean Sea. This paradise had fascinated all of us and I can highly recommend booking a cruise that includes a visit to the Cayman Islands.

We enjoyed yet another pleasant evening on board, which featured a delicious farewell dinner. Numerous guests were understandably sad about this dream vacation coming to its end. Comforting many of these passengers, I recommended they go to a travel agency and book the next cruise shortly after they had arrived at home. In those days the guests only had the option of booking trips in their home town. Nowadays cruise guests can easily pay a visit to the so-called 'cruise consultant,' a type of internal travel agency on board the cruise liner, where they can select and book the next cruise. This procedure is less expensive and included various considerable benefits for the passengers.

Once dinner was over, almost all of the guests went to the theater again to watch the last show which offered several highlights even on the last day. The guests marveled at the snake man, the mini-version of the 'Phantom of the Opera' and other thrilling performances. The cruise director entered the stage for the last time to entertain the audience with a final amusing delight. "Dear Ladies and Gentlemen," he began, "before we get on with the last part of our evening program, I have to reply to a question which a guest recently asked. He wanted to know whether passengers sometimes ask very silly questions that make us shake our heads. Patting the man's back, I asked him whether he had some extra time and a good sense of humor because he would hardly believe my response, although I am really telling the truth. At first he frowned, but then laughed and agreed. 'Okay, I am all ears. Are these questions actually very extraordinary?' I explained to him that we have a quiz show featuring the silliest questions. This quiz show starts with the question which is in eleventh place and ends with such banal questions that we in fact do not know how these guests could even manage to save enough money for a cruise.

'Shoot!' my very curious guest exclaimed in encouragement."

"Well, my dear Ladies and Gentlemen", the cruise director announced, "we will now introduce our quiz show highlighting some of the silliest questions and the replies which we would have liked to give. We have, however, refrained from a suitable answer since we didn't want to embarrass or annoy our guests."

I also don't want to deny you of the pleasure of this quiz show, my cherished readers! Come on, the countdown has begun!

11th Place:
"At what time is the midnight buffet served?"
Dream reply: "Approximately at 2.00 pm, Sir."

10th Place:
"Does this staircase lead upstairs or downstairs?"
Dream reply: "Only upstairs, Sir, in order to go downstairs you have to take the lift."

9th Place:
"Is this island completely surrounded by water?"
Dream reply: "No, Ma'am, the south is connected to Africa, while the northern part is connected to the Philippines."

8th Place:
"Does the crew sleep on board?"
Dream reply: "No, Sir, the crew leaves the ship by jet ski very late in the evening to spend the night in a hotel on an island and returns on board the ship early the next morning."

7th Place:
"Who is steering the ship, while the captain is having dinner?"
Dream reply: "His cabin waiter, Ma'am."

6th Place:
"Does the ship produce its own electrical power?"
Dream reply: "No, Sir, we've installed a very long power cable at the stern which connects our liner with an electric power station in Miami."

Place 5:
"What do the chefs do with the ice sculptures after they have melted?"
Dream reply: "The water is poured into plastic bottles and sold."

4th Place:
"Which elevator do I have to take to get to the ship's bow?"
Dream reply: "Simply press all buttons; someday you will have pressed the correct one and the elevator will move ahead instead of going up and down..."

3rd Place:
"Is fresh- or salt water used for the toilets?"
Dream reply: "Who cares? Put your finger into the toilet bowl and try the water! Afterwards let us know how it tastes and we will attach an appropriate label."

2nd Place:
"Do the outside cabins have a roof?"
Dream reply: "No, of course not! The guests in the outside cabins sleep out in the open every night."

1st Place, unique in its ingenuity:
"How do we know which photos in the photo gallery are ours, unless they are properly identified?"
Dream reply: "????"

These were the silliest questions... oh no, stop! I nearly forgot to tell you about an ignorant jerk I once had the pleasure of meeting. This book wouldn't be complete without the description of this incredible moment.

Our cruise liner was on the verge of leaving the port of Miami. I was making small talk with my colleagues while standing at the reception desk when a guest suddenly came hurrying. Banging his fist on the desk, he yelled: "What the hell is this bullshit? I didn't book a suite so I could stare at a parking lot for seven days!" He pointed at the enormous parking space in the harbor area which was at the guests' and harbor staff's disposal.

Gawking at the guest, we waited for him to burst out laughing, but he kept a straight face. The purser was the first of us who regained his composure. Taking a deep breath, he explained to the upset guest: "Dear Sir, I promise you that the panorama in front of your window will frequently change over the next seven days." "I should hope so!" he gruffly replied. He was unable to realize that we were still tied to the dock at that moment. Afterwards he went upstairs and never approached the purser's desk. It's your guess whether he ever realized he had made such an outlandish outburst.

But now let me again refer to the farewell show. The audience nearly died laughing; these questions were exactly the right way to end an already wonderful cruise. The cruise director bowed to the guests for the last time, while the orchestra played a cheerful melody. The stars of the evening's show once more entered the stage and took their bows. The cruise director, who had a beautiful voice, sang the farewell song before the curtain fell and the music finally faded away.

But the last evening was not over yet. As the bars and the casino were still open, the guests who had already packed their suitcases and had some time left met for another cocktail, a cigar or a last game in the gambler paradise. There was a lot of drinking, winning, losing and smoking until deep into the night. It was common for our guests to discuss the cruise while sitting comfortably in one of the numerous lounges and tell us what they enjoyed as well as what could be improved. They laughed about the funny waiters and their assistants, praised the delicious buffets and the food in general to the heavens, and saw themselves already booking the next cruise. Everybody had become aware of the following fact: nowhere else will you be offered more value for your money than on a cruise liner. At no other place will you experience delicious food, art and culture, combined with a touch of Las Vegas – at a price which almost anyone can afford.

As a closing word I can assure you of the following: Those of you who haven't yet gone on a cruise, do not know what you are missing. One of the very common comments is: "A cruise is interesting for old people who are unable to walk and have no other choice but to sail across the oceans."

My dear readers, after having read this book, you must certainly have become a bit curious. Don't hesitate, go to a travel agency and book a cruise today! However, if you're reading this book while you have already made yourself comfortable in your cabin and are enjoying the view to the sea while laughing, shaking your head or squinting by the light of your reading lamp, I hope that you have enjoyed reading the book! You have a choice: either make plans for your first cruise or look forward to your next one!

I am now aboard a cruise liner towards Alaska for the third time, a destination which no nature-lover should miss. Most of this book was written during such cruises. Should I ever again put pen to paper, I will start recounting my experiences which I've gathered in this last vestige of idyllic paradise of our beautiful planet.

THE END

The Grand Finale

On April 22 2014 the following tragic scene was witnessed in our
Spa Facilities on board.

Rated pg 6

Kids under the age of 6 should view the following only in the
presence of at least 2 adults and the grand parents.

Table of Contents:

Acknowledgements

Last, but not least I wish to thank the following people who have collaborated with me to put this book on paper:

- Mrs. Ute Hieksch for the perfect translation into American English for the American market and all those who like to read the book in American English,

- Mrs. Eva Hoppe of company "Gruenanlage" for the detailed and awesome book illustration

- The company "Print Factory" in Mönchengladbach for the professional formatting, edition and printing of the book.

If you have been at sea for more than 26 years, you're bound to have a lot of stories to tell!

This is particularly true for a man who has worked as waiter aboard cruise liners for more than two decades!

In this book Mr. Rade – Johannes in real life – allows us the luxury of participating in his various experiences over the years. He narrates in a very lively and vivid manner and is candid about what impressed him the most. No matter whether he is recounting an anecdote regarding his initial cruise employee application or taking us on a wild romp throughout his career, stories involving the world champion and record holder in eating lobsters, the 'esteemed' colleagues who are always good for a joke, the numerous international, sometimes bizarre guests – Johannes always strikes the right tone. He makes you feel as though you are actually at his side in the restaurants or on the various decks aboard the ship. You will frequently laugh out loud at his outlandish antics. And even when he refers to serious topics such as the 'Man overboard' alarm, he addresses these subjects with compassion.

Let this book take you away on an imaginary cruise to Jamaica, through the Panama Canal, to the Cayman Islands and numerous other destinations. And who knows – maybe this autobiographical tale will inspire you to take a real cruise someday.

In any case Johannes's book will undoubtedly arouse your interest in a cruise and perhaps even tempt you to book one!

Made in the USA
San Bernardino, CA
17 December 2017